THE PSYCHOLOGY OF SELF-CONFIDENCE

BY

THOMAS N. STANTON

<u>TABLE OF CONTENTS</u>

INTRODUCTION

Man is confronted with three fundamental natural truths in his attempt to comprehend the cosmos in which he lives: the presence of matter, life, and consciousness.

He created the sciences of physics and chemistry in answer to the first of these phenomena, the science of biology in response to the second, and the science of psychology in response to the third. It is well known that, up to this point, physics has seen the biggest breakthroughs in knowledge, whereas psychology has seen the least.

The differences in the comparative rates of advancement can be attributed, at least in part, to the difficulties that each of these three sciences provide. Man, fundamentally seeks to understand the principles of action displayed by things in their behavior in order to understand what they do and why in various settings when searching for natural laws. Given this objective, a physicist's job is easier than a biologist's since there are less variables to consider when investigating the activities of inanimate objects and a greater range of possible actions for inanimate objects than there are when studying the behavior of living things. A conscious living thing like a man, however, displays a complexity and variety of behavior that are far larger than those displayed by any other entity, alive or nonliving. This makes the task of a biologist easier than that of a psychologist.

Man has a strong yearning for self-intelligibility, which psychology aims to provide, and a fundamental need for a conceptual framework from which to see his own life and activity. Man is a being with the capacity for self-awareness—the capacity to reflect on his own being and behavior. We're offering this book as a step in that direction.

It is not my desire to engage in debates about modern psychology or to claim that it has failed to give man the necessary self-knowledge in this situation. I will therefore just state that this is my conviction and that as we go forward, it will become evident why I hold this belief and how it differs from the current schools of psychology.

If psychology wants to give a true picture of man, I believe that the anti-biological, anti-intellectual, robot conception of human nature that dominates modern thought must be abandoned. This implies that many of the most fundamental assumptions in psychology must be questioned and rejected. The biological entity that psychology is tasked with studying—the organism specifically distinguished by the capacity for conceptual thought, propositional speech, explicit reasoning, and self-awareness—does not resemble either the perspective on man as an instinctually controlled puppet (psychoanalysis) or the perspective on him as a stimulus-response machine (behaviorism).

The role of self-esteem in a man's life is the main issue of this book. It discusses the need for self-esteem, its nature, the circumstances in which it might be satisfied, the effects of its frustration, and how self-esteem (or lack of it) affects a man's values, actions, and ambitions.

Almost all psychologists agree that self-esteem is something that men desire. What they have not figured out, however, is the nature of self-esteem, the reasons why man needs it, and the requirements he must meet in order to obtain it. Almost all psychologists agree, if only in general terms, that there is some connection between a man's level of self-esteem and the state of his mental health. But neither the nature of that link nor its causes have been determined. The kind and level of a man's self-esteem and his motivation, that is, his actions in the areas of work, love, and interpersonal relationships, are somehow related, even if only faintly, according to the vast majority of psychologists. However, they have not given a justification or pointed out the guiding ideas. These are the topics that this book addresses.

In fact, for many years, I designated my system as "Objectivist Psychology" when presenting lectures on my psychological theories, despite the fact that I knew this was only a temporary label—a working title—and that it is inappropriate to name a system of psychology, or any science, after a philosophy. Even if a physicist applied principles of Objectivist epistemology or metaphysics, one would not refer to it as "Objectivist Physics," for example.

The name I ultimately chose resulted from my convictions that psychology must have a strong biological orientation, that studying the nature of life must come before studying the nature of man, that man's psychological nature can only be understood in the context of his nature as a living organism, and that man's nature and needs as a specific kind of organism are the source of both his singular accomplishments and his potential problems. The biocentric approach, which is biologically oriented and life-centered, is fundamental to my way of thinking and how I handle psychological issues. I refer to my approach as "biocentric psychology" for this reason.

When a science is still separated into schools, each with their own name, it is obvious that the field is still in its early stages of development. In this regard, I lament that my work needs to have any designation at all. In all honesty, I do not refer to what I am doing as biocentric psychology. I refer to it as psychology.

THE PSYCHOLOGY OF SELF-CONFIDENCE

PART ONE- THE FUNDAMENTALS

CHAPTER ONE

THE SCIENCE OF PSYCHOLOGY

The Definition of Psychology

With very few exceptions, there are two questions that every person asks themselves for the majority of their lives. Rare exceptions are people who, at the very least, have a good understanding of the answer to the first of these questions. But everyone asks the second, occasionally out of amazement and frequently out of desperation. These are the two queries: How am I to comprehend myself? and: How am I supposed to comprehend others?

These inquiries serve as the basis for and initial motivation for psychological research throughout history, in the growth of the human race and in the life of an individual.

These queries can be expanded upon to address a more general and abstract question: Why do people act the way they do? What would be necessary for him to behave otherwise?

Hermann Ebbingaus, a German psychologist, made the now-famous remark in the early years of this century: "Psychology has a long past, but only a short history." He was attempting to acknowledge the fact that, despite men's intense interest in psychological issues and issues of a psychological nature throughout recorded history, psychology as a separate scientific discipline did not emerge until the second half of the nineteenth century.

If "nature, to be commanded, must be obeyed"—then the purpose of science is to give man the intellectual means of his survival. Science is the rational and systematic study of reality's facts; its goal is to discover laws of nature, to achieve a comprehensive, integrated knowledge that will make the universe understandable to man. Man requires such knowledge in order to deal with reality successfully and in order to survive.

It took many centuries before physics, chemistry, biology, and physiology, for example, were conceptualized as specific sciences. A new science is born when, out of the countless questions that man asks concerning the nature of things, certain questions are isolated and then integrated into a distinct category—isolated and integrated by a defining principle that distinguishes these questions from all others and identifies their common characteristics.

What does psychology as a science entail? How should it be described? What is the exact scope of it?

Consider the following issues—these represent common psychological issues—and think about how one might determine that they are psychological by applying what principle.

A scientist finds it challenging to respond to a challenging question that has come up in his job. He feels no closer to a solution now than when he started working on it months ago. The answer then comes to him suddenly one day when he is out for a walk. What mental mechanisms underpin and explain the experience of unexpected "insight" or "inspiration"?

We observe among the people we know that one is typically calm, assured, and even-tempered; another is agitated, anxious, and unsure of himself; a third is tight, brooding, and emotionally unresponsive; and a fourth is emotionally explosive and volatile, elated one minute and depressed the next. What causes these variations? What factors influence a person's personality and character? What are personality and character?

In the middle of the night, a man wakes up, his body shivering and his heart racing. He has no need to be afraid, as far as he knows. However, he is terrified. The sense of impending doom remains throughout the restless night, as well as the days and weeks that follow. The dread overtakes him as if some alien force has taken possession of his body. Finally, he seeks out a psychotherapist's assistance. He discovers that millions of people, to differing degrees, have the same issue as him. We refer to it as pathological anxiety. What caused it? What does it represent? How can it be treated?

These illustrations relate to people, but psychology is not just the study of people; it also covers the study of animals. When a scientist looks into a canine's learning abilities, a monkey's response to rewards and punishments, or the chimpanzee's "family life," his interest and focus are distinctly psychological. On the other hand, it is obvious that a scientist's research is not psychological if they examine astronomical bodies' motions or a plant's heliotropic behavior. How can we spot this? What is the underlying difference's principle?

Only living things are studied in psychology. among all living things? No—of those sentient, conscious-exhibiting living things.

What are the specific facts of reality that give rise to that science? is the question to be answered if one wishes to comprehend the definition and unique characteristics of a particular science. For instance, the existence of certain living things in nature is a fundamental fact of reality that gives rise to the science of biology. Therefore, biology is the branch of science that investigates the traits and qualities that living things have.

The fundamental reality that gives rise to psychology is that some living things are conscious—that they are capable of being aware of their existence. The science of psychology investigates the qualities and traits that some living things have due to consciousness.

The study of motivation, conduct, and the composition, categories, and purposes of consciousness are all included in this definition. The domains covered by the classic definitions of psychology as "the science of consciousness," "the science of mind," "the science of mental activity," or "the science of conduct" are therefore incorporated into it.

Here, the term "consciousness" is used in its broadest and most general sense to refer to any capacity or state of awareness, including the sophisticated mode of cognition a human being is capable of and the significantly more constrained range of awareness a frog is capable of.

A species' range of consciousness—measured in terms of ability to distinguish, adaptability of action or response, and overall capacity to cope with the external environment—increases with the complexity and degree of development of its neural system. The chimpanzee's neural system is less developed, the cat's awareness range is smaller, and the frog's awareness range is smaller than that of a man.

Living species vary not only in their general levels of consciousness but also in the sensitivity of particular sense modalities; for example, a dog's sense of smell is more developed than a man's. When evaluating a species' range of awareness, one looks at the species' total ability to discriminate and to change its response to its surroundings rather than the sensitivity of a specific sense modality taken out of context. (Of course, in the case of man, his significantly better capacity for discrimination is a result of his conceptual ability.)

Is it alive or not? is the fundamental query to be posed to anything that is already in existence. Any living thing must first be assessed to determine whether it is conscious. What is the specific type of awareness that any conscious organism possesses? is the primary inquiry to be posed to it. The job and purpose of consciousness in a living entity is to guide the survival of every type of living thing that has awareness. Without consideration of the unique shape and range of consciousness of the given species, one cannot comprehend the distinctive behavior of that species. Therefore, the study of any species' psychology is the study of the traits and qualities that species possesses as a result of its unique form and range of consciousness. While psychology is interested in all sentient beings, the study of man is its main focus. The primary reason the psychologist is interested in studying other species is to provide insight on humans. The study of the traits and qualities that man possesses as a result of his unique shape and range of consciousness is known as human psychology.

Understanding the nature and effects of man's unique kind of awareness is the essential and fundamental work of psychology; this contains the key to understanding man behaviorally, motivationally, and characterologically.

The ability to reason is what defines man and sets him apart from all other living species. This entails broadening the scope of his awareness beyond the perceptual concretes that are immediately in front of him, abstracting, integrating, and grasping principles—to perceive reality at the level of consciousness conceptualization (Chapter Three).

The range of an animal is only as broad as its perceptions. The basic forms of inference that it is capable of are completely constrained by and reliant upon the physical inputs in its immediate sensory field (in the context, of course, of past experience). It is unable to think, ask questions, or project a series of inferences that are not dependent on current sensory input. However, man can map the movement of planets over the far reaches of space on the back of an envelope.

Man survives by the guidance of his unique type of consciousness, that is, by the guidance of his conceptual capacity, just like every other species that possesses awareness.

This is the first fact about human nature that needs to be understood and the foundation of any scientific study of man. It is the fundamental idea without which no part of what makes humans unique can be comprehended. Any analysis of man must start by recognizing the fact that he is a rational being with a distinctive form of conceptual consciousness, regardless of whether the subject of the inquiry is the nature of emotion, the psychology of family relationships, the causes of mental illness, the significance of productive work, the process of artistic creativity, or sexual behavior.

As a result, psychology as it relates to humans is correctly understood and described as the discipline that investigates the traits and qualities that man possesses as a result of his logical ability.

Consciousness

A quality of living things—a quality of existence at a certain stage of growth and organization—is consciousness.

A faculty and a state are both referred to as "consciousness."

"Consciousness" refers to the faculty that allows some living things to be aware of their existence. (I refer to a power or capacity as "faculty" in the Aristotelian sense.)

"Consciousness" is a state that can be defined as awareness, which is an organism's state of cognition, perception, or sensing.

There are no other notions to which the concept of consciousness as a state, the state of awareness, can be reduced. It cannot be further deconstructed or explained in terms of other conceptions. All other psychological terminology ultimately must be understood in the context of the phenomena of consciousness as one's root concept; otherwise, phrases like "thought," "idea," "perception," "imagination," "memory," "feeling," or "desire" will not make sense. One can look into the physiological underpinnings of consciousness (such as sensory receptors, afferent nerves, etc.); one can distinguish between different degrees and types of consciousness; and one can look into the neurophysiological mechanisms that underlie consciousness. However, awareness as a concept is a primary that cannot be reduced. It is a "axiomatic idea," as Ayn Rand put it. Axioms are typically thought of as statements identifying a fundamental, self-evident fact, according to the author. However, as they are composed of concepts, explicit propositions as such are not primary. Axiomatic conceptions serve as the foundation for all other concepts, axioms, assertions, and thought in human understanding.

An axiomatic concept is the identification of a fundamental truth about reality that cannot be dissected, that is, reduced to other truths or separated into its constituent elements. It is the basically assumed and directly felt or experienced, which needs neither justification nor justification, but on which all justifications and justifications lie.

"Existence," "identity" (which is a consequence of "existence"), and "awareness" are the first and fundamental foundational concepts. However, it is impossible to investigate (or "prove") existence or consciousness as such. Instead, one can research what exists and how awareness works. These primaries cannot be reduced. (Any attempt to "prove" them is futile because it amounts to "proving" existence via nonexistence and consciousness through unconsciousness.)

The fact that mental activities are linked to neuronal activity in the brain has no bearing on awareness' position as a distinct and irreducible primary. To claim that mental processes are "nothing but" neural processes—that, for instance, the perception of an object is a collection of neural impulses, or that a thought is a specific pattern of brain activity—is a type of what philosophers refer to as "the reductive error." Both a perception and the neurological mechanisms that govern it, as well as a thought and any accompanying brain activity, are distinct from one another. Such an equation is blatantly illogical and anti-empirical. According to one philosopher, "Reductive materialism holds that consciousness is a manifestation of brain activity; that it is either a fine and subtle kind of matter, or (more frequently) a form of energy, either kinetic or potential." . . . To employ meaningless language to imply that awareness is a type of substance or motion. Arguments against any given stance must frequently take the reductio ad absurdum general form. He is consequently in the fortunate position of being impervious to all arguments if he takes an initial stance that is as ludicrous as any that can be imagined. He is already absurd, thus he can never be "reduced to the absurd." Although consciousness and motion may be intricately associated, we mean different things by the two terms. Though awareness may be created by motion, we do not mean motion in the same way that we do not mean green cheese if he cannot understand this, there is no point in disputing with him. To paraphrase another thinker:

We describe a concept as being clear or unclear, appropriate or inappropriate, or clever or unfunny. Are these concepts understandable when used to describe the movements of electrons, atoms, molecules, or muscles, which, in the view of [the reductive materialist], constitute the entirety of consciousness? Can a motion be cogent, clear, or clever? What would a clear motion look like exactly? What kind of reflex is germane or cogent? Or a clever physical response? When used to describe thoughts, these descriptors are absolutely appropriate; nevertheless, when used to describe muscle or nerve motions, they instantly become ludicrous.

On the other hand, movements contain characteristics that, when applied to concepts, are unimaginable. What is the average velocity of one's opinions on a protective tariff? Movements have velocities.

Would it make appropriate to discuss the north-easterly direction of one's opinion on the ethics of retaliation? Movements have a direction.

It is true that while consciousness cannot exist independently from matter, i.e., a living body, matter can exist independently of mind. However, the idea that consciousness and matter are identical is in no way supported by this dependency of awareness on matter. Contrarily, it is only legitimate to speak of one object as dependent on another if they are not similar, as numerous critics of reductive materialism have noted.

Aristotle's depiction of awareness (and of life) in his writings is clearly superior to that of the majority of "moderns." In many ways, studying the development of philosophy from Aristotle to Descartes to the present feels like history is going backward rather than forward—almost as if most of Aristotle's followers throughout the ages were pre-Aristotelians. Aristotle does not consider consciousness to be supernatural, an incomprehensible, or an obtrusive presence in a mechanistic universe that should be exiled by reduction to the blind motion of inanimate particles, like an exile whom the authorities found obtrusive. Rather, he believes consciousness to be a natural phenomenon. According to Aristotle, consciousness is a property of some creatures and a fact of reality. In this case, he takes a much more "empirical" stance than the majority of "empiricists." His example ought to serve as a guide for others who want to engage in a rigorous scientific investigation of aware living things.

One's own consciousness is the only awareness of which one has direct and immediate knowledge. Only indirectly, inferentially, through their outward physical manifestation in action, do we know the consciousness of other entities. This does not imply that with simple introspection, one may fully understand the nature and laws of mental activity. It means that each man can only ever directly feel his own consciousness; he can never directly perceive or experience the consciousness of another being.

Because each man has his own internal psychological laboratory to which he can refer, men can communicate with one another about psychological conditions.

In order to make sense of this metaphor, let's say that a guy cannot be made to understand what it is like to see if he has never experienced it. For a man who has been blind from birth, no description of light waves, retinas, rods, and cones could have any relevance. The essential categories of consciousness can only be described extensively, or by reference to direct experience, just like the fundamental characteristics of physical objects like extension and mass. Introspective ostensive definitions are essential to any communication between men regarding the psychological realm, just as extrospective ostensive definitions are essential to any communication among men regarding the physical world. The foundation upon which all more complex concepts and subsequent, inferential knowledge are built is comprised of these extrospective and introspective observables.

The first place to learn about psychology is through introspection, and even if there were other ways to learn about psychology, none of them would be relevant or meaningful. If one didn't understand concepts like ideas, beliefs, memories, emotions, and desires to which one could relate their observations and in light of which they could interpret their findings, they would be unable to study behavior, descriptive self-reports of other men, cultures, or cultural products. (Strictly speaking, of course, it is ludicrous to think that someone could be studying anything if they were unaware of such categories.)

Although introspection is a necessary precondition and a source of psychological knowledge, neither one's own introspection nor the introspective reports of others are sufficient on their own. The study of behavior, which is one of the outer signs and expressions of mental activity, is essential to psychology. Action is regulated by consciousness. Man is neither a disembodied ghost nor an automaton; awareness cannot be fully understood without reference to conduct, and behavior cannot be entirely understood without reference to consciousness. The facts from introspection and the observations of beings in activity must be methodically combined to form cohesive knowledge in scientific psychology. A hypothesis must take into account all relevant evidence and data in order to be considered valid. This means that no significant information should be excluded from consideration.

In light of the aforementioned, it is appropriate to make a little comment on the doctrine of behaviorism, a peculiar occurrence in contemporary psychology.

The Uprising Against Consciousness

Behaviorism suggests the following program in order to purportedly establish psychology as a "genuine science," on par with the physical sciences: to do away with the idea of consciousness, to do away with any interest in "mythical" mental states, and to study only an organism's behavior—i.e., to limit psychology to the study of physical motions. Because of this, a historian of psychology who wrote on behaviorism appropriately titled his chapter "Psychology out of its Mind." 5

The terms "methodological behaviorism" and "radical behaviorism" are occasionally used interchangeably. Radical behaviorism, which maintains that the mind is a sequence of physical responses, such as muscular and glandular reactions, is an explicit kind of reductive materialism. This doctrine's obvious unacceptability has already been mentioned. Methodological behaviorism proponents commonly denounce this theory as "unsophisticated" and "philosophical." They insist that their version of behaviorism is purely procedural, holds that consciousness—whatever that might be—is not an object of scientific study, and that scientific psychology must limit itself to an analysis of observed behavior without reference to mentalistic data or any concepts derived through introspection. They claim that their version of behaviorism makes no metaphysical commitment whatsoever.

However, a methodology must be appropriate for its subject in order to be valid. As a result, it unavoidably implies an understanding of the nature of its subject. According to methodological behaviorism, behavior of the creatures that psychology examines can be understood independently of consciousness. And it is obvious that this is a metaphysical viewpoint.

Methodological behaviorists might want to downplay their materialism. The doctrine of epiphenomenalism, which holds that consciousness is merely an incidental by-product of physical processes (much like smoke is an incidental by-product of a locomotive) and that conscious events have no causal efficacy, neither with regard to bodily events nor to other mental events, i.e., one's thoughts do not have the power to affect either one's actions or one's subsequent thoughts, is what their doctrine ultimately amounts to. Epiphenomenalism's proponents are thus compelled to hold the view that human history would have been exactly the same if nobody had ever been conscious of anything, if nobody had ever had any perceptions, or if nobody had ever thought. Epiphenomenalism isn't any more logically sound than reductive materialism as a philosophical theory, and neither is particularly compelling when put through even a rudimentary logical investigation.

In all practical senses, there is no distinction between these two behaviorism variants. They both concur that consciousness has no bearing on psychology or behavior; this is the crux of their argument.

The behaviorist has been notably reticent to state the consequences that flow from his theory. He hasn't felt compelled to say, for example, "Nothing I may think, understand, or perceive (whatever these terms mean) bears any causal relation to the things I do, or the theories I advocate, since phenomena of consciousness are illusory or irrelevant to explanations of behavior, and since this includes my behavior."

The irresistible temptation is to agree with someone who professes a theory that essentially asserts either that he is not conscious or that it doesn't matter whether he is conscious or not to him (or to others).

Numerous authors, representing the widest range of perspectives, have revealed the arbitrariness, the inconsistencies, and the epistemic barbarism of the behaviorist theory. 6 It is not necessary to go over their objections again here.

In keeping with their typical practice of ignoring aspects of reality that they find it inconvenient to consider, behaviorists have largely chosen to disregard these objections rather than attempt to respond to them.

The psychologist's use of introspection is the main target of the behaviorists' criticism. They contend as follows: Because the physical sciences, which are far more developed, do not use introspection, psychology should give up on introspection and adopt their methods. It should, like physics, study the actions of material entities, i.e., study observable behavior. Psychology has failed to establish itself as a science or to produce any genuine knowledge; the fault lies in the psychologist's reliance on introspection.

This program has resulted in a plethora of "experiments" and "measurements" on the part of behaviorists, with just one distinction from the physical sciences: behaviorists are infamous for being unsure of what their experiments are meant to achieve, what they are measuring, why they are measuring it, or what they expect to know once their measurements are complete. Their program has had no real practical success. (This does not imply that every experiment carried out by a proponent of behaviorism has been worthless; rather, it means that any value it may have has no intrinsic connection to the behaviorist thesis, i.e., the experiment was not dependent on or required of the experimenter to be a behaviorist.) The first people to realize that psychology necessitates, among other things, the study of behavior under experimentally controlled conditions were hardly behaviorists.

It is true that psychology hasn't succeeded in becoming a recognized branch of science, and it is also true that traditional introspectionists like Wundt, Titchener, and those associated with the so-called Würzburg school had significant misconceptions about the goals, techniques, and nature of psychology. However, the behaviorist approach symbolizes the denial of psychology as such, not a solution or a step in the right direction.

Behaviorism, despite its pretense of representing scientific objectivity, actually reflects a retreat into methodological subjectivism. Being objective is focusing only on the facts and removing one's hopes, fears, or desires from cognitive attention. Objectivity is based on the idea that facts are what they are and are not influenced by the viewpoints of those who see them. Therefore, if a scientist decides to investigate a particular aspect of reality, objectivity demands that he adapt his research methods to the nature of the field being investigated; ends determine means; he does not, arbitrarily, because it suits his convenience, choose certain research methods and then rule that only those facts are relevant that are amenable to his methods.

Nobody, not even the behaviorist, can avoid the awareness that (a) he is conscious and (b) this is a reality about himself of the utmost significance, a fact that is essential to any meaningful account of his behavior. The behaviorist is not justified in trying to bring the entire field down to the level of his inadequacy if he is not up to the task of formulating scientific epistemological principles for the use of introspection and for the integration of introspective data with psychological data obtained by other means. Subjectivism is the arbitrary definition of the nature of conscious organisms in order to support a particular research methodology.

Behaviorists frequently make the claim that because states of consciousness are "private" and therefore not "publicly observable," they cannot be the object of objective, scientific knowledge. This is an epistemological fallacy that they did not invent but is now widely accepted among psychologists and philosophers.

Consciousness phenomena are "private" in the sense that was previously mentioned, i.e., a man can only directly experience his own consciousness. However, as was also mentioned, the conclusions a psychologist draws about the nature and functions of consciousness based on his introspection may be verified by his coworkers who also use introspection, just as one scientist verifies the reported results of another by duplicating the other's experiment in his own laboratory. Physical scientists also occasionally differ with psychologists regarding what they see or the proper interpretation of what they perceive. The approach to resolving such discrepancies is, in general, the same: conduct additional research, compare data more carefully, define terms more precisely, examine additional, potentially pertinent facts, assess their conclusions in light of their other knowledge, and look for inconsistencies or non sequiturs in their reports.

The truthfulness of one's conclusions—that is, whether they are consistent with reality's facts—and the soundness of one's reasoning behind them—rather than their origin in "publicly viewable" data—are what determine their objectivity. A conclusion reached via logic can be verified by other men, making it "publicly verifiable" in this sense. However, the terms "objective" and "publicly observable" (or "verifiable") are not interchangeable.

Despite what men may learn from one another, each man is an epistemic outlier; learning does not take place in a group setting. A hundred unreliable, non-objective judgements will not produce an objective, reliable conclusion if one man's judgment is faulty and subjective since it is his own.

The mystery surrounding the "publicly observable" is over.

In modern psychology and philosophy, there is a tendency to view consciousness or the mind with suspicion and hostility as a troubling, "unnatural" phenomenon that must be explained away or, at the very least, excluded from the domain of what is scientifically knowable. The behaviorist attack on consciousness is simply the extreme of this trend.

Mystics have maintained for ages that phenomena of consciousness are beyond the purview of logic and science. The proponents of the anti-modern mind's " science" theory concur. They declare that they are defenders of reason and opponents of supernaturalism, but in reality, they are giving man's consciousness over to mysticism by saying that only insentient matter is "natural." They've given the mystics triumph that they couldn't have obtained on their own.

A truly scientific psychology must recover the human mind as an appropriate subject of rational research in order to combat such neomysticism.

CHAPTER TWO

Man: A Living Being

Capabilities and Needs

All living things, from the simplest unicellular animal to man, the most complex of all organisms, have a distinctive structure, the parts of which work to maintain the structure's integrity and sustain the life of the organism.

It has been correctly stated that an organism is an integrate rather than an aggregate. An organism dies when it stops carrying out the processes necessary to preserve its structural integrity. Dissolution is what death is. When an organism dies, all that is left is a collection of chemical molecules that are decaying.

Action is essential for all living things to survive. Life is motion, a cycle of self-sustaining activity that an organism needs to maintain at all times in order to survive. Both the straightforward energy conversions of a plant and the extensive, intricate activities of a person demonstrate this principle. In terms of biology, idleness equals death. An organism must take action, both internally (such as during the metabolism process) and externally (such as during the food-seeking process).

In essence, all self-preserving behavior follows the same pattern: an organism maintains itself by using resources from its environment, modifying or rearranging them to create resources for its own survival.

Think of the metabolic processes—nutrition, respiration, and synthesis—and the associated bodily processes that make up metabolism.

The raw materials that the organism requires are introduced into its system through the process of nutrition; energy is then extracted from these materials through the process of respiration (oxidation); a portion of this energy is then used in the process of synthesis, which changes the raw materials into structural elements of living matter. The organism's ability to maintain itself is continued thanks to the remaining energy and all of the structural elements. All living things are characterized by metabolism.

The activity of harnessing a waterfall to obtain the electric energy required to power a factory engaged in the manufacture of farm equipment, clothing, automobiles, or drugs is a peculiar example of the larger principle involved. Although the action in this instance is behavioral rather than metabolic and external rather than internal, the fundamental idea of life remains the same.

Life is contingent, and the possibility of death always exists for an organism. It must meet a number of requirements in order to survive. It needs to come up with the biologically sensible course of action. The characteristics of the specific organism determine the appropriate course of action. Different species have different means of surviving.

By using its resources to meet its needs, an organism maintains itself. A species' capabilities and needs must be considered in order to fully comprehend the actions that are both possible for and distinctive to that species. These make up its fundamental behavioral context.

In this context, "need" and "capacity" refer to that which is inherent and universal to the species, not to that which is acquired and particular to the individual. "Need" and "capacity" are used in their basic, metaphysical sense (by "metaphysical," I mean: pertaining to the nature of things).

The things that an organism naturally needs for life and wellbeing, or for the efficient continuation of the life-process, are what are known as the organism's needs. The inherent potential for action within an organism is defined as its capacities.

The idea of capacities and needs is essential to both biology and psychology. Biology is concerned with the capabilities and needs of living things as physical beings. The needs and abilities of living things as conscious entities are the focus of psychology.

In the same way that man has particular psychological needs due to his distinctive form of consciousness, his conceptual faculty, he also has particular psychological capacities due to this same faculty. Some of these demands will be covered in Part Two.

When a physical or psychological need is not met, the organism is at danger of suffering discomfort, disability, or even destruction. The degree of the temporal urgency and the nature of the harm that needs may represent, however, differ amongst them. Although the principle holds for all wants, it is more readily apparent in the case of bodily demands.

(a) Man needs both food and oxygen to survive, but he can only go for a short period of time without one of them. While both are necessities, a man can go much longer without water than without vitamin C. Sometimes a need is unmet and the person dies right away, but other times it can take years.

(b) Man needs to keep his body temperature at a specific level, and he has internal adaptive mechanisms that allow him to respond to changes in the environment. If he is exposed to temperatures that are too high for his adaptive mechanisms to handle, he will experience pain and eventually pass away within a few hours. As with lack of oxygen, food, etc., the disastrous effects of need and frustration are immediate and obvious in such a situation. However, there are some cases of need-frustration where the path to disaster is much less clear-cut. Man, for instance, requires calcium, and there are parts of Mexico where the soil is devoid of calcium. Although these people do not completely perish, their growth is stunted, they are generally weak, and they are susceptible to a variety of diseases because of the calcium deficiency. Their general capacity to function is compromised. A need-frustration can therefore undermine an organism's overall ability to survive and make it more susceptible to destruction from a variety of sources rather than directly causing the organism's demise. (This idea is crucial to keep in mind when thinking about how psychological needs are frustrated; we will be reminded of it in Chapter Twelve.)

Science learns about human needs by observing what happens when those needs aren't met. Needs make their presence known by way of signs of discomfort, ailment, and death. (It is difficult to imagine how scientists would be able to isolate and identify something if a need were, in some way, always and everywhere satisfied automatically—if no one ever suffered from any frustration of the need.)

Even when symptoms do appear, identifying the underlying need-deprivation is frequently difficult. It took scientists a long time to link a lack of green vegetables to the deaths of men from scurvy, and only relatively recently did they discover that the essential component provided by the vegetables is Vitamin C.

Given that the human body is an integrated system, it is not surprising that, at times, physical needs are not met, which can lead to psychological symptoms as well as vice versa. As an illustration of the first, consider the hallucinations and memory loss that can be brought on by a thiamin deficiency. Any psychosomatic illness, such as peptic ulcers, migraine headaches, etc., serves as an illustration of the second.

The idea of need arises from the fact that life is conditional. If a being were unbreakable and did not face the choice between life and death, it would not require anything. The idea might not be appropriate for it. The idea of need could not exist without the idea of life.

"Need" implies the existence of a purpose, outcome, or end: the organism's survival. Therefore, one must show that something is a necessary condition for the organism's survival and well-being in order to maintain its status as a physical or psychological need.

While many psychologists are aware of this fact, biologists are not. They attribute to man a vast range of psychological requirements without providing any evidence to support their assertions, as if positing needs were a matter of free will. They hardly ever explain the criteria by which they determine what is and is not a need, nor do they explain how or why their lists of supposed wants are necessitated by the nature of man as a living entity.

Various psychologists have claimed that among the things that men have as inherent needs are the need to dominate other men, submit to a leader, bargain, gamble, gain social status, snub someone, be hostile, be unconventional, be a conformist, degrade oneself, boast, murder, and experience pain.

It is important to note that these so-called needs are believed by their proponents to be inherent and common to the entire human species.

A need is not the same as a wish or a desire. It is not always true that anything symbolizes a need that is fundamental in human nature just because many men may desire it. Needs must be tangibly discernible. This ought to be clear. However, few facts have been more carelessly disregarded by psychologists as a whole.

Sigmund Freud's theory of the "death instinct" was one of the most remarkable "needs" ever put forth by a psychologist. 1 Freud claimed that instincts—specifically, the life instinct and the death instinct—can be used to explain human behavior. According to Freud, the latter is more potent because all men do pass away in the end. The urge to "return" to an inorganic state, to "reestablish a state of things which was disturbed by the emergence of life," is present in every cell of the human body, according to the author, who claims that these instincts represent innate biological needs. Man has a biological need to suffer and die. 2

This theory serves as an extreme example of what can happen when psychologists allow themselves to make assumptions about needs without taking into account the context in which those assumptions are made and the criteria used to determine what constitutes a need. The postulate of a death instinct, a need to die, or a need to experience pain is utterly meaningless. A need is something an organism needs for its survival; the result of frustrating a need is pain and/or death. The idea of a biological need can only have meaning if life is taken as the ultimate goal. The idea of a need to die is absurd, just like the idea of a square circle.

Nature threatens man with pain and death if he doesn't meet his actual needs, but what does nature threaten him with if he doesn't meet his purported need for pain and death?

It is grotesque anthropomorphism to jump from the observation that all living things die to the conclusion that every cell in a man's body has the "will to die." An organism cannot "return" to non-existence, it cannot be "disturbed" by the emergence of itself, and it cannot feel the urge to "return" to an inorganic condition or "to re-establish a state of things which was disturbed by the emergence of life," which is the most egregious example of a logic error. One of the most embarrassing works in the entire body of psychological literature is without a doubt Beyond the Pleasure Principle, the monograph in which Freud outlines his theory of the death instinct.

Biology has made significant strides in this direction, but the process of isolating and classifying man's bodily demands is still far from being finished. Psychology is in a state of disarray when it comes to the duty of distinguishing and recognizing man's mental demands.

However, this disarray highlights the necessity to understand the nature of human desires. Not all needs are obvious. Alleged needs must be supported by comparison to the necessities for human survival.

It cannot be argued that man has psychological needs. The prevalence of mental illnesses is proof that both demands exist (and are being resisted) and that psychology has failed to comprehend the nature of these needs.

Needs, Objectives, and "Intuitions"

In his quest to comprehend the fundamentals of human behavior, the psychologist notices that (a) man has a variety of requirements as a biological being, and (b) that (c) man typically acts to satisfy a variety of ends or objectives.

The necessity of action, or goal-seeking, is a result of the existence of needs. This notion holds true even when a man chooses goals that are incompatible with his requirements, leading him to pursue a path toward self-destruction.

To bridge the gap between wants and goals, to trace the processes from the former to the latter, and to understand the connection between them, i.e., to comprehend how needs are converted into goals, may be stated as the fundamental problem of motivational psychology.

It should be clear that taking into account the unique abilities of man is necessary for finding a solution to this issue. However, motivated psychology's history largely represents an effort to ignore man's most distinctly human ability, his conceptual faculty, and to explain his behavior without taking into account the fact that he can reason or that his mind is his primary means of survival.

One variant of this effort is the behaviorist vision of man as a stimulus-response mechanism. Another is the idea that man is a conscious automaton that is driven by instincts.

Many psychologists use the notion of "instinct," a phrase that denotes nothing scientifically understandable while giving the appearance of causal insight, to serve the same purpose that the concept of "devil" served for the prehistoric savage and the concept of "God" serves for the theologian. When a primitive couldn't understand something, he "explained" it by positing a demon; when a theologian couldn't understand anything, he "explains" it by positing a God; when many psychologists couldn't understand something, they "explain" it by positing an instinct.

The idea of "instinct" seeks to connect wants and objectives without using the cognitive (i.e., reasoning and learning) faculties of man. As a result, it stands for one of the worst and most fruitless attempts to address the motivational issues.

The eighteenth, nineteenth, and early twentieth centuries saw a significant interest for instinct theory. It remains a key tenet of the (orthodox) Freudian school of psychoanalysis, despite the fact that it has been losing ground over the past few decades.

Instinct theorists concluded that the origins of some behaviors are innate, unchosen, and unlearned inclinations that compel man to act as he does after observing specific behaviors they considered to be typical of the human species. They discussed several instincts, such as a survival instinct, maternal instinct, acquisitive instinct, pugnacity instinct, and so on. They competed with one another to compile lists of the instincts their particular theory assumed man to possess, promising to account thereby for the fundamental causes of all human action. They rarely attempted to define precisely what they understood an instinct to be, much less to explain how it functioned.

The three most well-known of these theorists were Sigmund Freud, William McDougall, and William James. "Instinct is... the faculty of behaving in such a way as to accomplish particular goals, without foreknowledge of the ends, and without prior education in the performance," writes James. Then, writes McDougall, "We may," "Define instinct as an inherited or innate psycho-physical disposition that determines its possessor to perceive and pay attention to objects of a certain class, to experience an emotional thrill of a particular quality upon perceiving such an object, and to act in regard to it in a particular manner, or, at least, to experience an impulse to such action." If these definitions aren't particularly helpful, Freud's formulation stands out for its obscurity. Instinct, according to Freud, is "a borderland concept between the mental and the physical, being both the mental representative of the stimuli emanating from within the organism and penetrating to the mind, and at the same time a measure of the demand made upon the energy of the latter as a result of its connection with the body." This is the closest Freud ever gets to a definition, despite the crucial importance instincts play in his system.

That enigmatic power known as "instinct" is not a cognition, an action, an emotion, or a desire. It has been determined that certain theorists' attempt to classify an instinct as a "compound reflex" is illogical and has fallen apart. Reflexes are distinct, measurable neurophysiological phenomena whose existence can be scientifically shown; they are not merely a repository for unrecognized behavior.

The only thing that can be gained from explaining man's behavior in terms of intangible "instincts" is the admission that one does not understand why he behaves the way he does. When men engage in sexual activity, we can infer that they have a "sex instinct"; when men seek food when they are hungry, we can infer that they have a "hunger instinct"; when some men act destructively, we can infer that they have a "destructive instinct"; when men typically seek out one another's company, we can infer that they have a "gregarious instinct." But these inferences don't actually explain anything. Putting oneself in the same epistemic category as the doctor in the tale who "explains" to a devastated mother that the reason her infant won't drink milk is that "the child is just not a milk-drinker" is all it takes to qualify for this claim.

The history of instinct theory over the past 50 years is one of intense efforts on the part of its proponents to distort language, their formulations, and reality in order to defend their doctrines from science's growing recognition that traits and behaviors thought to be "instinctive" are either (a) not inherent to the species but rather a result of specific men's acquired attitudes or beliefs, as in the case of pugnacity; (b) not inherent to the species but rather a product of particular men's

The idea of "instinct" was first employed to explain intricate animal behavioral patterns that seemed to defy explanation, like migratory, mating, and maternal behavior. But when extended to animals, the idea is just as false.

Animal behavior can be classified into three general types, in theory. 1. Reflexes are actions that are neurophysiological reactions to physical stimuli and do not require the faculty of consciousness, as the patellar reflex (knee jerk) in response to tendon strain. 2. Behaviors that entail the faculty of consciousness but not a process of learning and are directly influenced by an animal's pleasure-pain sensory system, such as going toward warmth. (Some students of animal behavior use the term "instinct" exclusively to designate behavior of this second category; when so restricted in meaning, the use of the term may be justified; however, I am inclined to think it unwise, given the many other meanings historically associated with the term; at any rate, when I speak of "instinct" in this discussion, I refer to the term as it is commonly used by clinical psychologists and personality theorists—to cover a goo 3. Learning-driven behaviors, such as fighting and hunting. (Occasionally, and this is particularly pertinent to allegedly instinctive behavior, the learning is instantaneous, within a given context, and is practically inescapable to all normal members of a species; this is "one trial" learning; for example, avoiding a traumatically painful stimulus after one encounter.)

None of these categories, or (more frequently) any mix of them, have been used to describe animal behavior.

When one analyzes the intricate goal-seeking behavior of man, the shortcomings of "explanation by instincts" become even more clear.

Although man is born with needs, he does not come into the world knowing what those needs are or how to meet them. Given the right physical conditions, the function of his internal organs can automatically meet some of his more basic, vegetative body-maintenance needs. For example, his respiratory system can automatically provide oxygen when that need arises. However, the vast majority of his more complex needs—those that call for the coordinated action of his entire entity in relation to the outside world—are not met on an automatic basis. Food, shelter, and clothing are not things that man acquires "by instinct." To cultivate food, construct a shelter, or weave cloth, one needs awareness, freedom of choice, discrimination, and judgment. The body of a man is incapable of acting independently of his consciousness, knowledge, and values in order to pursue such objectives, to purposefully rearrange natural elements, or to reshape matter.

The realization of a value is the goal of every meaningful action. Only when something is chosen (in some way) as a value can it become an object of action.

Value and action are mutually implied and necessary: it is in the nature of a value to require action in order to realize and/or maintain it; it is also in the nature of a consciously initiated action to have the realization and/or maintenance of a value as its motive and purpose.

Values, however, are not innate. Man cannot have an innate understanding of what is true or false, what is for him or against him, what should be pursued or avoided, or what is beneficial for him or harmful.

Man may experience tension, unease, or pain as a result of unmet demands, which may lead him to take physiologically sensible measures like defending himself from the weather. But it is essential to understand what the right course of action is; this cannot be avoided.

Man's body only sends signals of pain or pleasure; it does not inform him of the causes of these sensations or how to get rid of them. His mind needs to learn that.

Man must learn what to do to survive since he lacks the "instinct of self-preservation." Man's ability to think is what allowed him to make fire, build bridges, perform surgery, and create a telescope—not an instinct.

And if a man chooses not to think—if he chooses to risk his life in needless dangers, to close his eyes rather than open his mind at the sight of any problem, to seek solace from the responsibility of reason in alcohol or drugs, to act willfully stubbornly against his own objective self-interest—he has no instinct that will force his mind to function, no instinct that will compel him to value his life enough to do the thinking and take the actions which will save it.

The eloquent denial and mockery of the idea that man has a natural instinct for self-preservation is provided by the blatantly self-destructive behaviors that so many men engage in as well as the suicidal course that has characterized so much of human history.

Freud sought to resolve the conundrum by asserting that, in addition to having a life instinct, man also has a death instinct after realizing some of the challenges that an alleged instinct for self-preservation presents. This theory has mostly lost its credibility. However, Freud's fellow instinct theorists have no right to mock him. If one is determined to explain human behavior using instincts and believes that man has a self-preservation instinct (as almost all instinct theorists do), one may feel compelled to propose a conflicting death instinct in order to explain men's actions.

If there is such a thing as an "instinct," it must be some kind of innate, automatic knowledge, some kind of frozen knowledge imprinted in the nervous system at birth. Thus, instinct theory amounts to a revival of the doctrine of innate ideas, which has been thoroughly debunked by biology and philosophy as a mystic legacy.

The mythology of instinct is harmful to scientific theory because, by providing a phony justification, it puts an end to future research and prevents us from truly knowing what motivates human conduct. As the final, dying convulsion of medieval demonology, it ought to be ignored.

Motivational psychology calls for an understanding of the consequences of the fact that man's rational faculty is his biological distinctiveness and fundamental tool of need-satisfaction instead of recourse to such archaic abstractions.

CHAPTER THREE
Man: A Rational Being

Mind

The term "consciousness" refers to a state, specifically the state of being conscious or aware of some aspect of reality, in its most fundamental sense. The ability to be aware of reality is a human faculty that is implied by the word "consciousness" in a derivative sense.

The idea of "mind" is more constrained than "consciousness" and is related with the "rational faculty" or "reason" in particular. This relationship is the key to understanding its significance and proper implementation.

Many animal species exhibit consciousness in varied degrees or forms (and perhaps all). But only a man can undertake explicit conceptual integrations while being directed by logic. Man's unique type of awareness is composed of his conceptual or intellectual faculties. The term "mind" refers to this type of consciousness.

In contrast to the types of consciousness exhibited by lesser species, "mind" refers particularly to man's consciousness (or form of consciousness).

The Level of Conceptual Consciousness

The listener is highly likely to assume that someone is interested in studying man with his head removed, that is, without reference to his mind or his capacity for conceptual reasoning, if they hear someone advocating for a biologically oriented or biocentric psychology.

The behavioristic, physicalistic, or "guillotine" approach to treating people, however, is fundamentally antibiological. The nature of a species' unique means of survival is of utmost importance to the biologist studying that species since, as he or she is aware, it is the key to understanding that species' behavior. In the case of man, it is evident that the use of his conceptual ability is his unique method of interacting with reality and of continuing to exist. His capacity for thought is the source and enabler of all of his singular accomplishments, including his understanding of science, his contributions to technology and industry, his work in the arts, culture, and social institutions, among others. His capacity for thought is what keeps him alive. Therefore, a biocentric perspective requires that the conceptual capacity of man be given top priority in the analysis of his behavior.

The ultimate source of all knowledge is the evidence of reality provided by one's senses. Man acquires knowledge by stimulating his countless sensory receptors, and this knowledge travels to his brain as emotions (primary sensory inputs). These sensory inputs do not, by themselves, constitute knowledge; rather, they are only the building blocks of it. The human brain naturally records and combines these events to produce perceptions. Perceptions, which are the cornerstone and basis of human knowledge, are the direct awareness of entities, their actions, and their attributes.

In Chapter Two's study of the nature of living things, we learned that an organism maintains its physical integrity by acquiring resources from its surroundings, rearranging them, and reaching a new integration that transforms these resources into the organism's means of survival. An analogous phenomenon can be seen in the way a consciousness perceives reality. Integration is the fundamental idea of knowledge, just as it is the fundamental idea of life. This principle is in play when, in the brains of humans or other animals, various sensations are automatically stored and combined (by nature's "programming," in effect) in a way that results in a perceptual awareness of entities—an awareness that both humans and other animals need to survive. However, in this case, the integration is not automated or "coded" by nature; rather, conceptual integration must be accomplished voluntarily by man. (The notion of integration is important, as we shall see, to the process of concept-formation as well.)

The question of whether any animals that serve as our subordinates are able to comprehend even the most fundamental ideas has been debated. In his scholarly work The Difference of Man and the Difference It Presents, Mortimer J. Adler presents a detailed examination and analysis of the facts and reasoning on both sides of the debate and advances a convincing argument against it. He has, in my opinion, made a strong argument for why no other animal should be given credit for concepts and that only humans are actually capable of conceptual reasoning.

That is extremely unlikely, even if the simplest conscious animals are capable of perception. They can only register and react to dispersed, unretained, and unintegrated experiences, which is the most plausible explanation.

The higher forms of conscious life, including man, have the ability to produce unique, unrelated percepts as well as "perceptual residues" and "perceptual abstractions." Perceptual residues (also known as perceptual traces) are "memory-images that work representatively, i.e., in place of sensory inputs that are no longer themselves operative." Perceptual abstraction is the ability of an animal to recognize similarities and distinctions among sensory details, to understand that some sensible details are of the same kind and are distinct from other sensible details. This skill enables animals under human control to exhibit the highest levels of "intelligence." This skill does not, however, by itself imply or necessitate the ability to construct concepts, which includes being able to both recognize and explicitly state what constitutes a category of sensible particulars that a set of particulars fall under.

In this excellent essay, Adler explores the idea of perceptual abstractions: When an animal, for example, has cultivated the disposition to distinguish between triangles and circles, regardless of variations in their size, shape, color, or location, as well as whether or not they are composed of continuous lines or dots, this cultivated disposition in the animal is the perceptual attainment I have dubbed a perceptual abstraction. In other words, when a triangular shape or a red patch is not truly present and perceptually experienced, the animal does not use its acquired disposition to classify those shapes as triangles or those hues as red. Never without an appropriate sensory stimulation, this disposition is inactive. Only when it is.

What is the nature of the enormous intellectual advancement that occurs as the human capacity for concept formation develops? What is the nature of the progression from the capacity to form the concept of "green," from the capacity to perceive various objects of various shades of green, from the capacity to perceive individual chairs and form the concept of "chair," and from the capacity to perceive individual men and form the concept of "man"?

It is important to understand the great limitations of an entirely perceptual type of awareness in order to fully comprehend the nature of the enormous boost in intellectual strength made possible by man's conceptualizing abilities. Any consciousness, whether it be human or animal, can only hold a limited number of units in its field of awareness at any given time. A consciousness' capacity to amass or broaden its knowledge is severely constrained if it is limited to the sensible particulars it can immediately observe. Under humans, all animals are in this condition.

The capacity to develop or acquire a system of symbols that represents these various classes, such that a single symbol, held in a man's mind, can stand for an infinite number of particulars, and the ability to organize numerous particulars into groups or classes based on a distinguishing characteristic (or characteristics) they share, are two related factors that aid in the rise to the conceptual level of consciousness.

Concept-formation is a method of categorization. Language is a system of symbols.

Let's use the notion of "chair," one of a child's first and most basic concepts, as an example. His visual perception of multiple things' similarities, particularly in shape, and how those similarities set them apart from all other objects constitutes the first stage. On a visual, nonverbal level, he is aware of the likeness, and his mind scrambles for a means to record it permanently. The first representation of that awareness is a hazy vision, which omits many of the differences between the chairs he has noticed (such, for example, color) while maintaining a rough idea of the crucial trait they all have. The next stage is when he picks up the term "chair" from his elders for that specific kind of thing (or class of objects). He can now hold that awareness in his mind in a far more solid way than he previously could, when it could only be captured as an image. When and if he discovers what a "chair" is, the process is complete. A definition directly and verbally states the basic characteristic(s) of a group of entities, based on which those entities are distinguished from all other entities and grouped into a single class.

Even though the concept at hand is extremely straightforward, we can still see the essence of the concept-formation process in the example above. It entails the mental act of categorizing a group of existing things based on a characteristic—an attribute—that those things exhibit and that sets them apart from all other existing things. (An aspect of an entity is said to have a "attribute" if it can be conceptually separated for identification purposes but cannot exist independently of the entity; examples include shape, color, length, and weight.) Although the notion in this case was initially signified by a visual image, this is not a necessary step in the concept-formation process and happens most frequently among young children (and in the mind of primitive men). The majority of concepts are learned directly through language, without the need for a visual or other non-linguistic sign as an intermediate.

Understanding the similarities and differences among existing things (entities, qualities, actions, and relationships) is the first step in the concept-formation process. Next comes an explicit identification of the nature of those similarities and differences. Concept formation entails a discrimination and integration process. Discrimination involves the mental ability to abstract, or to isolate, separate, and think about a certain quality or feature of something existing. The ability of the mind to remember several occurrences of these abstracted concretes, relate them, and combine them into a unified awareness that is symbolized in consciousness is what integration entails. As we've seen, this unification happens at a basic level via a non-linguistic symbol. It is accomplished using a properly defined word on a mature level, as a completely completed concept.

When a concept is established, it no longer only relates to the specific concretes that happened to give rise to it; it also refers to all concretes that have the implicated differentiating characteristic(s)—all concretes of this kind that exist now, have ever existed, or will ever exist.

At the first level, the concepts of man are divided into a number of categories of concretes that are perceptually visible.

This level is the foundation for the far more complex and extensive system of thoughts that grows from it. Man, on the other hand, continues to integrate his narrower concepts into wider concepts, and then his wider concepts into yet wider concepts (again, through isolating and integrating specific traits). On the other hand, he keeps honing his knowledge by classifying or grouping generalizations into more precise categories.

When a person progresses from the concepts of "chair," "table," and "bed" to the concept of "furniture," by integrating such additional concepts as "household goods," by integrating such additional concepts as "automobile," he eventually reaches the still wider concept of "manufactured utilitarian objects." This is an example of the first process, the integration of narrower concepts into wider ones. When a person proceeds from the generic notion of "tree" to the classification of different sorts of trees, such as "oak," "birch," "maple," etc., they are engaging in the second process, which involves subdividing broad concepts into more specific ones.

As we've already established, language serves as a tool for man to remember and communicate his thoughts.

Language is a systematic system of auditory-visual symbols that aids in the clear, concise retention of concepts. Words, i.e., single units that stand for an unlimited number of specifics, enable the human mind to keep and deal with broad categories of entities, qualities, actions, and relationships. If he had to create mental images of every concrete that fit under those categories, this achievement would be impossible. "Matter," "energy," "freedom," and "justice," which the human mind is unable to comprehend or hold if forced to envision all the perceptual concretes these notions indicate, are examples of enormous, intricate concepts that words help people understand.

Man requires symbols to remember and identify his ideas, but he also needs a structured system of language symbols. The exactitude, clarity, and complexity of his thought processes could never be achieved with a random collection of pictures or other non-linguistic symbols.

The capacity to view concretes as instances or units of the class to which they belong is a requirement of the conceptual mode of functioning and is crucial to the concept-forming process. The capacity to view entities as units is man's unique style of cognition, according to Ayn Rand in a stunningly creative explanation of the nature of concept-formation. . . .

A unit is an entity that is thought of as a distinct member of a group of two or more comparable individuals.

An idea is the mental integration of two or more components that are separated based on a certain characteristic (or characteristics) and joined by a particular definition.

There are certain things that a man can never have all of his conscious awareness focused on at once. His conceptual faculty's ability to condense a large amount of information into a manageable number of units is the essence of his cognitive strength.

Integration of sensations into perceptions is automatic, whereas integration of perceptions into concepts is not. This voluntary process must be initiated, maintained, and controlled by man (Chapter Four). Perceptual knowledge is the given and the self-evident, whereas conceptual knowledge is a freely started process of reason. I'll quote Miss Rand once more: "Reason" is the ability to perceive and integrate the data provided by a person's senses. Despite being a rational animal, man does not always act in a logical manner. Instead, it means that his ability to reason—his capacity to understand reality on the conceptual level of awareness—is his most distinguishing characteristic, the thing that truly sets him apart from other creatures. One quality that sets him apart in that talent is his ability to talk in propositions.

One of man's most important benefits from having a conceptual faculty is the capacity for self-awareness. No other species is able to analyze its own mental activity, to keep track of and consider its own thought processes, to decide that a certain thought process is irrational or unreasonable—inappropriate for the task of understanding reality—and to alter its following thought processes in response.

Man's capacity for conceptual thought, which gives him special stature, also drives him to meet special obstacles.

No other animal has a conscious awareness of the problem of life or death that all organisms face. No other animal is conscious of its own impending death or has the ability to lengthen its life by learning new things. No other animal has the capacity to think and plan in terms of a life span, and no other species has the obligation to consider its actions in terms of the long-term effects for its own life. No other animal has the capacity to constantly work to increase its knowledge and raise the level of its existence, much alone the duty to do so.

No other animal has to deal with the questions, "Who am I?" How should I approach living? What guidelines should I use to direct my actions? What objectives should I pursue? What is the purpose of my life? What kind of person should I try to become?

The requirement of dealing with these problems is fundamental to the "human condition"—to everything that makes man's life unique. The conceptual form of awareness is a result of all of man's singular accomplishments and all of his prospective issues. We'll talk about some of these repercussions on the pages that follow.

CHAPTER FOUR

Man: A Being with Free Will

The Concept of Volition

Apart from the arbitrariness of so many of their assertions, the majority of contemporary psychological theories share the trait of their frequent and ponderous irrelevance. The cause of their apparent exponents' apparent assumption that one may have a science of human nature while continually ignoring man's most important and distinguishing characteristics is the source of both their irrelevance and arbitrariness.

Epistemological rehabilitation is urgently needed in psychology today. For instance, it shouldn't be necessary to show out the flaws in the argument that all learning is random trial-and-error learning by putting a rat in a maze where only random trial-and-error learning is feasible and then using the rat's behavior as proof of the theory. It should be even less necessary to bring out the flaws in adopting the fundamental assumption behind these experiments: the illogical and blatantly irrational idea that human learning can be understood by examining the behavior of rats.

Man is the subject that is most obviously absent from the writings of contemporary psychologists, whether or not the authors have a penchant for studying rats (or pigeons, or earthworms). Even today's most comprehensive textbooks fail to mention that man is capable of thought; when they do, they dismiss the idea as irrelevant. These works would not teach one that man's unique type of consciousness is conceptual or that this is a fact of fundamental importance. One would not discover that the ability to reason is both a naturally unique trait of humans and their primary means of survival.

The first of two fundamental aspects of man's nature that are essential to comprehending his psychology and behavior is the relationship between reason and survival. The second is that using one's rational faculties is not automatic, unlike using one's senses in an animal, and that choosing to think is not physiologically "wired" in humans. These are the words that Ayn Rand used to express this idea:

The fact that man is a being with volitional consciousness is the key to "human nature," Thinking is not a mechanical process, reason does not operate automatically, and logic does not come to us pre-wired. Your stomach, lungs, and heart all work automatically, but your mind does not. You are free to consider or to avoid that effort at any time and in any situation of your life. The dilemma of "to be or not to be" is equivalent for you, a human being, to the question of "to think or not to think." This is because you are not free to escape from your nature, from the fact that reason is your means of existence.

Miss Rand doesn't elaborate on this assertion theoretically in her later writing. Let's continue to deliver it right here.

In order to fully explain the concept of volition, it is necessary to first place the problem in a larger biological perspective and take into account some fundamental truths about how living things function.

A persistent process of internally generated action defines and sustains an organism's existence. This can be seen in the way an organism develops and matures, how it heals itself, and how it interacts with its surroundings. The most noticeable characteristic of live action is its goal-directedness. This is not meant to imply that there is a higher level of life that is aware; rather, it is designed to emphasize the important fact that living things have a self-regulating action principle that moves toward and typically results in the continuation of the organism's life. For instance, consider the intricate metabolic processes, the amazing self-healing abilities of living things, or the coordinated orchestration of the innumerable discrete processes involved in the typical process of physical maturity of an organism. The unquestionable, intriguing, and difficult phenomenon at the core of life is organic self-regulation.

From a single cell to a man, there are various stages of development and complexity in life. One can identify three types or categories of self-regulatory activity as life develops from simpler to more complex levels. I'll refer to these as the vegetative level of self-regulation, the conscious-behavioral level, and the self-conscious level. The most basic phase is vegetative. This sequence describes every physiological-biochemical mechanism a plant uses to sustain its own existence. This self-regulatory activity pattern is present in every higher life form, including a single cell. It is active in unconscious physiological-biochemical processes that occur in both men and animals' bodies, such as metabolism.

As animal consciousness develops, the conscious-behavioral level of self-regulation occurs. The animal's body still functions at the vegetative level, but when it moves through its environment, a new, higher level is needed to safeguard and support the animal's life. The animal's strength of awareness is what allows it to reach this degree. Its sensors give it the information it needs to hunt, avoid barriers, avoid attackers, and more. The animal is able to control and direct its motor activity thanks to its awareness of the outside world. Animals without their senses cannot survive. The fundamental method of survival for all living things that possess consciousness, the action regulator, is consciousness.

Of course, an animal cannot understand the concept of life and death at the sensory-perceptual level of consciousness; yet, in the right physical context, an animal's sensory-perceptual system and pleasure-pain mechanism automatically work to defend the animal's life. Animals die if their range of awareness cannot handle the circumstances they are in. However, to the extent of its abilities, its consciousness works to control its behavior in a life-affirming manner. Thus, a new type of self-regulatory activity, a new expression of the biological principle of life, develops in nature with the ability to move and the development of consciousness in animals.

Life and consciousness are at their highest level of development in man. Animals and humans both share a sensory-perceptual form of consciousness, but man progresses past it to a conceptual mode that includes explicit reasoning, abstractions, principles, and self-awareness. Man has the capacity to be explicitly aware of his own mental activity, to question their veracity, to assess them critically, and to change or rectify them. This is in contrast to other species. Man is not naturally rational; he is aware that his thought processes may be suitable or unsuitable for the task of understanding reality. He does not view his thought processes as an unchangeable constant. Man demonstrates a third type of self-regulating behavior in addition to the first two: the ability to control his own consciousness.

The nature of this regulatory activity is very different from the two earlier ones in one very important way.

The ability to control one's conduct is "wired in" to the system at the vegetative and conscious-behavioral levels. A living organism is a complex system of structures and functions that are structured hierarchically. Both the regulators at the bottom of the hierarchy and the regulators at the top of the hierarchy have some power on the various components. For instance, the heart's own "pacemaker" system directly controls the heart's rhythm. The pacemaker system is governed by the autonomic nervous system and hormones, which are governed by brain regions. The life of the organism, or the requirements for the organism's existence, is obviously the ultimate regulative principle, inherent in and controlling the entire system of sub regulators, from the nervous system to the heart down to the internal action of a single cell. The implicit norm or aim of the organism serves as the organizing principle for its internal behaviors. The organism has no control over this ultimate regulator or any of the sub regulators; they are all "programmed" into the organism by nature.

The unique nature of self-regulation, the governing and integrating principle, is "wired in" to the system on the vegetative level, and this is also true—albeit in a different way—of the conscious-behavioral level in animals. The animal's life, which serves as the ultimate standard and purpose, is biologically "programmed" to control its behavior through its sensory-perceptual system and pleasure-pain mechanism.

Think about self-conscious self-regulation now.

In both animals and humans, awareness—the upkeep of sensory and/or intellectual contact with reality—is consciousness' fundamental purpose. The integrative process is automatic, that is, "wired in" to the neural system, on the sensory-perceptual plane of awareness, which humans and animals share. Sensations (basic sensory inputs) are spontaneously incorporated into perceptions in a typical human brain. By nature's "programming," consciousness is the controlling and regulating objective of the integrative process on the sensory-perceptual level. The conceptual level of consciousness is an exception to this rule. Here, the regulation is not "wired in" to the system or automatic. Although it is not innate to humans, conceptual awareness serves as the driving force behind all of man's mental activities and is essential to his optimal existence. It must be provided by man. He must decide on that goal. He must intentionally focus his mental energy and combine his mental activity toward the objective of conceptual awareness. Though conceptual functioning is a natural ability, it must be chosen to be used.

Man must concentrate on the work at hand in order to actively integrate his thoughts in order to abstract, conceive, relate, infer, and reason. The decision to make awareness—awareness of that which is significant in the given context—aim one's allowing one to choose to focus in every given circumstance.

By establishing the objective of awareness, one engages and guides the thought process, and awareness serves as the regulator and integrator of one's mental activity.

By essentially giving oneself the directive, "Grab this," one establishes the objective of consciousness.

It hardly needs to be argued that this objective is not "wired in" to a man's brain by nature as the automatic regulator of mental activity. It is not necessary to create particular laboratory studies to show that thinking is not an automated process or that a person's mind does not automatically "pump" conceptual knowledge when their body needs it. Man will not be compelled to abstract their common properties, integrate his abstractions, or apply his knowledge to every new detail he discovers simply because he is confronted with physical objects and events. It is all too simple to see how readily man might shirk his duty to think. He must decide to concentrate his thoughts and try for comprehension. On a conceptual level, he is accountable for self-control. The act of concentration has to do with how a man's consciousness operates, not what is included in it.

A man is in focus when and to the degree that his mind is focused on achieving awareness, clarity, and understandability with regard to the subject of his concern, that is, with regard to what he is thinking about, handling, or doing.

Thinking involves maintaining that concentration on a certain issue or problem.

Being out of focus is allowing one's thoughts to wander in will less passivity, guided solely by random impressions, emotions, or associations, or thinking about something without actually trying to grasp it, or taking action without thinking about what one is doing.

It is not a question of a man's level of intelligence or understanding at stake in this situation. It is also not a problem with the effectiveness or productivity of any one thought process. It also has nothing to do with the particular topic on which the mind may be focused. It is a matter of the fundamental regulating principle that controls the functioning of the mind: Is the desire for consciousness what controls the mind, or is it something else, such as desires, anxieties, or the pull of sluggish passivity?

To be focused is to make active cognitive integration your main goal. However, the choice that man must make is not just between the highest level of consciousness and complete unconsciousness. Depending on how focused a person is, they might reach different degrees of consciousness. This will show itself in (a) the clarity or fuzziness of his mental contents, (b) the degree to which mental activity is grounded in concrete details or includes abstractions and principles, and (c) the degree to which the appropriate larger context is present or missing during the thinking process. As a result, choosing to focus (or think) does not involve literally coming out of unconsciousness and entering consciousness. (This is obviously not possible. One cannot decide to start thinking when they are asleep.) Focusing involves raising one's level of awareness, changing from a state of (relative) mental inactivity to one of deliberate mental activity, and starting a process of directed cognitive integration. A guy can recognize the necessity of maintaining complete mental focus when they are in a passive (or somewhat passive) state of consciousness. He has the option of avoiding that knowledge or making an attempt to become more conscious.

A man's decision to concentrate and ponder does not automatically direct his thoughts moving forward without further effort once it has been made. Full consciousness must be initiated voluntarily, just as it must be sustained voluntarily. Every time a fresh issue or problem arises, the decision to think must be renewed. A man's decision to be focused yesterday won't force him to be focused today. A man's choice to concentrate on one issue does not compel him to concentrate on another. A guy may choose to seek a given value, but it does not mean he will put up the mental work necessary to realize it. Man must continue to keep an eye on and control his own brain activity during any particular thought process in order to "stay on the rails." He is free to put his conscious function on hold, give up trying, shirk the duty of self-control, and allow his mind to passively wander at any time during his life. He is free to keep only a partial focus, taking in what he can easily understand and choosing not to fight for what he cannot.

Man is free to avoid not only the broad effort of purposeful awareness, but also particular paths of thinking that he finds uncomfortable or hurtful. When he notices traits in his friends, his wife, or himself that go against his moral principles, he has the option of letting his mind go blank or quickly shifting his attention to another issue, refusing to consider the ramifications or meaning of what he has noticed. He can refuse to integrate his knowledge, he can refuse to pause on it, he can push it aside and continue to shout with righteous indignation despite dimly realizing during an argument that he is being driven by his emotions and is maintaining a position for reasons other than those he is stating, reasons that he knows to be untenable. He can effectively scream to himself, "Who can be sure of anything," as he realizes that the course of action he is taking is in obvious contradiction of logic. —sink into a veil of thought and keep walking.

In such circumstances, a man actively seeks unawareness as his objective rather than simply abdicating his duty to make awareness his goal. This is what evasion means.

Man is psychologically free when he makes the decision to concentrate or not, to think or not to think, to activate or not his conceptual level of consciousness, and only when he makes this decision.

Man's freedom to focus or not to focus, to think or not to think, is a special type of option that needs to be separated from all other types of choice. It must be distinguished from the choice to think about a specific topic because a man's thoughts depend on his values, interests, knowledge, and circumstances in each given situation. It needs to be differentiated from the choice to carry out a specific physical action, which again depends on a man's values, interests, knowledge, and circumstances. These choices entail causal antecedents of a different kind than the decision to focus.

Since it is the greatest regulator in the mental system and is directly under human volitional control, the primary decision to concentrate or set one's mind to the goal of cognitive integration is causally irreducible. All other judgments and options are subregulators in regard to it.

Volitional decision ability obviously requires a healthy brain. Any human faculty can become inoperative due to a disease. The brain and neurological system are assumed to be undamaged and to be operating normally in this examination.

Recognizing that a man has the choice to think or not to think means understanding that he has the choice to think or not to think in a certain circumstance. Man is the causal agent of an indivisible action that includes the process of focusing his thoughts and the decision to think (not the activity of thinking).

Just as the value sought, awareness, is a primary, so too is the decision to focus one's thoughts. Not any other values that come before and enable consciousness, but awareness itself, which makes all other values possible. Goal-directed (value-directed) human action has awareness as its foundation and prerequisite; it does not add another goal or value along the way, as it were. The choice of whether or not to focus one's thoughts (value awareness and make it one's aim) is a fundamental one that cannot be further simplified.

It is important to emphasize that volition especially relates to the conceptual level of consciousness. When and as a child begins to go from the perceptual to the conceptual level, when and as he learns to abstract, classify, comprehend concepts, and reason explicitly, he faces the requirement for cognitive self-regulation. He experiences cognition as an effortless process as long as he is operating at the sensory-perceptual level. But as soon as he starts to conceive, he is forced to acknowledge that this new level of consciousness demands effort and mental exertion, and that he must decide to exert this effort. He learns that, at this new level of consciousness, he is not perfect; mistakes might happen; and cognitive success is not always assured to him. (In contrast to the perceptual level, where seeing is the same as seeing, on the conceptual level, asking a question does not entail knowing the answer without further investigation, and vice versa.) He learns that he must constantly keep an eye on and control the activities of his mind. Of course, a child does not express this understanding orally or clearly. But due to direct introspective awareness, it is implicit in his consciousness.

Man cannot escape the implicit understanding that his mind has a volitional function, just as he cannot ignore the implicit information that he should think, that being conscious is preferable, and that his effectiveness as a living thing depends on it. He can, however, choose to act on that knowledge or to ignore it. To reiterate: He is not "programmed" to think automatically by nature.

(Sometimes, the "reason" for not paying attention or not thinking is anti-effort, or a reluctance to put up the work and take on the responsibility that thinking entails. In other situations, the "motive" is a wish, desire, or emotion that the person wants to indulge but that their reason will not permit. In these situations, the person "solves" the issue by losing concentration. In other situations, the "motivation" is running away from a fear that one knows they shouldn't give in to but yet does, suspending their awareness and invalidating their knowledge. These "motives" are merely sentiments that a man may choose to treat as controlling; they are not causal imperatives.)

As focusing entails widening the scope of one's awareness, evading entails doing the opposite: narrowing the scope of one's awareness. When one understands (clearly or dimly) that they should raise their degree of awareness or reduce it when they know (clearly or dimly) that they shouldn't, this is called evasion. On the implicit subjectivist tenet that if one does not perceive the fact, it does not exist, evading a fact is an attempt to make it unreal to oneself (or its existence will not matter and will not entail any consequences).

Man uses consciousness to perceive and recognize reality's facts. It serves as an integrative organ. By establishing awareness as the right aim, one may focus and start the integrative process moving in a meaningful direction. Integration lacks concentration. Evasion is the deliberate disintegration of one's self, the act of subverting the proper function of consciousness, the setting of the cognitive function backwards, and the reduction of one's mental contents into fragments that are not allowed to interact with one another.

Man's life and wellbeing depend on him maintaining a proper cognitive connection with reality, which calls for a constant state of complete mental concentration.

It is important to distinguish between problem-solving and the act of focusing, which constitutes a core mental set. The pursuit of an answer to a particular topic is what problem-solving requires; as such, it implies focus but is not the same as it. For instance, a man who goes for a walk on a sunny day with the sole intention of enjoying himself and without any immediate concern for any long-term issues may still be in mental focus if he is aware of what he is doing and maintains a basic alertness, a readiness for purposeful thought, should the need arise.

Not every waking moment needs to be spent working on a problem-solving project in order to be in focus. It implies that one needs to be aware of what their mind is doing.

The process gets easier and more "natural" the more regularly and consciously a man maintains a policy of being in full mental focus, of thinking, of judging the facts of reality that confront him, of knowing what he is doing and why. Every emotional motivation to keep thinking is strengthened by the continuously developing knowledge he gains as a result of his policies, the growing sensation of control over his life, the building self-confidence, and the conviction that he lives in an open world. They also lessen the chance of an inducement that might even tempt him to evade. He is too aware of the fact that reality is not and cannot ever be his enemy and that he stands to lose everything by choosing to remain oblivious.

However, he has "trained" himself to have every emotional motivation for reason and none for irrationality. This does not mean that for such a man, the policy of rationality becomes automatic; it will always remain volitional. He has mastered the art of making rationality "second nature," to use a phrase from Aristotle. That serves as his own psychological reward. His psychological condition, however—and this must be emphasized—must be upheld voluntarily; he still has the ability to betray it. He still has to decide to think in every new situation he finds himself in.

In contrast, a man's ability to think gets more challenging the more he practices a policy of paying as little attention as possible to his surroundings and dodging any realities that he deems unpleasant to ponder. Feelings of helplessness, inefficacy, or anxiety—the perception of living in an incomprehensible and hostile universe—are the unavoidable results of his non-thinking philosophy. These emotions undermine his belief in his capacity for thought and in the value of thinking, and he often feels intimidated by the scope of the inner turmoil he must sort out. The innumerable anxieties that his avoidance strategy would surely subject him to further tilt his emotional balance in favor of more deception, evasions, and a frantic flight from reality.

No, this does not imply that his avoidance and irrationality are automated; rather, they remain voluntary. However, he has "trained" himself to find it harder and harder to be reasonable, and to feel the temptation to evade it more and more. That is the psychological penalty his nature imposes on him as a result of his failure.

He still has the ability to alter his course, though. Every man still has that power on the other side of psychosis, if there are no interfering structural or chemical diseases, independent of his prior mental practices. Only one issue is covered by volition: Is the aim of one's consciousness awareness, or not? Instead of influencing one's ability to choose to focus, persistent avoidance and irrationality might have an impact on the effectiveness, quickness, and productivity of a particular thought process. The chronic avoider suffers from mental fatigue, slowness, and internal chaos when he does decide to think since he has spent his time undermining rather than improving the effectiveness of his intellect. He can improve his thinking and restore it if he persists. However, the mental effort he previously refused to put forth must now be put forth threefold.

A man may, at any given time, be so overpowered by a violent emotion—especially fear—that it may be difficult or impossible for him to think rationally. However, he has the ability to recognize that he is in this state and, unless immediate action is required, to postpone acting or reaching a decision until his mind has returned to normal. He can maintain control in this way even under extreme stress. (It is noteworthy to note, incidentally, that a man is more prone to becoming psychologically incapacitated and helplessly blinded under pressure if he consistently gives in to his emotions in nonacute situations, when he easily could have done otherwise. This is because he lacks a well-established "habit" of rational self-discipline to support him.)

A reward is not a necessary reason. A guy is not required to think about anything just because he has a strong reason to wish to; this is not a requirement. Additionally, a man's fear of thinking about a certain subject does not prevent him from doing so or force him to avoid it.

When seen in the context of the knowledge at his disposal, a man's conduct, or actions, follow from his values and premises, which in turn follow from his thinking or non-thinking. His actions can be regarded as free because they are managed by a free faculty, or one that acts voluntarily. A man is held accountable for his deeds because of this.

A man can't directly command his impulses and feelings into reality, but he is free to ignore them if and when he thinks they're unsuitable. The automatic result of an estimate (conscious or subconscious), which is the result of an individual's values and premises (conscious or subconsciously) applied to a particular scenario, is a desire or an emotion (Chapter Five). Only by changing the thinking or lack of thinking that gave rise to a person's values and premises can they change their desires and feelings.

The Social Environment and Free Will

Depending on the level of human reason or irrationality a man experiences, his social environment may offer incentives to think or may make the work more difficult. However, a man's thinking or lack of thinking cannot be determined by his social environment. It cannot force him to put forth the effort and take on the burden of cognition, nor can it force him to evade; it cannot force him to put his desires under the control of his reason, nor can it force him to give up his reason in favor of his desires. Man is indisputably a self-regulator in this matter. He may receive incentives for good or evil from the social environment, but an incentive is not a necessary cause.

The only thing in the environment that can be recognised by a man's thinking is the significance of those facts, the conclusions and convictions that can be made from them. The character of a man, including his level of reason, independence, and honesty, is determined less by what he perceives and more by what he thinks or doesn't think about it.

Man is not infallible; he might make sincere errors in knowledge or judgment at any point along the way. He may also mistakenly interpret the significance or meaning of the events he witnesses. His ability to choose not to act guarantees that he won't be helplessly trapped by his mistakes for the rest of his life. He can choose to keep his mind open to fresh information that might convince him that his initial assumptions were incorrect and that his conclusions need to be updated.

For example, if irrational parents raise their children in a confusing, terrifying, and contradictory way, the child may grow up believing that all people are inherently dangerous and unfathomable. If the child stops thinking at this point and never tries to question or get past this ingrained sense of helplessness and terror, he may live the rest of his life in a state of resentful paralysis. However, this does not have to be his fate: if he persists in working through the issue or, as he ages, decides to take into account the newer, broader evidence now at his disposal, he may realize that he has made an unwarranted generalization and reject it in favor of a fully reasoned and conscious conviction.

In the same situation, a different child might come to a different conclusion. He might decide that all people are dishonest and bad, and that he will beat them at their own game by acting dishonestly and viciously in order to injure them before they hurt him. Again, he has the option to change this finding in the future in light of additional data. He will have numerous chances to realize he is mistaken thanks to the facts of reality at his disposal. He will turn into a scoundrel if he doesn't make the decision to think, but not because his parents were unreasonable; rather, it will be because he neglected to take responsibility for actively constructing his beliefs and regularly comparing them to the realities of reality.

In the same situation, a third child may decide that his parents are unreasonable, unfair, and unjust, or at the very least, that they do not act logically, and that he must behave differently. He may suffer at home but continues to look for examples of better human behavior among his neighbors or in books and movies, refusing to accept the unreasonable and the incomprehensible as inevitable. Such a child will benefit greatly from his tragedy, though he won't realize it for many years: he will have built a strong sense of self-worth.

If a teenager is raised in a community where crime is rampant and cynically accepted as the norm, he has two options: he can give up his right to independent judgment, allow the dominant values to mold his character, and become a criminal himself; or, by choosing to think, he can see the absurdity and degrading self-talk of those who support a criminal lifestyle and fight for a better way of life for himself.

If a man is indoctrinated from an early age with the doctrine of Original Sin, if he is taught that he is flawed by nature and must live a life of penance, if he is taught that this world is filled with suffering, frustration, and disaster, and if he is taught that seeking pleasure is wrong, he does not have to believe it. He is free to think, to question, and to assess the nature of a moral code that condemns man and existence and places its standard of the good outside of both.

A man is free to inquire "why" about every value or proposition that is presented to him as the right or truth. Without his permission, other people's beliefs cannot breach that "Why?" threshold.

Of course, it is possible for a young child to be exposed to such extraordinary vicious irrationality from the first months and years of his life—such perplexing, contradictory, and terrifying behavior on the part of his parents—that it would be impossible for him to develop normally due to the limited evidence available to him; it might be impossible for him to establish any solid foundation of knowledge on which to build. It is possible for a youngster to have significant mental retardation or be mentally paralyzed.

In this way, intellectually. But those who assert that man is a product of his upbringing do not mean this; doing so would indicate the destruction of a child's psyche rather than its "conditioning."

Let's take a look at the situation of the person who does seem to be a product of his history and social milieu. Let's examine the case of the young boy who grows up in a dangerous area and ends up in trouble as an illustration.

The desire to "swim with the river" is the most overtly apparent purpose in the acts of a youngster who thus allows himself to be influenced by his environment. The desire to avoid the work and responsibility of making his own decisions is at the heart of this desire. To choose one's own activities, one must first choose one's own aims; to achieve this, one must select one's own values; and to select one's values, one must reflect. But the first and most fundamental duty that such a boy neglects is to think.

Since he lacks any personal standards or values, his quest for "security" forces him to embrace whatever ideals are presented to him by the social group he is a part of. To swim with the current, one must accept the ocean, swamp, rapids, cesspool, or abyss that the stream is specifically flowing toward. Such a youngster will desire to follow the crowd, take any path of action that has been predetermined for him by others, and "belong."

So, if the neighborhood boys create a gang at the corner pool hall, he'll join; if they start robbing people, he'll start robbing people; and if they start killing people, he'll start killing people. He is moved by his emotions. Once his thinking has been given up, all he has left are his feelings. He doesn't consciously or rationally decide to join the gang; rather, he just feels like it. He doesn't follow the group even though he truly believes they are correct since he would rather do so. If his mother opposes and challenges him to leave the hoodlums, he does not consider her arguments or draw the conclusion that she is mistaken since he does not feel like considering it.

If, at some point, he starts to worry that the gang might be going too far, if he shudders at the idea of killing someone, he realizes that the only other option is to split up with his friends and be left alone. However, he makes the blind decision to stay with the gang because he is terrified of the idea of being left alone. He may see people who live completely different lives across the river or just a few blocks away, as well as boys his age who somehow avoided becoming criminals; he has many ways to access a wider view of life's possibilities; however, this does not cause him to consider whether a better kind of life is possible for him, nor does it inspire him to ask or look into the matter because he experiences fear of the unknown. When asked what it is about leaving his comfort zone that terrifies him, he will essentially respond, "Aw, I don't know anybody out there and nobody knows me." However, it makes him feel satisfied because he has an immense fear of being alone and feelings are his only absolute, the only absolute that cannot be questioned. In reason, this is not an explanation because there is nothing objectively terrifying in that statement.

And if he is taken to jail at the age of twenty to await death for some monstrously gory and senselessly wanton crime, he will scream that he couldn't help himself and that he never had a chance. It is true, so he won't shout it. He feels it, so he will scream it.

Contrary to what he intended, there is some truth to his scream: given his fundamental anti-thought agenda, he was powerless to stop it and never stood a chance. No other person who lives their life according to such philosophy has existed. It is untrue, however, that he or any other person could not help eschewing the need for thought and riding irrationally on his emotions.

This youngster had the option of reflecting on his activities each day of his life and at each significant turning point. He has the information necessary to justify changing his policy. He got around it. Choosing not to ponder, he. He would be more justified in lamenting his inability to prevent his actions if, at every pivotal moment, he had exercised due diligence and care in his decision-making but had simply drawn the incorrect conclusions. However, reform institutions are not filled with helplessly perplexed, morally upright individuals who kill one another on the street because their reasoning is flawed.

The key to understanding what caused this boy's destruction rests not in his environment but rather in the fact that he let his emotions to move, direct, and inspire him. He attempted to replace his mind with his emotions. Nothing stood in his way of thinking, other than his lack of motivation.

In large part, a man is "the product of his surroundings" to the extent that he fails to think responsibly. However, this goes against human nature. It represents pathology in action.

The extent to which man is absent from and ignored by most current psychological theories is profoundly evident in the attempt made by most psychologists to explain a man's behavior without reference to the degree of his thinking or non-thinking—by attempting to reduce all of a man's behavior to causes in either his "conditioning" or in his heredity. Today's prevailing theory holds that man is nothing more than a walking recorder into which his parents, teachers, and neighbors dictate whatever they please—these parents, teachers, and neighbors themselves being nothing more than walking recorders carrying the dictations of other, earlier recorders, and so on. The origin of new ideas, conceptions, and values is not addressed; rather, it is said that the powerless piece of putty known as man creates them as a result of a chance combination of unidentified forces. The social determinist's shock, skepticism, and outrage at the idea that original, self-generated thinking has any substantial influence on a man's life contains an intriguing personal confession.

The Inconsistency of Determinism

In its broadest sense, the concept of "free will" refers to the idea that people are capable of acting in ways that are not influenced by external causes and that they may make decisions without being forced to do so. As one author puts it: "For an action to be free, it must be such that the agent executing it causes it, but such that no antecedent conditions were necessary for conducting just that action."

Different conceptions of free will disagree on the nature of these choices, to what human faculty they relate, how they work, and what their boundaries are. Theories of free will have frequently made the blatantly unpersuasive claim that particular desires or physical actions are "free," i.e., causally irreducible.

Man's ability to exercise free will is limited to one simple action, or decision: whether to think or not to think. It is a freedom brought about by his exceptional capacity for self-consciousness. This fundamental decision affects all other decisions made by man and determines the trajectory of his behavior in the context of his knowledge and the existential possibilities that he is faced with.

The idea of man as a being with volitional consciousness is in stark contrast to the psychological determinism theory that permeates contemporary culture in general and the social sciences in particular.

Psychological determinism rejects the idea that human consciousness possesses any sort of free will or volition. Man is merely a reactor to internal and external pressures, and those pressures determine the course of his actions and the content of his convictions, just as physical forces determine the course of every particle of dust in the universe. According to this theory, man is ultimately and fundamentally passive in relation to his actions, decisions, values, and conclusions. It asserts that, in any given circumstance or moment, only one "choice" is psychologically possible for man as a result of all the preceding determining forces acting upon him, just as only one action is possible for the speck of dust; this means that man has no actual power of choice, freedom, or self-responsibility. This perspective holds that man has no freer will than a stone; he is just presented with more complex options and is controlled by more complex forces.

This is the view of man's nature that the majority of modern psychologists embrace, despite the fact that they typically do not want to have it expressed so directly or accept its full implications. Many of them openly acknowledge that they accept it as "an article of faith." The majority, then, does not assert that this viewpoint has been established as true or rationally demonstrated. Because they view psychological determinism as "scientific," they claim to believe in it. The single most pervasive and harmful misconception in modern psychology is this one.

Any form of determinism, regardless of the purported driving powers whether physical, psychological, environmental, or divine, involves an essential and unsolvable contradiction—an epistemological paradox.

According to the determinist theory of mind, a person's ability to think, recognize reality's facts, prioritize feelings over facts, or do any of these things at all is determined by forces beyond his control. In any given situation or moment, a person's method of mental functioning is the inevitable result of an endless series of antecedent factors; a person has no control over it.

That which a man does, according to determinism proponents, he had to do; that which he believes, he had to believe; if he concentrates his thoughts, he had to; if he avoids the effort of concentration, he had to; if reason is his only source of guidance, he had to be; if feeling or whim are his primary motivators, he had to be; he couldn't help it.

However, if this were the case, man would not be able to have any conceptual knowledge. No hypothesis, including the notion of psychological determinism, could be said to have greater plausibility than any other.

Man is neither infallible nor omniscient. This implies that (a) he must put forth effort to acquire knowledge, and (b) the sheer existence of a thought in a person's mind does not necessarily imply that the idea is true. Many false ideas can enter a person's mind. But if man believes what he must believe, if he is not free to compare his beliefs to reality and decide whether to accept or reject them—if his actions and thought processes are dictated by factors that may or may not be related to reason, logic, and reality—then he will never be able to determine whether his conclusions are correct or incorrect. Knowledge is the accurate identification of reality's truths, and man needs a way to verify his findings in order to know that the contents of his mind do, in fact, represent knowledge and that he has correctly identified reality's facts. The method is the act of reasoning, which involves comparing his findings to the world around them and looking for inconsistencies. But only if his ability to judge is free, or non-conditional, can this be validated (given a normal brain). A man cannot distinguish between his beliefs and those of a screaming maniac if his capacity to judge is not free.

But how did determinism's proponents come to know what they did? What provides proof for it? On this issue, determinists are rather silent.

Determinism proponents cannot claim to know that their theory is true; they can only state that they are powerless to believe otherwise. This is because if they believe that their ability to think and accept reason is conditional and dependent on factors beyond their control, they are not free to compare their beliefs to the facts of reality. Furthermore, they are unable to assert that their hypothesis is highly probable; all they can do is admit the internal urge that prevents them from having any doubts about its likelihood.

Evidently detecting this epistemological conundrum, some determinism proponents have attempted to avoid it by claiming that while they are deterministic in their beliefs, logic is what drives them. However, how do they know this? They cannot control their beliefs any more than a maniac can. They are both equally the pawn of deterministic forces, along with the insane. Both are unable to evaluate their own conclusions.

Loss of volitional control over logical judgment is one of the features of psychosis, yet according to determinism, that is man's typical, metaphysical state.

The epistemological conundrum of determinism cannot be solved.

A mind that is unable to critically evaluate its own reasoning—a mind whose judgment is not free—cannot distinguish between what is logical and what is illogical, cannot determine what drives and inspires it, and cannot legitimately assert any form of knowledge. Such a mind is ineligible for such evaluations by its very nature. Only a volitional consciousness can even think of logic; an automated consciousness could not need it and could not imagine it.

Machines cannot apply the ideas of logic, thought, or knowledge. A machine cannot reason; it only carries out the commands that its creator gave it, and only those commands. It acts as if two plus two equals four if that is how it is programmed to act, and acts as if two plus two equals five if that is how it is programmed to act; it is unable to change the instructions or information sent to it. If "self-correctors" are integrated into it, it only executes the predetermined "self-correction" actions; if the "self-correctors" are set wrongly, it is unable to execute any autonomous, self-generated improvements to its performance. No idea reached by man could claim objectivity or truth if he were just a super-complicated machine, designed by his heredity and operated by his environment, pushed, pulled, shaped, and molded by his genes, his toilet training, his parental upbringing, and his cultural history. This includes the notion that man is a machine.

Those who advocate for determinism must either claim to have received their theory through mystical revelation, excluding themselves from the world of reason, or they must claim to be an exception to their own theory, excluding it from the sphere of truth.

Man's ability to acquire information cannot be denied without causing him to contradict himself. Even in the attempt to refute it, one must admit that it is true. Any hypothesis that requires the conclusion that man can know nothing automatically invalidates and refutes itself. However, this is the inevitable result that follows from the notion of determinism.

Any hypothesis about the structure and functioning of the human mind must be evaluated in light of the fact that it is a creation of the human mind and, as such, must be consistent with both its own existence and content if it is to be accepted as true. With the exception of Bertrand Russell's idea of types, the theory is incoherent and illogical. For instance, it would be clear that a guy was irrational if he claimed that "Man is incapable of knowing any facts" as a truth of reality. In a finer and more intricate fashion, determinism's epistemological paradox is of the same order.

The claim of determinism to be true is at odds with what it claims to be true. It demonstrates what is known as the self-exclusion fallacy.

Many intellectuals who disagree with the classical associationism theory have argued that there is no way to ever prove associationism to be true and that there is no way to have any knowledge under associationism theory of mind. However, associationism is only a particular type of psychological determinism. The fact that the same argument may be used against any form of determinism and renders it invalid has not been acknowledged.

Whether the human mind is said to be passively controlled by the "rules of association," conditioned reflexes, environmental forces, or Original Sin is irrelevant. Any theory of mind that undermines a person's ability to exercise free will over his or her faculties of judgment will fall apart due to this insurmountable conflict.

Conceptual knowledge—as opposed to inescapable, unchosen beliefs—is only conceivable to man because he is a being of volitional consciousness and because he is free to begin and maintain a reasoning process.

The Law of Causality and Free Will

Particularly helpful in spreading the myth of psychological determinism are two false beliefs. The first is the assertion that the law of causality logically follows psychological determinism and that volition defies the rule of causality. The second is the assertion that there would be no psychology as a discipline, no psychological laws, and no method to anticipate human behavior without determinism.

In the first of these claims, there is a blatant misunderstanding of the nature of the rule of causality at play. Let's start by thinking about what this legislation actually means. The law of causality is the concept of identity applied to action, according to Ayn Rand. Entities are responsible for all actions. The nature of the entities that act determines and determines the character of the activity; a thing cannot act against its nature.

The first thing that needs to be emphasized is that all activities are the products of entities. (The idea of "activity" logically necessitates and assumes something which acts; it is impossible without it. Not disembodied actions, motions, or changes, but actual acting, moving, and changing creatures make up the cosmos.)

The acts that an entity is capable of taking rely on what that entity is, or what it is. The fact that a seed can grow into a flower but a stone cannot, that electricity can run a motor but tears and prayers cannot, that actions consistent with their natures are possible to entities but contradictions are not, is due to their inherent inexorability, not to "chance" or the whim of a supernatural being.

In the same way that what something can do depends on what it is, so too does what something will do in every given circumstance. Iron expands when exposed to a certain temperature, water boils when exposed to the same temperature, and wood burns when exposed to the same temperature. Their different qualities are what lead to the variations in their behavior. It is not "chance" that an automobile collides with a bicycle and sends the bicycle flying into the air instead of the car, just as it is not "chance" that an automobile collides with a train and sends the car flying instead of the car. Identity leads to causality.

A relationship between entities and their actions is known as causality.

The law of causality is a very broad abstraction; in and of itself, it neither specifies the sorts of causal processes that are active in any specific thing nor implies that the same kinds of causal processes are active in all entities. Such an assumption would be unnecessary and gratuitous.

A stone, which moves by a mechanical sort of causality, cannot initiate activities; instead, it can only respond to the actions of other things or forces. It requires an external force—a man's hand, the wind, or another object—to start rolling down a mountainside. It cannot produce either goals or actions. However, an animal has the ability to move; it can start moving, moving in a goal-directed manner, starting to walk or run; the source of its motion is within itself. It makes no difference in this situation that the animal might begin running in reaction to the perception of some stimulus-object. What matters is that the animal has the ability to react in a way that a stone cannot: by initiating a running motion within its own body and going in the direction of a target. In these two examples, many causal mechanisms and principles of action are at play.

A living thing has the capacity for a type of action that lifeless objects are incapable of: self-generated, goal-directed action (in the sense defined above). The ability to initiate an action of consciousness—the ability to initiate an abstract cognitive process—is what sets man apart from all other living species.

Because this process of thought, which is essential to human survival, must be initiated voluntarily, man bears a special duty. The ability to choose, in the purest sense, is a psychologically irreducible natural reality that exists in man.

This freedom of choice is a category of causality, one that applies to man, rather than negating causality. A man is the cause of a cognitive process; it is not causeless. The entity that acts determines the actions that entity is capable of, and the nature of man (and of the man's intellect) requires the choice between focusing and non-focusing, between thinking and non-thinking. Man's inherent nature forbids him from evading this decision; it is solely up to him; it was not predetermined for him by the gods, the stars, the chemistry of his body, the makeup of his "family constellation," or the social and economic structure of his society.

One cannot overlook this special quality of human nature if one is to be constrained by a true "empiricism," which is a respect for observable facts without arbitrary commitments to which reality must be "adjusted." The issue of "reconciling" volition and causation is also revealed to be illusory if the law of causality is seen as a link between things and their acts.

But today, the law of causation is not viewed in this way. That is where the confusion comes from.

The Renaissance marked a turning point in history. According to Windelband's A History of Philosophy, it is as follows:

Galileo gave the concept of causation an entirely new relevance. The Platonic-Aristotelian notion claimed that causes were things or substances, whilst effects were either those things or substances' or things' activities, or other things and substances that were believed to result only from those activities. Galileo, on the other hand, reverted to the perspective of earlier Greek philosophers, who only applied the causal relation to states—in this case, to the motions of things—and not to the Being of the substances themselves. Both causes and effects are motions.

Post-Renaissance science and philosophy were dominated by this perspective, which saw causation as a connection between actions and activities rather than between entities and actions. The "model" of causation was mechanics: the relationship between impact and counter-impact, of action and reaction, was defined as the essence of the causal relationship.

A disastrous legacy remained long after physicists realized that the mechanical "model" was inapplicable to many aspects of the physical world, including many inanimate, deterministic systems within the universe (such as electromagnetic phenomena), leaving behind the deceptively persistent idea that every action, including every action by a person, is only a reaction to some prior action, motion, or force.

The idea that motions have a causal relationship is completely illogical. It is important to keep in mind that, if one adopts this perspective, there is no way to demonstrate or support the law of causality. If all that is happening is motion succeeding motion, then it is impossible to build the essential connections between subsequent occurrences. For example, one can notice that A comes after B, but not that B is the result or outcome of A. (This is incidentally one of the reasons why the majority of philosophers who subscribe to this causality concept have been unable to respond to Hume's claim that the law of causation cannot be proved. You cannot—unless you understand how it relates to the rule of identity. However, doing so requires disproving the motion-to-motion theory of causality.)

The motion-to-motion perspective also hides the explanatory function of the law of causation. If one wants to know why certain entities behave in a certain way in a particular situation, one must understand the characteristics of the entities in question. In reality, this comprehension is always implied and presumed in any explanation that makes use of preceding actions. For instance, if someone claims that the action of a lighted match being thrown into a wastebasket caused it to catch fire, this constitutes a sufficient causal explanation only if one is aware of the properties of paper and lighted matches; otherwise, a description of the action sequence would be meaningless.

The idea that every action is just a response to a prior action arbitrarily excludes the possibility of self-generated, goal-directed activity in opposition to the available evidence. This debate is not intended to address how this premise has slowed down biological research. The devastating effects of this premise on psychology are immediately relevant in this case; it is this premise that prevents men from understanding the existence of a volitional consciousness.

According to this theory, thinking or not thinking is only a necessary response to a prior necessary reaction to a prior necessary reaction, etc. Such a viewpoint renders man completely helpless. With the reality that man is a cognitive self-regulator, it is wholly irreconcilable. However, it is the incorrect assumption of causality that needs to be challenged, not the reality of cognitive self-regulation.

(It is incorrect to inquire as to "What caused one man to focus and another man to evade?" The incorrect idea of causation we just described is almost always reflected in this question. The question shows a lack of understanding of the concept of choice in its fundamental sense as it relates to the act of concentrating or thinking. "To what is the action of focusing or thinking a reaction?" asks the questioner.)

Determinism can be viewed—and frequently is—as being equivalent with universal causality when applied to physical nature. However, when used in relation to man, or in a psychological setting, the phrase has a more limited meaning that is not implied by the rule of causality and that is manifestly at odds with the facts. Let's now think about the topic of psychological law and prediction.

Man's awareness or mind has a distinct nature; it has a distinct architecture, distinct qualities, and distinct abilities. Its methods of operation display particular principles or rules, which psychology must find and define. None of this is in conflict with the reality that man uses reason in a voluntary manner. Man has a specific, finite amount of regulatory power over his mind. Man can choose to focus, to aim his cognitive faculty in a particular direction, but he cannot change or violate the psychological laws by which his mind functions, just as the driver of an automobile can steer the vehicle in a desired direction without changing or violating the mechanical laws by which the vehicle operates. A guy cannot avoid crashing his car if he does not drive it properly, and the same is true for him when he does not steer his mind.

For instance, a man is free to think or not to think, but he is not free to ignore the fact that, if he does not think, if he consistently avoids facing any facts or issues that he finds unpleasant, he will trigger a complex cascade of negative psychological effects, one of which will be a significant loss of self-esteem.

This can be proven to be a psychological law (Chapter Seven).

Or, alternatively, if a man develops particular values as a result of his thinking or non-thinking, these values will cause him to feel particular emotions in particular circumstances. He won't be able to use "will" to make these emotions go. When he realizes a certain emotion is unsuitable, he can change it by reconsidering the value(s) that cause it, but he can only do this in a certain, "lawful" way, not just on a whim (Chapter Five).

The concept of "free will" does not imply unrestricted, arbitrary control over one's own thoughts. Therefore, one may forecast the psychological effects of particular ideas, beliefs, conclusions, attitudes, and thinking policies to the extent that one understands the principles by which man's mind functions. For instance, it is possible to foresee that a man with genuine self-esteem will find intellectual stagnation intolerable, that a man who views sex, life, and himself as evil will not be attracted to a woman who is intelligent, independent, and free of self-guilt, and will not feel comfortable and "at home" with her romantically, and that a man whose guiding principle is "Don't antagonize anyone," will not be the first to advocate for and

It is impossible to say for sure that these folks won't change their minds. Predictions must therefore be made with the qualifier "all other things being equal" or "on the assumption that no new factors emerge." However, this also applies to predictions in the physical sciences.

Identification of the fact of volition is a crucial condition for mentally understanding man. A psychology that is truly scientific must reject the mythology of determinism and the fallacious notion of causation that it is based on.

CHAPTER FIVE

Emotions

Emotions and Values

I've emphasized throughout the talk that man's capacity for reason is his most important quality because it explains the most of his other traits.

The widespread misunderstanding of the nature and function of emotions in a man's life sometimes obscures this truth. The phrase "Man is not only a rational being, he is also an emotional being" is often heard, however it implies a dichotomy, as if man has two natures, one of which is opposed to the other. The truth is that, like all of man's other psychological traits, the content of his emotions is a derivation and a consequence of his rational ability and cannot be comprehended without reference to the conceptual strength of his consciousness.

Reason serves two fundamental purposes for man as a means of survival: cognition and appraisal. Finding out what things are, defining their nature, traits, and properties are all parts of the cognition process. Man must learn how things relate to himself in order to evaluate them and determine what is good for him and what is bad, what he should seek out and what he should steer clear of.

A "value" is anything that one works to obtain and/or maintain. It is something which one considers to be beneficial to their welfare. An action's target is a value. Man cannot avoid the need to choose values and make value judgments because he must act in order to survive, and reality presents him with a wide range of actionable objectives and options.

Value is a notion that refers to a relationship—the relationship between a certain component of reality and man (or to some other living entity). When a man values something, whether it be a person, thing, event, mental state, etc., he strives to acquire, keep, use, or enjoy it when it is possible and proper to do so. A man devalues something if he believes it to be bad for him, hostile, or damaging in some way. He therefore tries to avoid or destroy it. When something is insignificant to him, neither helpful nor detrimental, he is unconcerned by it and does nothing about it.

There are neither internal nor external factors driving man to choose values that are actually good for him, that is, values that are consistent with his nature and requirements, conducive to his continuous efficient functioning, even though his life and well-being rely on it. He is unencumbered by nature in this regard. He is not biologically "wired" to always make the appropriate value decisions because he is a being of volitional consciousness. He might choose values that are detrimental to his wants and wellbeing, values that will bring him pain and ruin. But regardless of whether a man's ideals are life-serving or life-negating, they are what guide his behavior. Man's primary motivational connection to reality is his set of values.

In existential terms, the choice between life and death is man's fundamental "for me" or "against me" alternative, which gives rise to the morality dilemma (Chapter Twelve). However, this identification is conceptual and mature. The first time a human faces the problem of values as a youngster is through the physical pleasure and pain they feel.

A conscious creature automatically perceives pleasure as a value and suffering as a disvalue. The scientific basis for this is that although pleasure improves life, pain signals danger or a disruption of the natural course of life.

A kid can also experience values, the desired and the unwanted, through another fundamental alternative in the world of consciousness. It has to do with how he perceives reality cognitively. There are times when a youngster feels cognitively effective in understanding reality, cognitive control, and mental clarity (within the range of awareness possible to his stage of development). He occasionally feels out of control, cognitively ineffective, cognitively powerless, mentally chaotic, and unable to process the information coming into his consciousness. When something is effective, we perceive it as a value; when it is ineffective, we perceive it as a disvalue. This fact's biological underpinning is the connection between efficacy and survival.

Man experiences the value of a feeling of efficacy as such introspectively, just as he experiences the value of pleasure as such. Why do you prefer pleasure to suffering is not a question one poses to a man. Also, no one questions him on why he chooses to be in charge rather than helpless. Man first develops preferences, or values, from these two sets of experiences.

A man may decide, as a result of his mistakes and/or omissions, to pursue pleasure through values that, in reality, can only lead to suffering; and he may choose to pursue a sense of efficacy through values that, in reality, can only render him impotent. However, the psychological basis for the phenomenon of valuation continues to be the value of pleasure and the devaluation of pain, as well as the value of efficacy and the devaluation of helplessness.

Values are the result of the thinking a man has done, or hasn't done. Values might reflect sane reasoning and mental stability or insane reasoning and psychopathology. They may be a sign of developmental stop or of psychological maturity. They might develop from self-assurance and kindness or from insecurity and dread. They might be driven by a desire to lessen suffering or to find happiness. They may result from a desire to use one's mind or a desire to go away from it. They can be obtained freely and consciously, or they can be naively absorbed from other men through what is essentially an osmosis process.

They may be held outright and consciously or implicitly and unconsciously. They can be either consistent or conflicting. They have the power to either improve or jeopardize a man's life. These are the alternatives to a being with volitional consciousness that are conceivable.

There is no method for man to revert to the status of an animal, no predetermined, stereotyped pattern of conduct he can mindlessly follow, and no "instincts" whose control he can cede his existence. The distortions, perversions, and corruption that constitute his values—regardless of whether he shirks his duty to reason or fights against the imperative of thought—remain distorted manifestations of the reality that his is a conceptual kind of consciousness. His ideals are still the result of his mind, but they are the product of a mind that is self-destructive, set against its own rightful function, and in reverse. Irrationality is a concept that only applies to humans, just like rationality does not apply to animals.

Nature has "programmed" an animal's biology with its core beliefs and objectives. What kind of entity should I strive to become is not a concern for an animal. What should my reason for living be? How should I approach living? Man does—and depending on the depth and caliber of their thinking, men respond to these concerns in radically different ways.

Men's core beliefs, basic conceptions of themselves, other men, and existence—their perceptions of what is possible for them and what they can expect from life—are reflected in disparities in their fundamental values.

A man's perception of himself has a significant impact on the values he chooses since values include the relation of some part of reality to the valuer, or the active entity. By way of a straightforward illustration, let's say that if a man were physically invincible, he would view the significance of the bomb differently than he does now since he is conscious of his own mortality. Whether one accurately assesses oneself or not, one's value judgments are implicitly influenced by one's (conscious or unconscious) perception of one's own nature, person, and abilities.

The goals a man sets for himself, the scope of his ambition, the range of his friends, the type of art he will love, etc. will unavoidably depend on his level of confidence or lack thereof and the amount to which he views the universe as open or closed to his understanding and action (Chapter Seven).

The process by which a man's perception of himself influences his value judgments, for the most part, does not occur on a conscious level; rather, it is implicit in his evaluations, reflecting prior judgments that are essentially "filed" in his subconscious.

The subconscious is made up of all mental processes and information that are hidden from or below conscious awareness. Two fundamental functions of a person's subconscious are essential to his intellectual growth and effective operation. Because it is obviously impossible for a person to retain all of their knowledge in their focused awareness, the subconscious functions as a repository for past knowledge, observations, and conclusions. It also functions, in essence, like an electronic computer, performing extremely quick integrations of sensory and ideational material. Man can therefore instantaneously access his prior knowledge (assuming it has been adequately assimilated) while freeing his conscious mind to deal with the new.

Each and every human learning follows this pattern. Once upon a time, learning to walk required a man's complete mental focus; however, once the skill was automated, he was free to pursue other interests. Initially, learning to talk required a man's complete mental focus; however, after the skill was automated, he was able to advance to higher levels of achievement. As he progresses through knowledge, man automates his identifications and discoveries, making his brain an ever-more effective tool—if and to the degree that he continues the growing process.

Man is an autonomous computer. This same concept applies to the growth of his cognitive abilities as it does to the formation of his values. As he develops values and dis-values, these too become automated; he is not required to recall all of his values to his conscious mind in every circumstance he comes across in order to construct an estimate. His subconscious is triggered into a lightning-like process of integration and appraisal in reaction to his perception of some component of reality. For instance, if a skilled driver notices an approaching truck veering toward a collision, he doesn't need to use new conscious reasoning to understand the fact that the situation is dangerous; rather, he recognizes the significance of what he sees and reacts immediately by slamming on the brake or quickly turning the wheel.

These lightning-like assessments manifest to man's conscious consciousness in a variety of ways, including through his emotions.

Man's ability to feel things automatically serves as a gauge for whether anything is in his favor or not (within the context of his knowledge and values). Value judgments and emotions have a cause-and-effect relationship. A value-response is a feeling. It is the automatic psychological outcome of an extremely quick subconscious appraisal (including both mental and bodily elements).

The psychosomatic manifestation of a person's perception of the favorable or unfavorable relationship of a certain part of reality to himself is called an emotion.

The order of psychological activities is: perception, assessment, and emotional response. But on the level of immediate consciousness, perception comes before emotion. The interim value-judgment may or may not be conscious to the person. The tremendous velocity of the sequence may necessitate a distinct effort of focused awareness in order to understand it. Men's confusion regarding the nature and source of emotions is made possible by the possibility that an individual may fail to recognize either the judgment or the elements involved in it, being only aware of perception and emotional response.

A person may not be aware of the evaluative processes that underlie his emotions for a variety of reasons. The following are a few of the most crucial of these explanations:

1. The ability to reflect on and recognize one's own mental processes is something that must be learnt. Most people have not developed the practice of trying to explain their feelings, thoughts, and desires to themselves; as a result, when they do, they typically fail and give up.

2. The majority of people do not hold their beliefs and values in a formally defined manner. A large portion of their mental contents are cloudy and obscure. Their views and values have never been expressed in precise, objective language and are just approximate representations of them that are stored in the subconscious using pre-verbal symbols like images that their owners find difficult to transfer into precise, articulate speech.

3. An feeling and the values that underlie it can occasionally be extraordinarily complicated. For instance, let's say a lady is sad and she knows it's because of her spouse. She knows she is prone to being oversensitive, but she also wants to be honest with him about how she feels without upsetting him and possibly making the situation worse. He may have been unkind to her in some way, but he is working very hard and is under strain. She, too, is carrying the emotional weight of his work pressures. It's possible that her subconscious is battling these competing ideas. She experiences a vague sense of annoyance with the universe in general and with her spouse in particular, along with some remorse, but she is unable to piece together why.

4. There are occasions when one emotionally reacts to something they are unaware of. For instance, one might meet someone who almost immediately makes them despise you, but if you search your memory, you can't come up with anything unfavorable that he has said or done. It's possible that one was only dimly aware of the speaker's affectations in their posture and movement, their voice's subliminal sincerity, or the potentially harmful connotations of their statements, and as a result, their subconscious responded accordingly.

5. Repression is the single greatest impediment to discovering the causes of one's emotions. The roots of such reactions may be hidden from consciousness because the ideals that underpin them are repugnant to the self-respect and conscious convictions of some people. An artist who is unable to acknowledge his feelings of jealousy toward a more talented competition may be completely unaware—and fiercely unwilling to acknowledge—that the joy he is experiencing is being brought on by hearing that his rival's art display was a flop.

It's interesting to note that people who are most unable to reflect on their actions and who are least aware of the origin of their emotions are also those who are most likely to wax poetic about their feelings and criticize reason. For them, emotions are a given, mystical revelations, the voice of their "blood" or "instincts," which must be blindly obeyed.

As an illustration, think about D. H. Lawrence's assertion that "My great religion is a belief in the blood, the body, as being wiser than the brain." Mental errors are possible. The brain is only a small and bridle, but what our blood feels, believes, and says is always true. What does knowledge matter to me? All I want is to directly answer to my blood, free from mindless or morally ambiguous interference.

Lawrence presents the viewpoint in an extreme manner. However, many individuals live by—or, to be more precise, die by—this concept on a more subdued, less showy basis every day.

Reason and emotion—thinking and feeling—are not faculties that are mutually antagonistic because man is an integrated organism and his nature (as a living thing) does not contain opposing aspects. However, the tasks they carry out are utterly dissimilar, and they cannot be substituted for one another. Emotions are not cognitive tools. Treating them as such poses the greatest risk to one's life and general wellbeing. The question of whether one's judgment is accurate or inaccurate is unrelated to how one feels about any fact or situation. Realization of reality does not occur through emotional perception.

One of the main traits of mental illness is the tendency to let one's feelings, such as one's hopes and anxieties, drive one's thoughts, behaviors, and standard of judgment. This is a treatment for neurosis, not just one of its symptoms. It is a policy that entails destroying one's capacity for reason.

The fact that melancholy, guilt, misery, and terror are the main emotions an irrational is left with after putting this philosophy into reality is not coincidental; rather, it is logical and unavoidable. As any psychotherapist can attest, the idea of the joyful irrationals is a myth, much as the idea of the happy psychotic.

Whether they think of some of their emotions as primaries or merely "there," most people tend to view some of them as trustworthy guides to behavior. However, there is a wealth of easily accessible material that contradicts such a mistake.

Man cannot experience an emotion simply by perceiving an object, much alone know what that emotion would be about. Except in terms of the value-significance of the object to the perceiver, the emotional response to an object is unexplainable. And this inevitably entails an evaluation procedure. For instance, when three men view a scoundrel, the first man sees how much this person has compromised his humanity and feels contempt; the second man wonders how he can feel secure in a society where people like this can prosper; and the third man secretly envies the scoundrel's "success" and feels admiration. The same thing is perceived by all three persons. Their differing assessments of the significance of what they observe account for the disparities in their emotional responses.

Emotions are not the result of any kind of innate concepts, just as they are not produced by objects of sense as such. Man cannot have an innate knowledge of what is beneficial or bad for him since he lacks an understanding of what is true or false. Again, a man's values are a result of how much and how well he thinks.

A person's values, as they are seen to relate to a particular situation, are the source of an estimate, which is always the reflection and outcome of an emotional response.

This final point must be emphasized. In addition to the matter of whether his values are objectively legitimate, a man may misapply them in a particular situation, making his assessment inaccurate even by his own standards. For instance, a man can misunderstand the nature of the relevant information. Alternatively, he can concentrate on a single feature of a situation while overlooking its overall context, resulting in an utterly misguided judgement. Or, his evaluation process might be skewed by internal conflicts and pressures that have little to do with the problem he is facing. He can also fail to see that his previous assumptions and judgments are insufficient for a judgment of the current circumstance, which includes novel and unfamiliar factors.

Man does not automatically keep in mind the complete, suitable context while forming value judgments. Out-of-context, succinct responses are typical. One of the consequences of improperly relying on one's emotions is a propensity to give such responses excessive weight. Sometimes people blame themselves for fleeting feelings they had out of context or that mean absolutely nothing. Imagine, for instance, that a happily married man who is madly in love with his wife meets another woman for whom he feels a sexual desire. He is briefly tempted to have an affair with her, but as soon as the full scope of his life returns, he loses the desire. Only the abstract sexual appreciation remains; there is no temptation to act. Such an experience may be benign and completely typical. However, many men would erroneously criticize themselves and speculate about potential character flaws shown by their sexual response. Unresolved conflicts are indicated by enduring and persistent emotions that conflict with one's conscious convictions. It's not necessary to be constantly emotional.

If one understands the nature and source of their emotions, one can use enduring and persistent feelings that run counter to their beliefs and/or other values as a tool for self-improvement. A man can learn about values that he has established without vocal identification, conceptions that he has accepted without consideration, and views that represent the opposite of his stated conclusions by looking at the origins of his feelings and desires.

Though it may appear that reason and emotion are at odds, what is actually happening is a conflict between two competing ideas, one of which is unconscious and only manifests as an emotion. Such disputes are not always easily resolved; it depends on how complicated the pertinent topics are. Resolutions are possible, though, and the first step is to identify the true nature of the issue that has to be fixed. A proper and attainable goal is the guilt-free emotional spontaneity that men yearn for—the liberation from torturous self-doubts, enervating sadness, and paralyzing worries. But only a reasonable understanding of emotions and how they relate to thought makes it possible. It is only feasible if one's emotions are not mysterious and if one does not worry that they will destroy one. A person who has taken on the duty of recognizing and affirming the values that underlay his emotions—the person for whose emotional freedom and openness do not imply the suspension of awareness—has the right and the reward to do so.

Emotion and Actions

In terms of man's survival, the pleasure-pain mechanism of consciousness—the ability to feel happiness and suffering—performs a vital role. The psychological function of motivation is involved in this process.

Imagine a living thing with a constitution that caused it to feel pain whenever it performed a life-affirming action and joy whenever it performed a life-harming one. Such a thing could not possibly exist; it would be biologically impossible. But even if it were to suddenly and miraculously appear, it would disappear very shortly. It was unable to live since its pleasure-pain system was set against its own life. Nothing could compel or inspire it to take the acts that were necessary for its existence.

A byproduct of effective activity, pleasure (in the broadest sense of the word, as both a bodily and emotional sensation) is a byproduct of life. Pain is a harbinger of impending danger and an indicator of ineffective behavior.

The biochemical basis for pleasure and pain is as described above. The reward for a successful (life-serving) action is pleasure, which serves as motivation to take additional action. Pain is a deterrent to acting differently since it is the consequence of ineffective (life-negating) behavior.

What a man perceives as pleasant or unpleasant on a bodily level, or on the level of senses, depends on his physiology (although psychological factors are often involved). A man's values determine what makes him happy or unhappy on an emotional level. His body does not allow for free will. His principles.

Man programs his emotional mechanism through his values, as I mentioned previously. Man can temporarily tamper with this mechanism by programming illogical values. He will eventually be unable to avoid the logic inherent in its biological function. The law of contradiction serves as a guardian of the biological function of the human emotional mechanism. A man could not continue to live if his values were continuously illogical (that is, at odds with his necessities and nature). Most men mix their rational and irrational values, which inevitably leads to internal conflict. In such a situation, one value must be frustrated in order for another to be satisfied.

The 'joy' of becoming intoxicated, followed by the agony of a hangover, is the most basic illustration of the aforementioned. Irrational values always have some sort of "hangover," whether it be the loss of one's health, career, marriage, intellectual ability, sexual prowess, or self-esteem. This is one of their defining traits. The rewards—or demons—of a man's emotions depend on the ideals he chooses. The final say always belongs to nature and reality.

The emotional state that results from achieving one's values is happiness or joy. The emotional condition that results from having one's values rejected or destroyed is suffering. Happiness or suffering may be viewed as an incentive system built into man by nature, a system of reward and punishment, designed to progress and protect man's life, since the activity of pursuing and obtaining values is the essence of the life-process.

Physical pain's biological utility, or benefit in ensuring survival, is well acknowledged. Man is alerted to bodily danger through physical pain, allowing him to take the necessary corrective action. The biological purpose of psychological distress, such as worry, guilt, and sadness, in relation to a person's consciousness is not properly understood. It serves as a warning that he needs to take action to change the way his mind is currently operating. Of course, he has the option to disregard the advice, but not without consequence.

The biological usefulness of emotions has another component. Man is capable of inferring conclusions and acquiring numerous implicit values and premises without being aware of doing so. He would be in danger if he had no way of knowing about them, if they had an impact on his behavior without giving him any warnings. However, man receives the proof of these subconscious presumptions through his emotions, allowing him to adjust or amend them as needed.

Every emotion has an intrinsic action tendency, or an incentive to take some action related to that particular emotion, which is indicative of the motivational force and function of emotions. A man's emotional response to something he loves highly, such as love, include the action propensity to make touch with the one they love, to seek out their presence, to engage in intellectual, emotional, physical, etc. interaction. The feeling of dread is a man's reaction to something that puts his values in danger; it includes the propensity to avoid or run away from the feared object. Values require action by their very nature. Emotions and value-responses are both valid. There may not necessarily be physical activity involved. For instance, there are peaceful contentment sentiments that make a guy want merely to sit quietly and think about what makes him happy or how beautiful the world is; his desired ideals have been attained and all he wants to do is focus on and experience the truth of their existence. However, each emotion has some implications for behavior. (Of course, this does not imply that the action must be executed; it may not be feasible or appropriate in a particular situation.)

Some emotions have a negative action implication, meaning that they tend to explicitly slow down or hinder activity. In the case of acute depression, this is obvious. The individual believes that nothing is worthwhile, that effort is pointless, and that he is powerless to find happiness. The tendency is to remain still, be passive, or withdraw.

Every emotional reaction has a dual value assessment that has ramifications for both the action and the response. The judgment "for me" or "against me"—as well as "to what extent"—is reflected in every feeling. As a result, emotions vary depending on their intensity and content. In actuality, these are not two distinct value judgements; rather, they are essential components of a single value judgment that can only be distinguished through the process of abstraction. They are felt as a single reaction. However, it is clear that the intensity factor affects both the strength of the action-inspiring impulse and, occasionally, the type of action that is executed.

A tendency to take action can be separated from the larger emotional field in which it arises as an emotional experience. It is the want or aversion emotion when viewed as a separate experience.

While not every value assessment results in an emotion, every emotion flows from one. Only when the participating person believes the value judgment to be significant for his own life and relevant to his actions will an emotion be felt.

Consider the case of a research scientist who reads about a recent finding in a field unrelated to his own, unrelated to his professional or personal interests, and unrelated to his own plans or objectives. He might rate the discovery as "excellent," but he wouldn't feel anything particularly strong or obvious as a result.

Let's say that he recognizes a potential lead in the discovery that could help him solve one of his own research problems. In this case, his evaluation of "good" is accompanied with excitement and a desire to follow the path.

If he believes the discovery holds a clear-cut, significant key to solving his own problem, his feelings of happiness and need to go to his lab will be much stronger.

Think about a different kind of example now. A man has a sexual yearning for the woman he is in love with. Then he becomes impotent due to a bodily injury. Although he retains the ability to feel sexual desire, it has drastically changed in emotional quality as a result of the change in his physical state, which also had an impact on the action implications of his judgment of the lady. Her value as a whole has not changed in his estimation; what has changed is how it relates to him and his own behavior.

A man must be able to do some sort of action in relation to an object in order to feel love for it, whether it be a person, a pet, or a new house. If not, his assessment of what is "good" is just an abstract judgment without any personal importance.

The application of the same theory to the feeling of terror is amply demonstrated. A person experiences terror when he perceives a threat to his beliefs because he knows there is a course of action he could, should, or might be able to pursue. If he were absolutely certain that taking any action was impossible, he may experience regret or sadness but not terror. (Note that fear always implies uncertainty; if a person is certain of what to do and is capable of doing it, he or she does not experience fear.)

Sometimes, a person's feelings and the actions they inspire are highly ethereal; in this case, the value response is essentially metaphysical. A person may be moved to tears by a significant accomplishment or a masterpiece of art because he perceives in it a manifestation of human creativity, the victory of human efficacy, the heroic, the noble, and the commendable. This sight serves as emotional fuel for the pursuit of his own values.

It's noteworthy to note that great joy and profound sorrow are both perceived as "metaphysical." The perception of living in a "benevolent" cosmos, or one in which one's values are achievable and in which one's efforts are open to success, is implicit in a sensation of genuine satisfaction. A sense of living in a world where one's values are unattainable, a world in which one is impotent, a world in which no activity is worthwhile since nothing can succeed, is implicit in intense sorrow.

Unresolved conflicts in a man's values have negative psychological effects. Understanding this problem requires consideration of the natural tendency toward action that underlies emotional responses.

Reality cannot include contradictions. However, a man is capable of having, with or without awareness, opposing thoughts, beliefs, and values. Contradictory concepts cannot be reconciled; instead, they undermine the mind's capacity for integration and the general certainty of man's knowledge.

Short-circuiting of the value-emotion-action system is the devastating result of holding opposing values. Two opposing and conflicting desires to act strike a guy. In essence, he feels or knows that he is being asked to perform the impossible. If the disagreement is avoided and suppressed rather than acknowledged and resolved, the psychological disaster will be more greater the more profound the values involved.

Consider the following scenario as a classic example of this issue. A priest who has committed himself fully to his vows of celibacy. But he starts to feel attracted sexually to a member of his church. One Sunday as he approaches his pulpit, he sees her and instantly experiences a violent sexual yearning. He briefly feels propelled toward a course of action that is intolerably at odds with the one to which he has dedicated his life. He immediately collapses. He has suppressed his desire for the woman, so when he comes to, he has no memory of it. However, he feels acute, seemingly pointless anguish.

When there is a value conflict, the emotional mechanism that converts assessments (conscious events) into actions short-circuits the process of consciousness to actuality (events of reality).

The programming of a man's emotional mechanism determines whether he experiences happiness or misery. It depends on how true and consistent his values are. He is a machine with an emotional apparatus. It is driven by man. He makes the motivating power of his emotions work for or against his life depending on the values he chooses.

Repression and Emotions:
The Suppression of Negatives

Certain thoughts, memories, identifications, and evaluations are prohibited from coming into conscious awareness through the subconscious brain process known as repression.

Repression is an automated avoidance response in which a person's attention is unintentionally drawn away from any "forbidden" content coming from subconscious or less conscious areas of their mind. Repression is the most dangerous and powerful of the many things that can make a guy feel cut off from his own feelings.

But what is suppressed is not feeling per se. A true feeling cannot be suppressed; if it is not experienced, it does not exist. Thoughts are constantly the target of repression. In the case of emotions, what is either blocked or suppressed are evaluations that would produce emotions or identifications of the characteristics of one's own emotions.

The knowledge of the emotion a man is feeling might be suppressed. Or he can suppress his understanding of its breadth and depth. The awareness of the source of the emotion, i.e., who or what sparked it, can also be suppressed. He can also suppress the causes of his emotional reaction. Or he can convince himself that he has no feelings by suppressing conceptual awareness that he is feeling any emotion at all.

For instance, a man could convince himself that he is feeling happy when, in reality, he is feeling jealous anger after learning of a friend's success in business. Another option is for a student to downplay how devastated he feels after being rejected from the college of his choice and persuade himself that he is "just a little upset." A young person may blame their despair on the idea that no one understands them if they feel sexually rejected by their sweetheart and suppress their hurt out of embarrassment. Or, a wife can rationalize her anxiety and anger by believing that her husband has no interest in her or their house while suppressing her guilt about an affair. A man could also deceive himself into believing that the topic doesn't interest him at all if he is secretly angry and frustrated over being rejected from a particular club. In contrast to evasion, which is initiated voluntarily and consciously, repression is unintentional and subconscious. Certain thoughts are barred and hindered from accessing conscious consciousness when someone is repressed; they are not evicted from focal awareness.

Three facts about the human mind need to be taken into account in order to comprehend the mechanism of repression.

1. Every awareness must be selective. A man can never focus on everything that is going on around him at any given time, therefore he must choose which things to focus on in order to ignore everything else. This holds true for both introspection and extrospection.

Focused awareness involves separating specific facts or aspects from the larger context in which they emerge and giving them their own consideration. Both the perceptual and intellectual levels of awareness share this.

2. Awareness might vary in intensity. Along the spectrum from focused awareness to peripheral awareness to complete unawareness or unconsciousness, there is a gradient of deteriorating mental clarity. For example, the area of pure blue (focal awareness) shades off by virtually imperceptible degrees to blue-violent (peripheral awareness), which shades into pure violet, to use a visual metaphor, the continuum involved is like that between two adjoining hues on the spectrum (unconsciousness).

Because of the phenomenon of degrees of awareness, a guy can keep his left hand from knowing what his right hand is doing. A man may be only very dimly aware of something, but nevertheless be aware enough to realize that he does not wish to be more fully aware.

A man may or may not choose to perform this action, but the mind may contain information that is currently neither subconscious nor in focal awareness but rather exists in a wider field of consciousness. This information must be distinguished and identified by a directed effort that will bring it into focal awareness.

3. Man is an autonomous computer. He can retain, integrate, and automate knowledge to an immeasurable degree larger than any other living species.

The amount of programmed data in a man's brain increases immensely as he matures, learning to construct concepts and then wider concepts, broadening the scope and effectiveness of his thinking. All of these functions are programmed and automated as part of normal human growth, including cognitions, assessments, and physical abilities. Man's continuing intellectual development as well as the quick cognitive, emotional, and physical responses that are necessary for survival are all made possible by this subconsciously held programming.

The objective or purpose a man has established affects what information, out of the entirety of his knowledge, will be fed to him from the subconscious while his mind is actively focused. The information pertinent to that specific subject will typically flow into a man's conscious mind if, for example, he is thinking about a physics problem. By establishing the proper goal(s)—by understanding the circumstances and, in effect, giving the subconscious the proper orders—focal awareness regulates the subconscious process.

The subconscious is governed by the "standing orders" it has received, or a man's long-term interests, values, and worries, in addition to the orders it gets in any given instant. These have an impact on how information is stored and organized, how it is reactivated, and the connections that the subconscious mind makes in reaction to fresh information or stimuli.

This is particularly clear when it comes to creative thinking. The foundation of creative thinking is the creation of a routine for observing and incorporating any information that might be pertinent to a particular area of interest. Though a thinker's primary worry may not always be on his mind—he may occasionally give attention to other matters—his subconscious is in charge of keeping him alert and calling for the conscious mind's attention if any important information arises. A last, split-second integration that is built on countless earlier observations and connections stored in the subconscious and held in anticipation of the final connection that would sum them up and give them significance is what causes the phenomenon of the sudden "inspiration" or "flash of insight."

Let's now discuss repression's psychological basis.

Mechanically, repression is merely one of several applications of the automatization principle. Repression entails an automated standing order that forbids integration, the exact opposite of the one engaged in creative thought.

The simplest form of repression is the suppression of unpleasant or frightful memories from conscious consciousness. In this instance, an unpleasant or terrifying incident that was present at the time and would be painful or terrible to recollect is prevented from coming to mind.

Of course, forgetting as a phenomenon is not unhealthy; memory, like awareness, is naturally selective, and people typically recall the things to which they give importance. Repressed memories, however, are deliberately suppressed; they do not merely "fade away."

Consider the case below. The temptation to steal money from a friend's locker at school convinces a 12-year-old boy to give in. The child is left feeling ashamed and guilty after the incident, and he is shaking with fear that he will be discovered.

His behavior goes undetected for a while. He tries to erase the memory and quickly diverts his attention, telling himself, in effect, "I don't want to remember," but every time the recollection of his theft returns, he relives the excruciating embarrassment and remorse. I hope it will leave me alone and disappear! It eventually does.

The memory is prevented from entering conscious awareness, so he no longer needs to push it out. It is stifled. The process of erasing memories has been automated.

The recollection is stopped before it can reach him if it ever starts to float near the top of awareness. The memory is then once again buried by a psychological alarm-signal.

He may run into the friend he took the money from twenty years later and greet him warmly; he has no recollection of his crime. Or he might feel a little uneasy around his friend and be reluctant to rekindle the friendship—without knowing why.

Not all repressed memories are as localized and precise as this one. Repression has a propensity to "stretch out," to include additional events connected to the upsetting one, so that the repressive mechanism may have an impact on recollections of entire regions or epochs in a man's life.

People who experienced traumatically terrible childhoods can occasionally display early upbringing amnesia. They don't just suppress specific episodes; they feel the need to forget the happenings of an entire decade, and they frequently succeed to an amazing degree. They may experience a strong wave of pain or depression if any issues concerning their upbringing are brought up, with very little, if any, ideational material to explain it.

Like memories, thoughts and judgments might be kept from awareness because of the suffering they would create.

For instance, a religious person might be horrified to discover that he is entertained questions about his professed beliefs; he then condemns himself as wicked and, in essence, commands these doubts to "Get thee behind me, Satan," causing them to vanish from his awareness. He initially avoids these uncertainties, but later on it is unnecessary because he has repressed them. Then, in order to distract himself from any leftover unease he is unable to completely eliminate, he may go on to deepen the repression through increased religious fervor.

Or think of a woman who is neurotically dependent and marries a nasty, despotic person. Because she has given her life to him and the idea that her owner and lord is irrational and malicious would terrify her, she dares not allow any criticism of him to penetrate her consciousness. She deliberately keeps her thoughts out of it as she watches him act. She has made a standing order prohibiting evaluation automated. She is aware of how she would evaluate her husband's actions if they were displayed by any other guy, but she does not allow this awareness to be integrated with the actions she sees in her husband. Her repression is strengthened and sustained in large part by evasion, but evasion is not the sole factor in her blindness; to a significant extent, she has set herself up to be blind.

Children whose parents are horrifyingly insane often exhibit a similar pattern of repression. Children frequently suppress their bad opinions of their parents because they find it easier to blame themselves in a fight than to ponder the prospect that their parents might be monsters. This same phenomenon can be seen in the citizens' attitudes about the rulers in a dictatorship.

The attempts to suppress feelings and impulses are perhaps the most difficult cases of repression. The repressive mechanism can be used to combat an emotion in one of two ways: either before the feeling is felt by blocking the appraisal that would cause it, or during and/or after the emotional experience, in which case the repression targets the man's awareness of his own emotional state. (Since it was already mentioned that emotions cannot be suppressed as such, I refer to "emotional repression" in the context of the preceding paragraph whenever I use the term.)

A man tries to suppress a feeling if he perceives it as threatening in any way. The threat could be merely physical discomfort, a sense of helplessness, or a setback to his self-esteem.

Think of a sweet, gentle woman who is frequently forced upon and taken advantage of by her friends. One day, she snaps into a tremendous wrath at them, and she is startled and shaken by her own emotion. She is terrified for three reasons: first, she thinks that only a highly immoral person could feel such wrath; second, she fears what the rage would cause her to do; and third, she fears that her friends will find out about her feelings and leave her. Do not evaluate their activities, and especially do not judge their behavior toward you. Be amenable to everything, she admonishes herself vehemently. This order paralyzes her evaluative mechanism when it is subconsciously automated; as a result, she no longer feels fury, but she also feels very little else. She is unaware of the true significance of any events for her. She then goes on to intensify her repression by creating a new barrier to keep her from realizing her own emotional depravity; she reassures herself that she experiences all the feelings she thinks are suitable to experience.

Or: A man notices that he is hanging out with a married couple who are his pals more and more. He ignores the reality that he is much happier in the presence of the wife than when he and the husband are by themselves. He is in love with her, but he is unaware of it. His sense of self-worth would suffer if he knew; first, because he would perceive it as betraying his allegiance to the spouse; and second, since the love is hopeless and would reflect poorly on his realism and "hardheadedness." If fleeting feelings of love or want run through his mind, he doesn't stop to consider them or analyze their importance; as a result, the usual integration process is disrupted. He can no longer pinpoint the exact moment when the first faint romantic notions entered his mind and were violently suppressed before they could fully awaken him with a "No!" that lacked any context or justification. He also doesn't understand why his life seems to become abruptly unjustifiably, desolately barren when he leaves his friends' house.

Or: A man who has never achieved much is jealous and resentful of his talented, aspirational younger sibling. However, the man has always expressed love for him. There is one fleeting moment when the man feels triumphant delight when his brother is drafted into the army. Then, in the following instant, he conceals the nature of his feeling—which is later suppressed—and makes a joke with his brother about how the army will "make a man of him." He later learns that his brother has been killed in action and is confused as to why all he feels is a heavy numbness and a diffuse, objectless guilt. He tells himself that his grief is too great for tears and drags himself around, strangely exhausted, not realizing that all of his energy is going into never letting himself identify the repressed wish that some enemy bullet has fulfilled. Then, after some time, she occasionally has a horrifying outburst of loathing for her children. Except for the occasional instances when she is irrationally and uncharacteristically negligent of her children's physical safety, she suppressed these feelings and is not conscious of them again. She then discovers sentiments of disdain for her spouse, which horrifies her. She suppresses them and commits herself wholeheartedly to playing the part of devoted wife, but their sex with each other becomes monotonous and meaningless. She goes to great lengths to portray to their friends the image of a happy, "well-adjusted" wife and mother—apart from the fact that she starts drinking when she is by herself.

Or: A man has strived to never admit that he is terrified since, since boyhood, he has thought of fear as a sign of his power. He has put in place a block that prevents him from acknowledging the emotion when it arises. Although he presents a calm exterior, his speech is sometimes stilted and monosyllabic, and he tends to shy away from any form of close connection. He doesn't seem to react in any way to any values. He expends a tremendous amount of effort just to keep up the appearance of inner balance—to keep his face pleasantly opaque and his mind cautiously empty. He feels most secure during "small chat" or other neutral topics in which no moral expectations are placed on him or are communicated by others during social interactions. At home, he exercises stolidly and earnestly to build his body, admires the hollowness of his face in the mirror, and feels manly—except that he usually steers clear of women because he is almost impotent.

Two particularly dreadful mistakes that can push someone into repression are listed below.

1. A lot of people think their moral character is judged by the feelings they experience.

However, a man's moral worth should be determined by his level of intellect rather than the substance of his emotions, as only the latter is directly under his volitional control (Chapters Seven and Twelve).

A man may make mistakes, whether intentionally or unintentionally, which lead to emotions he recognizes as inappropriate and unwanted; it is possible that some of these improper emotions are the result of mistakes or irrationality from the past. But the approach someone takes to such feelings in the moment affects his moral standing.

He will have ample reason to condemn himself if he continues to behave against his reasons and conscious judgment, to follow his emotions blindly, and to act on them despite knowing that doing so is wrong. Regardless of his previous transgressions, he is acting in the present as a man of integrity if, on the other hand, he refuses to act on them and truly works to recognize and repair his fundamental flaws.

Repression is essentially inescapable if a man uses the substance of his emotions as the yardstick of his moral worth. Though a guy believes, for instance, that having a sexual desire for his neighbor's wife is morally similar to having an affair with her, he will feel forced to suppress that want, even if he never intended to act on it.

All of the aforementioned ideas also apply to suppressing "immoral" thinking.

Freudian psychoanalysts assert that man cannot escape from his irrational and immoral wants because they are part of his nature (i.e., they are contained in his purported "id"). Instead, he can only repress them and transform them into "socially acceptable" forms. Repression is a life need, according to Freudians. They are forced to do so by their secularized interpretation of the Original Sin theory. Since they believe that some immoral and destructive desires are ingrained in human nature from birth and do not understand that a man's emotions and desires are the result of acquired (not innate) value-premises that, when necessary, can be altered and corrected, they are left with no other option but to repress him.

Please take note that the (neurotic) symptom is not produced by suppression, but rather by the failure of it, to repress, to cite psychoanalyst A. A. Brill from his Lectures on Psychoanalytic Psychiatry. People frequently misunderstand Freud's assertion that repression causes illness, leading them to conclude that the best way to stay healthy is to never repress. Now, only a total moron would think or utter something like that. No one, not even an animal, is free to act however they like, and Freud and his school of thought never supported such lunacy. 3 This brings us to the second significant mistake that causes males to repress:

2. A lot of individuals think that one must act on a feeling or desire if they feel it.

The quotation from Brill above implies this idea. Take note of the choice he presents: either a man suppresses certain urges, rendering himself oblivious of them, or he does "exactly what he pleases," yielding to each impulse that arises. That's ridiculous.

A logical individual doesn't act on his emotions irrationally or suppress them. A man's conviction that he won't act on an emotion just because he feels it is one of the best defenses against repression; this enables him to calmly identify his emotions and assess their justification without fear or guilt.

The paradoxical relationship between emotional self-indulgence and suppression is intriguing. Man, who suppresses his emotions out of fear will be driven by unconscious motivation, which means he will be subject to emotions he is reluctant to acknowledge. The man who heedlessly indulges his emotions also has the best reason to fear them and is, at least in part, compelled to repress as a means of self-preservation.

Therefore, a man must be ready to face any thought and any feeling and to consider them rationally, confident in the knowledge that he will not act without knowing what he is doing and why. This is the only way for a man to avoid repression.

In every aspect of a man's existence, including his understanding of the contents of his own mind, ignorance is not bliss. Repressed material doesn't go away; it's just forced underground, where it might continue to affect a person in ways they are unaware of, leading to actions they are unable to explain, and occasionally bursting into neurotic symptoms.

There are times in a man's life when he must repress his thoughts and emotions. But there are differences between repression and suppression. In order to direct one's attention elsewhere, suppression is the conscious, deliberate, non-invasive expulsion of particular thoughts or feelings from primary awareness. Suppression entails the underlying assumption that one will pay attention to the suppressed material later, when it is suitable, rather than denying any facts or pretending they do not exist.

For instance, when preparing for an exam, a student might have to hide his thoughts and feelings about a much-anticipated vacation. He is not avoiding or suppressing these thoughts and feelings; rather, he understands that his focus is currently needed elsewhere and behaves accordingly. Or, imagine a man who finds himself getting upset during a conversation; he controls the anger, though he does not deny it, in order to think more clearly and devote all of his attention to the problems that need to be handled.

However, there is occasionally a risk associated with suppression: a man may do so when there are still unresolved problems present that need for additional consideration and analysis. He might do it without intending to be dishonest. However, a suppression that is routinely applied can develop into repression; in other words, the suppression becomes automated.

Evasion is frequently used to precede and reinforce repression, but it is not a required or fundamental aspect of the repressive process. It is possible for someone to mistakenly—but not necessarily dishonestly—believe that he can order painful or unpleasant emotions to disappear. If this is done frequently enough, it can lead to an automatized block.

However, a man becomes more prone to the rapid repression of negatively charged data the more he engages in evasion, that is, the more firmly he sets in his mind the idea that the disagreeable or unsettling need not be looked at. In such a scenario, the repressive strategy generalizes and develops into a recognizable, instinctive reaction.

Emotions and Suppression
The Suppression of Positives

The Freudian understanding of human nature has led to the idea of repression being predominantly connected with negatives, i.e., the repression of the immoral and irrational. However, there are a lot of terrible examples of males suppressing sensible and positive emotions.

Because he perceives them as being threatening to him in some manner, a person suppresses parts of his ideas, feelings, or memories. In particular, when a person suppresses certain emotions or desires, he does so because he believes that they are wrong, unworthy of him, inappropriate, immoral, unrealistic, or evidence of some sort of irrationality on his part—and that they are dangerous due to the potential actions that they may inspire.

Repression is not a logical answer to the issue of upsetting or undesired mental contents, as we have already established. However, it is especially regrettable when the suppressed thoughts or emotions are actually right, good, normal, and healthy.

A person may hold themselves to an incorrect standard, condemning feelings and needs that are totally legitimate, and if he does this, he will try to suppress virtues and necessary needs rather than vices.

This misconception holds that a placid, uncondemning expectation and acceptance of irrationality in people is a requirement of maturity and "realism." As an illustration, consider the psychology of a man who suppresses his desire to find rationality and consistency in people, and who suppresses his pain and frustration at their absence.

Childhood encounters with human irrationality are among the psychological traumas and initial instances of repression that many people experience. When a young mind is trying to establish a solid grasp of reality, it is frequently exposed to what seems to be an incomprehensible cosmos by the behaviors of parents and other adults. People, unlike inanimate objects, seem to be beyond comprehension. Not nature, but rather people, seem to be a menace. And more often than not, he represses, denies, never addresses, never comprehends, never overcomes the issue.

The irrationality to which the individual we are considering was exposed as a child was not an act of deliberate cruelty or malice. It was just his parents acting in a "regular" way, which is something that most adults take for granted.

There were arbitrary rules and arbitrary, unexplained exceptions; unexpected rewards and unprovoked punishments; arbitrary promises made and broken; over solicitude when the parent was in one mood and callous remoteness when the parent was in another; pleasant responses to questions one day and irritably dismissing them the next; sudden expressions of love followed by sudden explosions of resentment; subtle pressures, etc.

It wasn't a single incident or moment that caused the trauma; rather, it was a series of blows that were delivered over time to a victim who was not yet ready to comprehend that he was a victim or of what. He was unable to comprehend the actions of his elders; all he knew was that he felt entrapped in a dangerous and incomprehensible environment.

As he became older, numerous other individuals he came into contact with, as well as his illogical playmates, instructors, etc., affirmed and strengthened this view.

Early on, he started suppressing his emotions. He disliked feeling confused and apprehensive since they were painful. He was unable to comprehend the reasons behind his emotions and his feelings themselves. His judgements lacked the conviction of certainty, thus he could not yet be completely secure in his ability to assess his parents and other people accurately. He described his sense of fear as being at times overwhelming and paralyzing. He therefore made an effort to ignore the existence of the issue in order to lessen his suffering and to keep himself under control. This meant becoming emotionally inert in the face of dishonesty, hypocrisy, inconsistency, and evasiveness. This had the meaning of deactivating his ability to render moral judgements.

He has now acquired the ability to "accept" human irrationality as an adult. In this sense, "acceptance" does not mean knowing that many men behave irrationally and that he must be ready to deal with this issue; it implies accepting irrationality as the usual and natural, ceasing to view it as an anomaly, and refraining from condemning it.

When a friend he had every reason to believe in betrays him in some way, he can't help but feel wounded and astonished. He then blames himself for his response, thinking that he is unrealistic and naive.

He feels terrible because he can't completely suppress his frustrated, tortured longing for rationality. His mentality has been so severely corrupted by suppression.

Now consider a different scenario: a man who suppresses his idealism, or his aspire to any ideals higher than the banal.

When he was a young lad, no one shared or understood his feelings regarding the books he read or the things he liked; no one shared or understood his feeling that a man's life should be significant and that he should accomplish something challenging and outstanding. People kept saying, "Oh, don't take yourself so seriously," to him. You are illogical. He gave up because he was offended by people's attitudes, felt like an outsider, and did not want to feel that way. As a result, he did not make an effort to understand his own desires and values or to analyze the situation carefully and objectively. He would say indifferently to his pals after watching a love film about a man's bravery: "Not bad. although that was really cheesy, didn't it?" — and suppress the recollection of the emotions he had been hiding out in the dark for two hours in the theater. As a middle-aged man, Babbitt now listens to his own soul as it talks about the wonderful things he wants to achieve when he grows up. He then tells his son to mow the grass and sits alone, wondering, "Why am I crying?"

Or: The man who had experienced excruciating loneliness in his youth. He had not been able to find somebody to like or admire or to converse with. He only had one girl in his care, and she had gone off with another boy. A really strong, independent man could not have such a need, he grew to believe. He believed that his loneliness was a weakness and that the anguish of his unsatisfied longing for someone he could value was a flaw he must overcome in himself. He suppressed his emotions more and more. His demeanor in public changed to one that was detached and upbeat. He now meets a woman at the age of thirty with whom he immediately falls in love. However, a subconscious barrier prevents him from knowing how much he loves her since, should their love not be returned, it would cause him to relive his past misery. His repression prevents him from knowing her significance, thus he is unable to share it with her. He visits her frequently but adopts a posture of amused, detached fondness because he believes it shows strength. She first responds to him. But gradually she pulls back, repulsed by a passionless distance that she views as frail and feminine.

Or: The man who suppresses his desire for the respect and adulation he has gained because he incorrectly sees it as a sign of independence failure and does not comprehend the feelings of loneliness and an odd, undesired bitterness that occasionally overtake him.

Or, the woman who suppresses her sexual arousal out of fear of upsetting her conservative, timid husband—and does not recognize the apathy that permeates more and more aspects of her life.

Or: The woman who suppresses her femininity because she believes the stereotype that femininity and intellect are incompatible, and who does not comprehend the tension and animosity that results in the sex world as a result. (Or: The woman who suppresses her intelligence out of acceptance of the same dichotomy and the resulting resentment.)

Or, the man with genuine self-esteem who controls his urge to assert himself out of deference to the neurotic sensibilities of those who are psychologically less secure and do not comprehend his sporadic outbursts of rebellious, seemingly unwarranted rage.

Repression is an attempt to strengthen one's sense of control over one's life, yet it always and inevitably has the opposite effect. Be aware that in each of the aforementioned situations, repression exacerbates irritation and pain rather than relieving it. Facts cannot be eliminated by self-made blindness, regardless of a person's motivations. Instead, the person who attempts it just succeeds in undermining his own consciousness.

Repression has terrible repercussions on a man's ability to think clearly and effectively in addition to destroying his emotions. Men tend to have unmanageable minds and confused thinking when they try to think about any issue in an area that has been affected by their repression. His intellect is restrained; it is not free to consider every detail that might be relevant; it is not allowed access to essential data. He feels incapable of drawing conclusions as a result, or the conclusions she draws are unreliable.

This does not imply that a man is forever disabled if he suppresses certain thoughts or sensations because he is still capable of doing so with prolonged effort. The unblocked section of the repressors' mind is still able to work on eliminating the restrictions because they only completely impair his thoughts.

Repressed material does not totally disappear; instead, it constantly makes an indirect appearance. The presence of emotions and desires that seem unrelated to and incomprehensible in light of one's conscious convictions and the presence of contradictions in one's responses—contradictions between one's desires, or between one's emotions and one's actions—are the two broad categories of clues by which repressed material can be traced, respectively. Successful de-repression requires an awareness of these paradoxes, and this awareness serves as the foundation for one's introspective efforts to break down mental barriers.

The specifics of the de-repression process are not the subject of this discussion. However, it should be mentioned that the procedure might be very challenging. Sometimes the complexity is so great that a man may need the assistance of a skilled psychotherapist.

It is essential that a man adopt the policy of being aware of his emotions: that he takes note of, conceptualize, and understand the causes of his emotional reactions. This will help him avoid repression—or help him de-repress. The main reason it is frequently so simple for males to repress is their policy of lack of interest for and ignorance of their own mental states and processes. When this policy is constantly maintained, repression becomes practically impossible.

Man must learn to think about his emotions if he wants them to bring him pleasure rather than pain. The "cold hand" that kills is not rational knowledge; rather, it is the power that liberates.

CHAPTER SIX

MENTAL WELLBEING

The Mental Health Code

Definitions of mental health and mental illness are one of the main objectives of psychology as a discipline.

It is widely acknowledged that psychological illnesses are the biggest health issue facing the country. In terms of the number of victims, monetary expenditures, and overall devastation of life, these disorders considerably outnumber any group of medical ailments (such as cancer or the heart). The mentally ill occupy more than half of the hospital beds in this nation. More than half of the physical ailments that patients seek medical attention are thought to have psychological causes. One in every twelve people in the population is predicted to spend some time in a mental institution during their lifetime. (Some predictions are one in ten.) A much higher proportion of people seek psychological assistance from therapists in private practice.

However, there isn't a consensus among psychologists and psychiatrists as to what constitutes mental health or sickness; there aren't any widely accepted definitions or fundamental benchmarks by which to compare one psychological state to another.

Many authors claim that it is impossible to develop a fundamental, generally applicable concept of mental health and that there can be no objective definitions and standards. They claim that all standards are subject to "cultural bias" since behavior that is considered healthy or normal in one culture may be seen as neurotic or abnormal in another. According to the theorists that uphold this view, cultural conformity is the closest thing to a definition of mental health that can be offered. To the extent that a man is "well-adjusted" to his culture, they claim that he is psychologically well.

The concept of "social adaptation" is likely the most frequently encountered one in talks of mental health, regardless of whether the speakers are outspoken proponents of cultural relativism. We are never provided a rationale or scientific reason for why social adaptation is the definition and gold standard of mental health; we are only given the assumption.

Such a description begs the obvious question: What if the standards and beliefs of a certain culture are irrational? Can being able to cope with the absurd be considered mental health? How about, for instance, Nazi Germany? Is a happy Nazi state employee who enjoys his social surroundings and feels calm and at peace with it an example of mental health?

Extreme cultural relativists typically avoid talking about these issues. However, if pressed, they must admit that the individual is cognitively sound; our own cultural prejudices are the only ones making him appear abnormal.

The moderates provide a different response because they are not as eager to completely break their ties to reality. They claim that such a man is not mentally healthy because he is not truly happy; he cannot be; no one could be well-adjusted to a culture that is so abominably crazy. Their response is undoubtedly accurate, but note that it also indicates a different definition of mental health than just social adaptability; it also implies a criterion that the speakers are not directly mentioning.

Numerous authors have pointed out the absurdities that result from the unreasonable arbitrariness of associating mental health with social adaptability. Different psychologists and psychiatrists have offered a range of standards for evaluating mental health in an effort to find more defensible definitions.

For instance, it is said that the mentally healthy person has an unhindered capacity for "growth, development, and self-actualization," "knows who he is," that is, has a strong sense of identity, insight into his own motivation, a high tolerance for stress, is "self-accepting," is free from paralyzing conflicts, has an integrated personality, etc.

These may be accurate descriptions, but they are not mental health definitions, and it is not always apparent what they exactly mean. In general, one can concur with the characterizations above, yet they fall short of the issue. A fundamental principle, or an explanation of the essence of mental health, must be offered. Effects or consequences are traits like the ones mentioned above. But why do they exist?

Placing the problem in a biological context—remembering that man is a living organism and that the concepts of health and disease are inextricably linked to the fundamental alternative confronting all organisms: the issue of life and death—is the key to the problem of defining the concepts of health and disease, as they pertain to man's mind.

This fact is well understood in the context of physical health and illness. A body that is healthy has organs that effectively support the organism's survival; a body that is ill has organs that do not. Any portion of a man's body might be considered healthy or diseased based on how effectively or poorly it performs its survival role. The measure of judgment is life.

There is no other plausible sensible standard. The concept of health or disease is only meaningful or possible when life or death is an option. An inanimate item cannot be healthy or unhealthy; the notions do not apply. The concepts of health and sickness are incomprehensible without life as the reference point.

Psychology must use the same criteria to determine if a man's mind is healthy or ill, just as medical science uses this standard to determine whether or not a man's body is operating as required for man to live. How well a man's mind carries out its biological duty must be used to assess its state of health.

What role does the mind play in biology? Evaluation, action control, and cognition.

The fundamental purpose of a man's consciousness is cognition, or awareness and knowledge of reality's facts. Man must behave, so understanding reality is essential to his existence so that he can control his conduct.

Evaluation is a key connecting factor between cognition and the control of action. Evaluation is the process of determining if a particular reality element is good or detrimental to oneself. Evaluations serve as the basis for and produce goals, feelings, and wants. The goals a man sets for himself and the methods he uses to try to accomplish them are determined by his assessments of what is in his favor and what is against him.

Man unknowingly moves toward self-destruction if his values and aspirations conflict with reality's facts and with his own needs as a living organism. Thus, in order for man to survive, the cognitive function of consciousness must rule over the evaluative function of consciousness, requiring that man choose his values and goals in the complete context of his logical knowledge and understanding.

Man is not perfect, and having a healthy mind does not necessitate never making a mistake in knowledge or judgment. The idea of mental health has to do with how the mind operates. It has to do with how a mind functions in relation to the elements of reality. It has to do with "psycho-epistemology" of men.

The idea of "psycho-epistemology" is essential to the topic of this book as a whole and to the issue of mental health in particular. Therefore, let's think about what this idea means.

Psycho-Epistemology

Psycho-epistemology should be categorized as a subfield of psychology since it is an area of scientific research. It could be referred to as the psychology of thought (or of cognition). Of course, epistemology is a subfield of philosophy; it is the field of study concerned with the nature and sources of human knowledge. Its main goal is to set the standards for knowledge, rules for evidence, and proof so that man can discriminate between what he may and may not consider to be knowledge. A normal (i.e., healthy) consciousness is assumed by epistemology, as is an undamaged intellect that is seeking to understand the truths of reality. Insofar as it is concerned with how the mind functions internally, it is only interested from the position of how relevant it is to establishing the standards of knowledge. Its primary focus is not on mental processes per se, but rather how thoughts relate to reality.

The field of psychology, and notably the field of psycho-epistemology, is responsible for studying mental processes as such.

In order to distinguish the study of mental processes on the conscious and subconscious levels of the human mind, the term "psycho-epistemology" is introduced. The topic is very broad and encompasses a lot of things that are outside the purview of this debate. In this context, I'll limit my discussion to the vitals that directly relate to the issue of mental health.

Mental processes might be voluntary or automated, conscious or subconscious. Conscious, volitional activities and subconscious, automatic ones constantly interact during each thought process. For instance, when addressing a certain problem is the desired outcome, knowledge that has been stored subconsciously is immediately awakened and integrated into the subsequent thought process. On a conscious level, the mind sets goals, divides problems into smaller ones, checks the thought process for coherence and relevance, etc. On a subconscious level, the mind's enormous integrative machinery works to provide the information that will enable the achievement of those selected goals by drawing on previously acquired knowledge, memories, observations, associations, etc.

All goal-directed mental activity—whether the purpose is to acquire knowledge, evoke a memory, or visualize an event, etc.—is characterized by this interaction between the subconscious, automatic, and conscious aspects of the human mind.

The study of the nature of and interaction between the conscious, goal-setting, self-regulatory, and autonomic mental processes is known as psycho-epistemology.

This area of psychology is concerned with all forms of mental processes that the human mind is capable of, both normal and abnormal, as well as with individual variations in how men's brain function.

I've emphasized how self-programming occurs in humans and how conclusions, values, and standing instructions control the automatic integrative mechanism of the subconscious (Chapter Five). As a person grows, he develops a distinctive way of thinking—a distinctive way of solving problems, considering ideas, "processing" real-world information, etc. He may develop the practice of seeking the utmost level of mental clarity possible with relation to whatever problem he is thinking about, or he may start to accept some degree of ambiguity or uncertainty as "normal." He may decide to follow the principle of always trying to understand problems in terms of principles, or he may try to solve issues in terms of the specifics of a particular circumstance without making any attempt to separate the important things from the irrelevant ones or to connect his observations to more general abstractions. His thinking may be receptive to new information, ideas, and arguments, yet it also may be rigid, restrained, or dogmatic. He may develop the ability to distinguish clearly between thinking and feeling, or he may have a propensity to use emotions as cognitive aids. He can develop the habit of depending on the opinions of others or he can regularly use his own first-hand judgment in whatever topic he chooses to consider. He may develop the ability to intellectually recognize his feelings and desires, or he may automate a policy of repression in any situation involving conflict, uncertainty, or self-doubt.

A person's own psycho-epistemology, or self-programmed manner of thinking, is made up of the mental routines and rules they develop through time. These routines and standing orders are crucial in controlling the mind's automatic, subconscious processes because they determine whether or not integrations will be made, what will or won't come into one's conscious awareness, what implications one will or won't understand, how quickly and effectively one will think through a particular problem, etc.

The aforementioned shows that a person's psycho-epistemology may or may not be suitable for the task of accurately appreciating reality, or it may be suitable to a greater or lesser extent. This brings us to the topic of mental health and sickness and how psycho-epistemology relates to it.

The Definition of Mental Health

The objective of consciousness or cognition may be the direction (or the major direction) of a man's psycho-epistemological processes, i.e., they may operate in a reality-oriented manner. Or his psycho-epistemology might be controlled (or predominately controlled) by objectives involving reality-avoidance strategies, that is, objectives involving the subversion of his cognitive system.

The alternative at the heart of the mental health problem is this. If there were no other way for the human mind to function, there would be no need to worry about mental illness.

Mental health is the ability to function cognitively that is reality-bound and the exercise of this ability. The persistent impairment of this ability is mental disease.

As we have seen, the biological function of consciousness serves as the justification for this concept.

Therefore, a man is mentally healthy to the extent that his psycho-epistemological processes are under the control of cognition, or awareness of and touch with reality, and that they satisfy its standards. When a man's psycho-epistemological processes conflict with the demands of cognition and undermine his cognitive efficacy, he is considered to be mentally ill.

Since the essential function of awareness is cognition, which is also the function that governs the other mental processes as intended, any actions or routines that are harmful to this fundamental task are either psychiatric illness' agents or their causes.

The core of biological well-being—the ability of an organism to successfully carry out its duty of survival—is the integration of an organism's physical integrity and the integration of its behaviors in the direction of life-serving purposes. Any factors that prevent integration also prevent life; disintegration is a death-moving force.

The cognitive process and mental wellness depend on integration. Conflict and disintegration are the hallmarks of mental disease.

Evasion, repression, rationalization, and their many derivatives are reality-avoidance techniques that are disintegrative by their own nature and goal. They undermine cognitive function as a result. They are the main causes of mental illnesses.

Healthy consciousness is one that is unhindered, integrated, and in unbroken cognitive contact with reality. Unhealthy states of consciousness include those that are obstructed, fragmented, paralyzed by dread or depression, impaired in their ability to operate by reality-avoidance techniques, and disconnected from reality.

A mental disorder is a thinking disorder, and mental sickness is ultimately a psycho-epistemological condition.

This is usually apparent when the patient has hallucinations, delusions, "word salads," neologisms, time-space disorientations, etc. as their main symptoms. However, it also applies to situations where the patient's symptoms are less obviously cognitive or psycho-epistemological in nature, such as when they are caused by pathological anxiety, depression, hypochondria, conversion responses, sado-masochism, etc. (Chapter Nine).

The signs and effects of a dysfunctional mind are neurotic and psychotic manifestations, such as improper emotional reactions or deviant behavior. But the mind's separation from reality is always the fundamental issue (in some form, to a greater or lesser extent).

Take a pathological instance of depression as an illustration. When a secretary's employer asks her to produce some office reports by the end of the day, the secretary interprets the request as a criticism of her abilities and self-worth and collapses in severe melancholy. To imply that she has "an emotional condition" is inaccurate. She has a psycho-epistemological condition. Her issue is with the way she thinks about and interprets what she sees and hears. Her issues are caused by the mental processes that cause her emotions.

Once such unbalanced emotions start to arise, they frequently have a detrimental impact on a person's thinking, which in turn causes more unbalanced emotions, and so on. One way that detrimental psycho-epistemological policies reinforce and perpetuate themselves is in this way. Emotions reflect evaluations and interpretations; inappropriate or disturbed emotions follow from inappropriate or disturbed judgments; these follow from inadequate or disturbed thinking. However, disturbed emotions do not cause the initial problem; the initial problem creates the disturbed emotions.

The same idea also applies to actions. If a man engages in dishonest, parasitic, and exploitative behavior in his interpersonal interactions, it is his psycho-epistemological policies—not his behavior—that define his mental illness.

We can identify the presence of mental illness by its symptoms, which include irrational thoughts, feelings, and behaviors. They serve as diagnostic assistance. They should not, however, be confused with their psychological bases or causes. Arguments made by cultural relativists who note that ideas, feelings, and actions deemed healthy in one culture may be viewed as neurotic in another are based on the propensity for such confusion.

These findings are irrelevant to the nature of mental health. A modern guy who acted in this way would very surely be psychotic, whereas a primitive man who spoke to trees and believed they were inhabited by conscious spirits would not necessarily imply mental illness. When evaluating the psychological meaning of a man's behavior, it is important to consider his environment and the knowledge that he has at his disposal. We can't always tell from a behavior observation taken out of context whether or not it indicates an anomaly in a person's thought processes. This is a crucial fact that the diagnostician must keep in mind, but it has nothing to do with the issue of what qualifies as mental health.

It should be highlighted that a man's brief lack of cognitive awareness of reality, such as what might happen when they are experiencing a violent emotion, does not signify mental disease. Mental illness suggests that there are lingering barriers to a person's ability to think clearly. The presence of automated (or partially automated) barriers to conceptual integration is implied by mental illness.

The patient's condition is classified as a mental illness merely because there is a breakdown in his cognitive function, even in situations where the physical causes of mental illness (genetic, biochemical, etc.) are present. It is not a mental disease if this breakdown has not occurred.

A person does not display symptoms like pathological anxiety, depersonalization, obsessive-compulsive behaviors, conversion hysteria, or delusions of persecution if his cognitive contact with reality is unbroken, his perceptions, judgments, and evaluations are free of blocks and distortions, he is willing and able to look at any fact relevant to his life, and his integrative powers are unimpaired.

It is difficult to avoid the conclusion that there is some degree of victim complicity in the majority (and possibly all) cases of mental illness with a psychological basis. He didn't directly will his disease, but he voluntarily started reality-avoiding practices that led to it. Small avoidances, indulgences in irrational wishes, capitulations to insurmountable anxieties, and deliberate acts of self-blindness are how the infection begins and are then perpetuated as the illness progresses over time. It must be acknowledged that there are instances where the element of evasion appears to be mostly or completely absent; in these situations, the "complicity" may not even involve any element of dishonesty but rather only involve a repressive policy that has extremely negative effects.

Injurious environmental factors can and frequently do contribute significantly to the emergence of psychological disorders. Many parents actively work to hinder their child's healthy cognitive growth as opposed to supporting it. However, they very rarely, if ever, succeed without the victim's assistance.

Some youngsters withstand these demands by being steadfast in their desire to comprehend and develop cognitive clarity. They do not compromise their mental well-being in an effort to "adapt" to a crazy upbringing.

Worse than wrong, the idea that mental health and social adaptability are to be equated actually promotes the onset of mental illness.

A person's mental health may depend on how clearly and consciously they can discern the truths of a situation when they are faced with unfairness and irrationality from people around them. The cost of his "adjustment" is the corrosion of his awareness if he suppresses his judgment, his revulsion, or his disgust in an effort to end his suffering or attain "social peace."

Many adults are caught between their desire to "belong" and their still-struggling critical judgment, which tells them that other people's values, beliefs, and way of life are incorrect and should not be accepted. They have not found a resolution to this conflict. They are in dispute, and the fact that they haven't given up shows that they're still healthy. However, these people frequently fall prey to the "health as adjustment" school. Their psychotherapists force them into a swamp of conformity by pushing them over the chasm of intellectual self-abnegation.

Unhindered cognitive effectiveness is a sign of mental health. Intellect independence is necessary for unhindered cognitive efficiency. A theory that undermines intellectual autonomy also undermines mental health.

Psychological Development

Psychological maturity is a term that is closely tied to mental health.

In its broadest sense, "maturity" refers to the condition of being fully developed or grown. A living thing is mature when its regular growth process is through and it performs at the degree of "adulthood" that is appropriate for its species. Therefore, the term of "psychological maturity" refers to the successful maturation of man's consciousness and the achievement of a degree of functioning consistent with man as a human being.

Man is a rational being, and among living species, his ability to be motivated by a conceptual kind of consciousness makes him unique. His psychological development is a matter of his conceptual faculty's correct growth and development; it is a psycho-epistemological issue.

A child's early knowledge is limited to perceptual concretes; he is not yet familiar with principles or abstractions. He can only think, plan, and act in the here and now; the future is mostly illusory to him. His world is only the now and now. He must be a dependent at this point since his way of functioning, albeit biologically necessary at this point in his life, is insufficient for the conditions of survival as an independent being.

As a child develops, his intellectual horizons broaden: he picks up language, starts to understand abstractions, generalizes, makes ever-more-subtle distinctions, searches for principles, and gains the ability to imagine distant futures. In other words, he moves from the sensory-perceptual level of consciousness to the conceptual level. With his growing knowledge and increasing mastery of conceptual brain functioning, his ability to deal with the outside world and the realities of life also grows.

The capacity for principled thought is the first and most fundamental indicator of psychological maturity.

The fundamental indicator of effectively achieving maturity, more generally speaking, is conceptualization policy. This is defined as "an actively sustained process of identifying one's impressions in conceptual terms, of integrating every event and observation into a conceptual context, of grasping relationships, differences, and similarities in one's perceptual material and of abstracting them into new concepts, of drawing inferences, making deductions, and coming to conclusions, of asking new questions and finding new answers, and expanding one's knowledge into a sum that is constantly growing. 2

It must be emphasized that this strategy only demonstrates maturity when it is applied to all facets of a person's life, not just to his or her line of employment. There are men who, when focused on, say, current politics or a problem in their personal life, become helplessly insecure, concrete-bound children who are blind to abstractions and principles and see nothing but the immediate moment. These men are brilliant at conceptualizing and thinking in principles when their focus is on higher mathematics, some distant galaxy, or some business activity. The capacity to think about oneself in terms of principles is a sign of maturity.

The development of one's conceptual faculty has an impact on all other facets of psychological maturity. These factors are listed in order of importance:

1. A guy who interacts with reality's facts conceptually has embraced the duty of living in a human manner, which includes accepting accountability for his own life and deeds.

A youngster is unable to take on such responsibility since he is still developing the knowledge and abilities required for independence. However, an adult who relies on others to take care of him—or who frequently laments, "I couldn't help it!" as the results of his actions catch up with him—is an instance of self-arrested growth, a person who has failed to complete the process of human maturation.

2. Accepting responsibility for one's own actions necessitates a strategy of long-term planning and action, ensuring that one's past, present, and future are all interconnected. A young person "lives for the moment" in

significant part. A mature adult in good health thinks and acts in terms of a lifespan.

The readiness to postpone instant gratification or rewards when and if required, as well as tolerating unavoidable irritation, is a corollary of this approach.

Crying is a typical newborn response to frustration. A child may reasonably feel disappointed if he is informed that he cannot go the circus on the day he had anticipated; next week may seem like an eternity away to him. A healthy adult, however, does not see his life and objectives in this way. When he can, he finds a method to get over his irritations; if he can't, he moves on; he doesn't let them paralyze him. He doesn't suppress his irritations.

3. Emotional stability is a fundamental sign of adulthood. This characteristic is the result of one specific feature of the conceptual functioning policy: the capacity to maintain the entirety of one's knowledge under stressful circumstances, such as frustration, disappointment, fear, anguish, and shock. It is the capacity to maintain one's ability to think when under the burden of such emotions. Going to pieces is the phrase used to describe the antithesis of this state.

Being routinely overwhelmed by the immediate problem in such a way as to lose one's abstract or long-range perspective, the larger context of one's knowledge, and be completely overcome by sentiments of rage, terror, or despair that paralyze thought is one of the telltale indications of immaturity.

Under stressful circumstances, a young person's grasp of an abstract perspective is, at best, shaky because it is still forming and solidifying. However, the perspective of an adult who has reached their full development has become more resilient to stress.

(This type of emotional stability needs to be clearly distinguished from the phony form of stability attained through emotional repression. The repressor is not an example of maturity since he dares not express his feelings out of fear of losing control.)

4. Finally, there is a crucial component of psychological maturity that only a small percentage of individuals truly attain. It has to do with how one feels about the unknown—not knowledge that has yet to be found by anyone, but knowledge that is already out there but that one does not already possess.

A toddler naturally perceives the world as a vast unknown. He is aware that there are many things he is still unable to understand and that grownups have knowledge much above his own. He is aware that he is still learning the bigger picture of his life and his deeds. He effectively tells himself: "I'll have to hold off till I'm older. I still find a lot of things difficult to understand. Others are aware of them, but I am not yet capable of understanding them."

A truly mature adult would not have an attitude like this. Of course, an adult may also realize that there are things he needs to learn and that he still needs to learn, and must frequently be ready to do so. However, he does not consider falling into the category of something that is understood by others but is, in theory, unknown to him. This does not imply that his objective is to have exhaustive knowledge. It implies that he views himself as capable of knowing what he needs to know and acquiring whatever knowledge his interests and purposes require within the context of his first-hand concerns, of his own actions, and of his own ambitions. When and if the knowledge is available and pertinent to his activity, it signifies that he does not accept the unknown as a given. In other words, he does not see himself as a psycho-epistemological second-class citizen. A man enters complete adulthood, or full self-responsibility, when he adopts and maintains this mindset.

PART TWO

THE PSYCHOLOGY OF SELF-CONFIDENCE

CHAPTER SEVEN

The Source and Nature of Self-Confidence

What Self-Confidence Means

No value judgment is more significant to a person—no element is more crucial to his psychological growth and motivation—than the assessment he makes of himself.

This estimate is typically perceived by him as a feeling rather than a conscious, verbalized judgment. Because it is a constant experience for him and a component of every other feeling and emotional reaction, it can be challenging to isolate and identify.

An emotion is the result of an evaluation; it expresses an assessment of the positive or negative impact that a reality component has on oneself. So, all of a man's value-responses must obviously include his perception of himself. Any decision including the question "Is this for me or against me?" involves an opinion about the "me" that is being considered. Man's psychology is permeated by his constant examination of himself.

The way a guy evaluates himself has a significant impact on his thoughts, feelings, desires, values, and ambitions. It is the single most important factor influencing his behavior. Understanding a man's self-esteem, its level, and the criteria by which he evaluates himself are necessary for psychological understanding.

Man perceives the need for self-esteem as a fundamental need and an urgent demand. He can't help but feel that his opinion of himself is crucial to his survival, whether he expresses this feeling clearly or not. Since man's nature forbids it, no one can be apathetic toward the issue of how he views himself.

Man's need for a favorable vision of himself is so strong that he may avoid facing facts that might have a negative impact on it by evading them, suppressing them, distorting his judgment, and even disintegrating his intellect. In order to convince himself that he has a high self-esteem when in reality he does not, a man who has chosen or accepted unreasonable standards by which to measure himself may be pushed to pursue blatantly self-destructive goals throughout his life (Chapter Eight).

The frantic belief that to stand before the universe without self-esteem is to stand naked, defenseless, and subject to destruction drives men to fake it, to manufacture the illusion of self-esteem, and thus to consign themselves to ongoing psychological deceit.

The sense of personal efficacy and a sense of personal worth are two intertwined components of self-esteem. It is the total of one's self-esteem and regard for oneself. The conviction that one is capable of life and deserving of living.

Man's intrinsic nature includes a need for self-esteem. However, he must learn it because he is not born knowing what will satiate that need or the yardstick by which self-esteem is to be measured.

Why is self-esteem important for men? (The fact that men want it does not prove that they need it.) What does it have to do with how man survives? What prerequisites must be met before achieving it? What accounts for its strong motivating power? These are the issues that need to be thought about.

The explanation can be found in two facts about the nature of man. The first is that man's primary method of survival is reason. The second is that man is a being of volitional consciousness in the conceptual world and that the use of his rational power is volitional.

The majority of men are unaware of the function and significance of reason in their life. However, once a child develops the capacity for self-awareness, he is forced to become implicitly aware of the fact that his consciousness is his fundamental tool for interacting with reality, that he cannot possibly exist without it, and that the success of his mental processes is crucial to his wellbeing. No one can escape understanding the value of reason at some basic level. Consider the fact that if someone thought themselves to be "dumb" or "crazy," they would inevitably view this as a terrible judgment on their capacity to deal with reality.

As soon as a youngster has the ability to think conceptually, he starts to become more and more conscious—implicitly and sub-consciously—of his responsibility for controlling the activity of his mind. He must use focused mental effort to keep his consciousness at the conceptual level. He learns how to distinguish between the states of mental focus and mental fog and can then choose one or the other.

Let's now explore how these facts relate to a man's quest for self-confidence.

Self-assurance:
The feeling of effectiveness

Man's life and happiness depend on him making the proper decisions since reality constantly presents him with alternatives and forces him to choose his goals and deeds. But he is unable to go beyond the bounds of his nature; he is also unable to claim or expect omniscience or infallibility. What he needs is something he can control: the conviction that his style of decision-making, or more specifically, his preferred way of using consciousness (his psycho-epistemology), is correct, correct in principle, and appropriate for reality.

An organism whose consciousness develops spontaneously does not have this issue because it is unable to contest the accuracy of its own mental processes. There can be no more pressing issue for a man, whose consciousness is volitional. Sole man is capable of rejecting, undermining, and betraying his own brain, which is his only means of existence. He is the only living thing that must make himself capable of existing by using his logical faculty in the right way. He owes it to himself first and foremost as a living thing. The psychologically most important characteristic of a man is how he decides to handle this problem because it is fundamental to his identity as a biological being.

If a man is devoted to cognition—if awareness, or understanding, is the main factor governing how his consciousness functions—then the mental operations that are activated by his decision will point in the direction of cognitive efficacy. The outcome is cognitive inefficacy to the degree that he fails or refuses to make awareness the regulatory purpose of his consciousness—to the extent that he avoids the effort of thought and the duty of reason.

Man's primary act of volition, the one action immediately within his volitional capacity, is to think or not to think, to concentrate or to suspend his thoughts. Three essential psycho-epistemological alternatives—alternatives in his core cognitive functioning pattern—are affected by this decision. They depict the position that logic, comprehension, and reality hold in a man's thinking.

1. A man has two mental concentration options: he can activate and maintain a sharp mental focus, aiming to elevate his understanding to the highest possible level of accuracy and clarity, or he can maintain a blurry approximation, in a condition of passive, undiscerning, aimless mental drifting.

2. A man has two options: suspend his intellect under the pressure of strong feelings (desires or fears), and submit himself to the direction of impulses whose validity he doesn't care to consider. He can also

distinguish between knowledge and feelings, letting his judgment be guided by his intellect rather than his emotions.

3. A man has two options: he can independently analyze whether a claim is true or incorrect, right or wrong, or he can accept uncritically the claims and opinions of others, putting their judgment ahead of his own.

Man enjoys a sense of control over his existence—the control of a mind in correct relationship to reality—to the extent that he consistently makes the right decisions in these matters. Self-confidence is faith in one's own mind and its dependability as an instrument for thought.

Such assurance does not imply that one is incapable of making mistakes. It is the conviction that one is capable of reasoning, judging, and knowing (and that one is able to remedy one's mistakes)—that one is capable in theory—and that one is unwaveringly devoted to maintaining unbroken contact with reality to the maximum extent of one's volitional ability. It is the assurance that nothing is more important than the truth, and nothing is more important than one's regard for the truth.

This fundamental kind of self-assurance must be separated from other, superficial, and specialized forms, which express a person's perception of their own effectiveness at specific tasks or in specific contexts. This fundamental self-assurance is a judgment of that which learns information and abilities rather than a judgment of one's knowledge or specific skills. It is psycho-epistemological self-assurance; it is a judgment (an implicit judgment, not always conscious judgment) given on one's own way of confronting and interacting with the realities of the world.

Man must have this level of self-assurance because if he does, he will be halted in his tracks, rendered immobile, doomed to fear and impotence, and declared unfit to exist.

Self-Respect:
The Perception of Worth

The concepts and ideals that direct a man's conduct when faced with moral decisions make up his character.

A youngster experiences the urge to feel right about himself as a person, correct in his typical method of acting—that he is good—very early in his development, as he becomes aware of his ability to choose his behaviors and as he develops the sensation of being a person. He is only aware of this question in respect to the choice between joy and suffering; he is not aware of it in relation to the question of life or death. Being morally upright enables one to experience happiness; being incorrect puts one in danger of suffering.

No other living species, I have emphasized, must answer the question, "What kind of being should I strive to become?" What moral standards should I use to govern my life? However, there is no way for man to avoid these inquiries.

Man cannot escape the world of moral standards and moral judgements. Every human being judges himself by some standard, whether those standards are conscious or subconscious, consistent or contradictory, life-serving or life-negating. To the extent that he doesn't live up to that standard, his feeling of personal worth and self-respect suffer.

Man needs self-respect because he must act to fulfill his moral obligations, and in order to act, he must value the person who will benefit from his action.

Man must feel deserving of pursuing values in order to do so. He needs to believe that he deserves happiness in order to fight for it.

Though conceptually distinct, the two components of self-esteem—self-confidence and self-respect—are intertwined in a man's mind. When a man dedicates his thoughts to the work of learning what is true and what is right, and when he governs his actions appropriately, he makes himself competent to live. Man will lose his sense of worthiness if he fails to uphold his duty to reason and thought, undermining his capacity to live. If he compromises his moral principles, undermining his sense of worthiness, he does so by lying, betraying his own (incorrect or accurate) judgment. As a result, he will lose his sense of competence. Both components of self-esteem have a psycho-epistemological foundation.

These are the characteristics and reasons of man's need for self-worth.

It is important to keep in mind that self-esteem is a moral evaluation, and morality only applies to the volitional, or to that which is up to man's free will. The only real yardstick for virtue (Chapter Twelve) and the only basis for real self-esteem is an unbroken rationality, which is defined as a decision to use one's mind as fully as possible and a reluctance to ever evade or act against it.

The Fundamentals of Self-Confidence

The first and most important condition for man to attain and retain self-esteem is that he maintains an unwavering desire to comprehend. Man's mental wellbeing and intellectual development are protected by his need for clarity, intelligibility, and comprehension of what is inside his field of awareness. The extent of a man's intelligence, or the breadth of his abstract capacity, determines the possible scope of his consciousness. On all intelligence scales, however, the fundamental requirement of the will to understand is the same: a person must identify and integrate all that enters their mental area to the best of their knowledge and abilities.

Sadly, this mindset is frequently abandoned or broken very early in a person's existence, and the individual "adjusts" to the idea that they are living in an opaque, confusing, and terrifying cosmos where cognitive self-confidence is impossible. Sometimes the cause is a volitional default on the side of the child, such as a reluctance to produce mental energy or a passive, careless attitude. Sometimes the cause is the desire to indulge in desires or behaviors that he is aware are irrational, necessitating the implementation of an evasion policy and the suspension of the will to comprehend.

A child who encounters human irrationality and is unsure of how to handle it is one example of a situation where the causes are more complicated. A young kid may view the world around him, including the world of his parents and other adults, to be confusing and scary. He may also regard many of the adults' behaviors, feelings, thoughts, expectations, and demands to be oppressive, contradicting, and bewilderingly hostile. The child gives up after making numerous futile attempts to comprehend their rules and behavior—and accepts responsibility for his sense of powerlessness. Whether consciously or unconsciously, he interprets his lack of understanding as a reflection on himself; he accepts an undeserved guilt; and he comes to the conclusion that something is wrong with him, that he is intellectually or morally lacking in some unnamed way. He may react with anger, hostility, anxiety, depression, or withdrawal. He gradually loses hope that he will ever be able to understand the world around him and accepts the fact that it will always be unknowable.

A youngster is vulnerable because he is not yet able to understand definitively that his elders are unreasonable—especially when they are occasionally attentive, considerate, fair, and affectionate instead. He is unable to understand their motivations and is aware that they are more knowledgeable than he is, but he senses, painfully, passionately, and inarticulately, that something is badly wrong—either with them, himself, or something else. He believes that he will never be able to comprehend other people, fulfill their expectations of him, or discern between what is right and evil.

No matter how distressed or perplexed a child is, as long as he persists in trying to comprehend, he is psychologically safe because he retains his mind and his desire for efficacy. He forfeits the chance to achieve complete self-esteem when he gives up the hope of becoming effective.

Every child is aware that there are some things he cannot hope to understand till he is older; this is not the child's fault. The issue is that he believes he will never know something but still wants to know it in order to function well. Because of this, he perceives himself as an outcast in the distant country of reality.

If a young child who is clings tenaciously to the will to understand is caught in an irrational environment, he or she may suffer greatly in the early years, but psychologically, he or she will survive; he or she will continue to struggle to find his or her way to the rational view of life that should have been exemplified by his elders, but wasn't; he or she will doubtless feel alienated from many of the people around him—and right He won't believe that he lacks the ability to survive.

There are further ways a young person can lower his self-esteem by accepting the unknowable. For instance, a student may come across some courses during his academic career that he finds extremely challenging. The explanation may be that he lacks interest in the subjects, doesn't see the value in learning them, has bad instruction, or faces a mental barrier in those areas; alternatively, it might be that he hasn't put in the necessary effort. However, if a young person comes to the conclusion that the problem is "just me—I can't understand certain things—my that's nature," they run the risk of psychological harm.

If someone recognizes the root reasons of his problem, he is not in danger; yet, depending on other circumstances in his particular environment, he may or may not decide to overcome them. But if he merely accepts the idea that some portions of reality are incomprehensibly inaccessible to him, he undermines his cognitive self-confidence. Once this concept is established, it spreads quickly and readily, including an increasing number of difficulties and issues.

The objectives that a person sets—in other words, the tasks they allocate to their consciousness—control the activity and development of their mind. If he maintains the will to comprehend and views cognitive efficacy as an absolute that cannot be compromised or given up, he will start a process of growth and development that will steadily increase the strength of his mind. His mind responds correspondingly if he loses the desire to understand; it stops improving its capacity for cognition.

The policy of conceptualizing—of seeking for and thinking in terms of principles—as the necessary tool for cognitive clarity will be forced onto a young person if they retain the desire to comprehend as they age. Understanding is impossible without integration, and integration is impossible without concepts and principles.

The foundational quality of psychological development is the practice of conceptualizing—of thinking in terms of principles. It is invariably a corollary to fully realized self-esteem.

So, maintaining the desire to comprehend in all facets of one's life constitutes the fundamental precondition for achieving self-esteem.

Let's now look at a further requirement for developing self-esteem.

A difficulty arises throughout a person's growth that, depending on how he chooses to handle it, might have a significant impact on his sense of self. It is a difficulty that everyone encounters at some point in their lives, usually as a child. When a man encounters desires or concerns that conflict with his rational knowledge, his intellect and emotions do not always quickly and fully align. In these situations, he must decide whether to act on his rational understanding or his emotions.

One of the most crucial lessons a child must learn is that emotions are insufficient motivators for behavior. The fact that he wants to do something does not mean that he should do it, and the fact that he is afraid to do something does not mean that he should not do it. Emotions are neither cognitive aids nor judging standards. A crucial component of a mind's healthy development is the capacity to tell knowledge from sensations. It is essential for achieving and maintaining self-esteem.

Cognitive self-assertiveness, which is manifested via the practice of thinking, judging, and directing behavior accordingly, is a prerequisite for and an element of self-esteem. One's self-esteem is undermined when the authority of their rational knowledge is challenged, when they give up their reason in favor of emotions they cannot rationalize or defend.

Emotions are the passive, reactive, automatic byproduct of subconscious integrations that, in a particular circumstance, may or may not be relevant to reality; reason is the active, starting factor in man—the process that he must develop voluntarily. One of the proper functions of man's reason is to evaluate the propriety or authenticity of his emotional responses. A man loses control over his existence and the sense of self-regulation that is necessary for self-esteem if he abdicates the power of his reason and allows himself to be swept along passively by feelings he does not judge.

Repression or the dismissal of one's emotions as unimportant do not constitute or entail healthy self-regulation. It entails realizing that feelings are effects—consequences of value judgments—and caring about what those judgments are and how much of a context they are valid in.

A policy of unbridled emotionalism necessarily leads a man to disasters and eventually causes him to fear his emotions as sources of danger and guilt. In contrast, a policy of rational self-regulation is most conducive to healthy emotional spontaneity in contexts where spontaneity is appropriate (which only reason can judge) (Chapter Five).

A youngster is first unaware of the concept or dichotomy between valid and invalid desires; this distinction is based on information that has not yet been attained. He learns from his experiences and his parents' lessons that some of the things he wants are good for him and some are not. Later, he discovers another, deeper distinction: he is entitled to some of the things he wants, but not to others. He discovers as a result that his aspirations must be evaluated for their validity.

Think of a young toddler who is tempted to steal a friend's toy when he is old enough to understand what theft is. He is hesitant to steal the toy since he is aware that he has no legal claim to it and that he would be furious if his friend took one of his toys. But he favors this specific toy. In order to steal, he hides his knowledge.

In a short period of time, he forgets the occurrence. But the effects of it are still being felt. A specific concept that was indicated and implicated by his behavior wordlessly registered in his mind: the principle that it is sometimes acceptable to disregard knowledge and facts in order to satisfy a desire. This, together with a residue of nebulous, unnamed remorse, the feeling of some inner uncleanliness, and the state of a mind coming to mistrust itself, is the legacy of this theft.

Therefore, he is free to consciously reject and remove this principle from his psychology. But if he doesn't, if he instead supports it through persistent deception and illogical emotional indulgence, he further damages his self-esteem. The frequency, extent, and kind of his knowledge evasions as well as the nature of his indulged needs will all affect how badly his self-esteem is affected.

When a person grows up in a healthy way and develops a comprehensive set of values, his mind and emotions are in harmony; he is no longer constantly divided between his desires and his knowledge.

However, regardless of how highly integrated a person may be, the process of holding and applying correctly the whole, long-range context of his knowledge is not automatic, and the subconscious integrations that give rise to his emotions are not faultless. Therefore, it is a man's duty to constantly assess and evaluate his impulses; it is never proper for him to see them as self-justifying motives.

As adults, the majority of males experience a severe lack of self-esteem. The senseless tragedy of their lives is that the majority of them betrayed their minds, not to sate some violent if irrational passion, but to indulge in senseless or pointless whims that they can no longer recall, to be free to act on whim or spur of the moment, without the responsibility of awareness or thought.

If rejecting one's intellect under the burden of irrational impulses is psychologically destructive, rejecting one's mind under the pressure of fear is arguably even more disastrous. However, giving one's thoughts to fear is pure self-abnegation. Pursuing irrational desires may nonetheless reflect some twisted, neurotic type of self-assertiveness, a grasping for pleasure or delight.

Of course, experiencing fear is not abnormal or disordered in and of itself. Fear frequently serves a purpose: it can motivate people to confront danger. The way a person views and responds to fear is vital to his or her psychological health.

For instance, young toddlers frequently encounter the experience of being startled by a barking dog. However, a child's response to this event may vary. When a youngster learns that the dog is playful rather than dangerous, he may force himself to approach and pet the animal until his fear is completely gone. Another child may be cautious to avoid the dog out of practical caution and stop feeling any further anxiety. After the initial meeting, a different child might avoid the dog, but he might continue to whimper and complain anytime he sees or hears the dog, even from a great distance; no amount of proof that the dog is nice will make him change his mind.

Their divergent responses are a reflection of the various approaches they choose to facing their anxiety. The first child, despite being terrified, maintains cognitive control; he does not allow the fear to overwhelm and swamp his consciousness. As a result, he does not see his fear of the dog and his avoidance of it as a reflection on himself or on his value as a person. Instead, he is able to understand, once the evidence suggests that the dog is not a threat to him, and his policy toward the dog adjusts as a result. The second child, however, is paralyzed and overcome by fear, paralyzed and overcome psycho-epistemologically; his self-awareness is reduced to a sense of all-encompassing helplessness; nothing is real to him, nothing matters, except that he is afraid; as a result, he views his avoidance of the dog as humiliating; as a result, his mind is closed to information that might change his policy toward the dog. It goes without saying that wise parents may help their children develop normally by teaching them how to effectively deal with their worries.

Since a young child understands so little and the world is foreign and unfamiliar to him, there is a certain level of fear to be expected in his existence. In a healthy and normal way, as his knowledge and skills improve, these anxieties are conquered and left behind, and as he becomes adulthood, fewer and fewer things have the power to frighten him. The approach a child takes to overcoming his concerns will determine how far he pursues this path till reaching full development.

A child's development poses a variety of difficulties; every day offers him fresh chances to broaden his knowledge and abilities, to investigate the environment, and to become more adept at navigating it. A child may feel some apprehension in the face of some difficulties—doubt about his capacity to handle them, fear of failing—for instance, when faced with the challenge of acquiring a new subject or skill.

Again, children might respond to their own concern in this situation in a variety of ways. One child's main focus is the importance of succeeding and developing his abilities; he disregards his anxiety and moves forward, and the fear vanishes. Another child is more preoccupied with his fear than he is with the potential to learn and grow from the unfamiliar; as a result, he withdraws and the dread ultimately takes control of him. (I am not referring to obstacles that are actually beyond the child's capacity to handle; rather, I am referring to challenges that are within the child's range of success.)

Now think about the next illustration. When a young person expresses a viewpoint that to him seems completely logical (and possibly is reasonable), his father reacts in shock and with severe fury. The young child is afraid that his father would hit him, as he has in the past. It's normal and understandable to be afraid. But the child can respond psychologically in a number of different ways.

He can continue to be conscious and judging even though he is afraid and realizes that trying to reason with his father is pointless. He can continue to have the desire to understand even though he is confused and upset. His father has not responded to him and has not provided any evidence to support his disagreement. Or he can allow the fear to mentally overtake him, making truth and understanding irrelevant; he can start to doubt the truth of what he said; he can decide that he must be mistaken; or he can give in to a single desire: to get out of this terrifying situation and prevent it from happening again—and be willing to put aside his independent judgment in order to accomplish this goal.

If a youngster struggles to maintain mental clarity in such circumstances, he will discover as he gets older that his vulnerability to terror drastically decreases; what he will frequently experience in its stead is a totally appropriate scorn. However, if he consistently gives into fear—surrenders psycho-epistemologically—fear obtains an increasing amount of control over him, making each future surrender seem more and more inevitable. This has an impact on his perception of his own effectiveness.

On an adult level, the same ideas are applicable. For instance, if a man retreats from life's challenges and bury himself in the "safety" of the routine, the familiar, and the undemanding out of a fear of failing or of making mistakes; if a man compulsively pursues meaningless sexual adventures out of a fear of being regarded (or of remorse); or if a man hides from life's challenges and avoids them altogether out of a fear of failure or of making mistakes;

Of course, there are moments when a fear-experience is so strong that thinking becomes temporarily impossible. However, such panicked reactions are unavoidably transient and only apply to urgent, short-term situations. When this happens, a person's behavior after the panic subsides reveals his attitude and approach to terror. After that, does he reflect on the event, process it, and become ready for future instances that may be similar—in other words, does he try to regain mastery and control over his life? Or does he only shudder at the thought of the terror, seek to avoid the situation, and hope he won't run into these issues again, surrendering himself to the idea that, should these issues reappear, he will only be able to be helpless?

Whether a man maintains the will to efficacy; whether he maintains the value of self-confidence as a goal not to be abandoned; and, as a result, views a state of fear as the temporary and abnormal, as that which he must overcome—or whether he gives up the expectation of achieving efficacy, resigns himself to a sense of impotence, and accepts fear as a fundamental, unalterable "given" of his existence, to deal with The will to efficacy demands that a person never abandon himself to living in constant fear, just as the will to understanding demands that a person never accept the unknown as an intrinsic aspect of his life.

It is important to note that the idea of giving in to fear refers to a psycho-epistemological process, which involves subverting one's awareness and consciousness in order to prevent or lessen a terror experience. The logical avoidance of actual and present risks to which there is no justification for exposure is very different from this practice. In truth, opposing principles are at play in these two situations: in the one, reality is being fled, whereas in the second, reality is being properly recognized.

A profound respect for facts, a strong sense of reality and objectivity, a recognition that existence exists, that A is A, that reality is an absolute that cannot be avoided or escaped, and that the primary duty of consciousness is to perceive it are all necessary for the preservation of the will to understand and the supremacy of one's rational judgment.

This principle is at stake in a choice that is essential to a man's self-esteem: whether to judge what is true or untrue, right or wrong, independently with his own intellect, or to delegate cognition and assessment to others and unquestioningly accept their judgments.

Again, the fundamental decision is whether to think or not to think.

Man cannot think inside another man's head. One man can learn from another, but knowledge requires understanding rather than just repetition or imitation; it must involve autonomous thought in order to be considered one's knowledge. The desire to understand implies the necessity of intellectual independence. The idea of "understanding" only applies to a certain mind.

The fundamental sense of control over one's life that self-esteem is based on is psycho-epistemological—it has to do with the efficacy of one's consciousness—so to give up the duty of independent thought is to unavoidably give up self-esteem.

Two very distinct questions—"What are the facts of reality?" and "What do people say, believe, or feel are the realities of reality?"—reflect fundamentally different psychologies and modes of psycho-epistemological functioning.

The decision to accept or reject man's nature as a rational entity who must utilize his mind to survive is implicit in the decision to think or not to think. Man may react with terror to the duty of thought and intellectual self-reliance because thinking costs effort and because man is imperfect. In an effort to escape from this fear, he may try to shift the cognitive load of his life onto others. However, if he does so, it leads to a feeling of disassociation from reality—a feeling of being "a stranger and terrified, in a world I never made" (Chapter Ten).

Self-Confidence, Pride, and Undeserved Guilt

The rules that a man uses to judge the level of his self-esteem are developed gradually over time; they are not the result of decisions made in response to one particular event or problem. The collapse of self-esteem does not occur over the course of a day, a week, or a month; rather, it develops over time as a result of repeated defaults, avoidances, and irrational behavior—that is, repeated failures to utilize one's thinking appropriately. The reputation a man develops with himself depends on his level of self-esteem (or lack thereof).

Humans form their own personalities as part of their psychological growth and development; they achieve this through the volitional decisions they make every day, not by self-awareness or intentional intention. His brain works like an electronic computer, subconsciously summarizing the ramifications of these decisions and their nature. The result is his personality and perception of who he is.

A young youngster does not expressly pledge his will to understand. However, he works to gain the greatest degree of clarity and understanding that is within his grasp in each matter that comes under his consciousness. As a result, he develops a mental routine, or approach to dealing with reality, which is philosophically known as the will to understand. For as long as he lives, he must voluntarily affirm this principle in each new situation he faces; it is always a matter of choice.

A youngster does not, for similar reasons, decide under the influence of fear to give up his will to efficacy and abdicate his mental authority. But in a long series of particular circumstances, given the choice between exerting effort to maintain mental clarity and control and allowing his mind to be consumed and overcome by a fear he had the ability to overcome, he defaults on the duty of thought and grants emotions the upper hand. As a result, he instills in his psychology a sense of helplessness that becomes more and more "natural" and is perceived as "just me."

The decisions a person makes regarding the functioning of his consciousness do not just disappear and leave no mark. These decisions have lasting psychological repercussions. A man's response to reality leaves an impression on him, for better or worse: either it reinforces and builds up his self-esteem, or it weakens and erodes it. Man's ability to self-awareness—the fact that he is the only species capable of evaluating and regulating his own mental processes—implies that he cannot escape the judgment of his own ego.

It's important to distinguish between the concepts of pride and self-esteem. Although they are linked, the two have very different meanings. Self-esteem is the belief in one's inherent value and effectiveness. The enjoyment a man feels for himself as a result of and in response to particular accomplishments or deeds is referred to as pride. Self-esteem is the belief in one's ability to uphold moral standards. Pride is the feeling that comes from achieving a certain value (s). "I can" is self-esteem. "I have" is pride. A man might be proud of both the traits he has developed in his own character as well as the actions he has taken in reality, or his existential accomplishments. The greatest pride a guy can feel comes from achieving self-esteem because it is a value that must be acquired and the man who achieves it is proud of his success.

However, if he is sensible, his self-esteem is untouched and unimpaired. If a guy, despite his best efforts, fails in a specific undertaking, he does not feel the same sensation of pride that he would if he had succeeded. Since these are not always in a man's direct, volitional control and/or not in his sole power, his self-esteem is not dependent on—or shouldn't be—depending on—certain accomplishments or failures.

Untold amounts of unneeded suffering and self-doubt result from not understanding this principle. If a man evaluates himself based on standards that include elements beyond his volitional control, the inevitable outcome is a fragile self-esteem that is constantly in danger.

For instance, a man might find himself in a situation where it would be highly advantageous for him to have certain knowledge, but he does not have it—not out of deception or irresponsibility, but rather because he did not see a need for it, did not know how to acquire it, or did not have access to the means to do so. Such a man has no justification, in reason, to criticize himself for moral deficiency or inadequacy. But he persists in doing so, convincing himself that "somehow" he should be aware of the facts; as a result, his self-esteem falls.

Or, a man is doing the best he can to think about a particular issue while he struggles to find a solution. He fails; he is unable to solve it or is unable to do it within a certain amount of time. Though he doesn't know how, he criticizes himself morally, believing that he should have been able to accomplish it "somehow." As a result, his self-esteem is damaged.

Or, a guy makes a mistake of judgment after thoroughly and diligently considering a matter, and negative effects result. Despite not knowing what he could have done differently given his information at the time of the decision, the guy feels guilty because he believes he should have avoided the mistake "somehow," and as a result, his self-esteem suffers.

It would be shallow and inaccurate to assume that these men's mistake is that they are "perfectionists," as many psychiatrists do nowadays. Men who place unattainable, unreasonable standards on themselves are not being "perfectionists," but rather are measuring themselves by an unrealistic, flawed standard of perfection that is at odds with the very nature of mankind. A logical standard of moral excellence calls for a person to apply his or her intellect to the utmost extent possible and to engage in unwavering rationality; it does not call for omniscience, omnipotence, or infallibility (Chapter Twelve).

Accepting unjustified guilt on the basis of a "somehow"—"Somehow I should know," "Somehow I should be able to accomplish it"—when there is no cognitive content to that "somehow," only an empty, undefined charge supported by nothing, is one of the worst wrongs a man can do to himself.

However, there is one specific reason why many guys are prone to making this mistake. Even while a man may not be at fault in the current circumstance, prior irrationalities and cognitive failures may have contributed to a general sense of self-distrust, making it difficult for him to feel completely confident in his moral standing. The answer to this issue is to identify this particular type of confusion for what it is, label it as a symptom, and make an effort to be objective and factual in one's self-evaluation. The battle to develop a logical strategy for handling guilt can help people rebuild their self-esteem on its own.

Self-confidence and Successful Work

One of the most crucial factors to take into account when examining the psychology of self-esteem is how self-esteem relates to successful work and, in a broader sense, to the development and exercise of a man's mental faculties.

When I first articulated the idea of efficacy, I was referring to what might be called metaphysical efficacy, or the kind of efficacy that has to do with a man's fundamental relationship to reality and that shows how reality-oriented his thought processes are. However, there is another way to use the word "efficacy": it could be used to describe a person's success in a given field of endeavor as a result of the unique knowledge and abilities he has attained. This latter kind will be known as particularized efficacy.

A guy may have a wide range of practical skills and self-assurance in a number of defined areas, showing some degree of particularized efficacy, yet he may be severely lacking in the fundamental efficacy related to self-esteem. For instance, a man might be assured in his ability to do his job but scared of any requirement for independent thought beyond what his "significant people" have set as the norm. He has a fundamentally reliant personality, not in a materialistic sense but rather in a psycho-epistemological one.

On the other side, a guy can have a strong sense of metaphysical effectiveness and self-worth, but because of the extreme specialization of his interests, he might lack many of the everyday abilities that most men take for granted, like the ability to drive a car or carry out some basic home repairs. In the event that he must perform such duties, he is not afraid of them and is confident in his capacity to learn the necessary skills. This is because a feeling of metaphysical efficacy implies faith in one's capacity to learn anything for which one has a good reason.

Men develop different sorts of particularized efficacy, or specific skills, depending on their interests, values, context, expertise, etc. Since using one's rational faculty requires interacting with a particular aspect of reality, metaphysical efficacy is inextricably articulated through various forms of particularized efficacy. However, metaphysical effectiveness is applicable to and expressible in all forms of rational endeavor and is not restricted in its expression to any specific form of action.

Self-esteem (or metaphysical efficacy) is not a value that is readily and unconsciously preserved once attained. Like with any value in a living thing, action is required to not only acquire it but also to maintain it. Similar to how breathing today won't keep a man alive tomorrow, thinking today won't keep a man's self-esteem tomorrow if he chooses to avoid, become mentally stationary, arrest, and sabotage his reasonable faculty.

Man keeps up his particularized effectiveness throughout his life, i.e., his capacity for knowledge, comprehension, and aptitude, in order to retain his metaphysical efficacy. Life is a process of self-sustaining and self-generated action, therefore continual intellectual growth is necessary for man's life as well as for self-esteem. 2 Man's ability for growth and self-development is significantly greater than that of any other living species, as is the character and range of acts he is capable of. Physical maturity marks the end of an animal's capacity for development; after that, its life consists of the actions required to maintain itself at a fixed level. After reaching maturity, an animal does not continue to grow significantly in efficacy, i.e., it does not improve its capacity to adapt to its environment. But human growth is almost unlimited, and it does not stop with physical adulthood. Man's primary means of survival is his mind, and his capacity to think, study, find new and better ways to cope with life, broaden the scope of his abilities, and develop intellectually opens up an endless array of options.

Man does not survive by adapting to his physical environment like an animal would, but rather by changing his environment via useful activity. If life is a series of self-sustaining actions, then the uniquely human way of acting and surviving is to think, to generate, to confront the problems of existence with a never-ending effort and ingenuity.

When man learned to make fire to keep himself warm, his need for thought and effort did not end. Likewise, when he learned to make a bow and arrow, then a shelter out of stone, brick, glass, and steel, his need for thought and effort did not end. When he increased his life expectancy from nineteen to thirty to forty to sixty to seventy, his need for thought and effort was no longer necessary.

Every accomplishment of man is a value in and of itself, but it also serves as a springboard for even bigger accomplishments and ideals. Life is growth; failing to advance is falling behind; life only continues as long as it makes progress. Every advancement gives man access to a broader spectrum of action and accomplishment, as well as the need for such action and accomplishment. There isn't a "plateau" that lasts forever. The issue of survival is never "settled," with no further consideration or action necessary. More specifically, the issue of survival is resolved by the realization that it necessitates ongoing development and creativity.

A man's dedication to the life process—and to the condition of being human—is expressed in his desire to advance his knowledge, abilities, comprehension, and control. A man has effectively "lived enough" if and when he thinks that he has "thought enough," that no further education is required, that he has nowhere to go and nothing to accomplish. Self-esteem and stagnant inactivity are incompatible.

The aforementioned should not be interpreted to imply that a psychologically healthy man's life consists solely of solving problems, performing useful work, and pursuing long-term objectives. The essential components of human existence are leisure, recreation, love, and human contact. But the method by which a man gains that sense of control over his life, which is a prerequisite for his being able to fully appreciate the other values available to him, is productive work. Guy who lacks direction or purpose in life, man who has no worthwhile goals, man who feels helpless and out of control, man who feels inadequate to and unfit for existence, man who feels unsuited for existence and is unable to appreciate it. A necessity for psychological well-being, a creative purpose is a psychological need.

Observe that the joy of acquiring a sense of control and efficacy is the first self-generated pleasure of a human being's life. The infant displays the joy of a living thing acquiring control over its own life as he learns to move his body, to crawl, to walk, to smash a spoon against a table and make a sound, to build a building out of blocks, and to speak words. The fact that a child begins his life with the sensation of virtue and the sense of efficacy as a single, indivisible emotion is vitally relevant psychologically and morally; pride is inexorably linked to success.

A mentally sound man never loses this kind of pleasure; it always serves as the major driving force in his life. The occurrence of the mentally active man who is young at 90 is explained by this attitude, just as the phenomenon of the mentally quiet man who is old at 30 is explained by the absence of this attitude.

It should be emphasized that both men and women must take into account the aforementioned factors. The enormous harm caused by the traditional wisdom that women should not aspire to any roles or functions other than those of wife and mother and that the pursuit of a successful profession is exclusively a male prerogative is beyond the scope of this analysis. In order to maintain her psychological health, a woman must pursue a long-term career; she is not, metaphysically speaking, some sort of second-class citizen for whom mental passivity and reliance are a normal state of affairs.

The extent of a person's productive ambition is a reflection of both his intelligence and, more importantly, how highly he values himself. A guy tends to set greater objectives for himself and look for more difficult challenges the higher his degree of self-esteem. (Of course, I'm talking about healthy, rational forms of ambition here; not the pretentious aspirations of a self-conscious person trying to hide and downplay his own shortcomings.) On any level of intelligence or ability, a man's eagerness for the novel and the difficult, for that which will enable him to use his capacities to the fullest extent, is one of the characteristics of self-esteem, just as a fondness for the familiar, the routine, the undemanding, and a fear of the novel and the difficult, is a virtually unmistakable indication of a self-esteem deficiency. A man with self-confidence wants to face challenges, achieve success, and develop professionally, while a man deficient in self-confidence wants to feel "secure." It is important to note that healthy self-esteem is not its cause, but rather its effect and expression in creative success. Genuine self-esteem is a result of a person's reasonable, reality-focused thought processes, or psycho-epistemology. The following is the causal progression: A reasonable psycho-epistemology contributes to the development of self-esteem; the two work together to produce accomplishments under normal circumstances; accomplishments produce pride. Particularized effectiveness follows from metaphysical efficacy.

Many men make the terrible mistake of trying to base their self-esteem on their existential accomplishments—the mistake of determining their value as people by how well they succeed in reaching certain productive goals—because they are unaware of this causal chain. As was previously said, a man does not always have direct, volitional control over and/or exclusive control over success of this kind. A man's feeling of self-worth is deeply damaging to his psychological wellbeing if he allows it to depend on variables outside of his control because he is neither omniscient nor flawless and because other men are participating in many constructive undertakings.

Sometimes, this mistake is unintentionally committed due to a sincere lack of comprehension. However, there are times when it is driven by neuroticism. For example, a man who is brilliantly talented and successful at work but blatantly irrational in the way he lives his life may desperately want to believe that the only measure of virtue is one's ability to produce results, that nothing else matters, and that no other area of activity has moral significance. Such a man may lose himself in his work in an effort to escape guilt and humiliation he may be experiencing in other areas of his life. As a result, productive work ceases to be a healthy passion and instead becomes a neurotic escape, a haven from reality and the criticism of his own ego.

Self-confidence and Gratification

Man's urge for pleasure is a fundamental psychological need rather than a luxury.

As pain is the emblem of failure, destruction, and death, pleasure (in the broadest sense of the word) is a metaphysical companion of life, the reward and result of successful effort.

Man experiences the value of life, the conviction that it is worthwhile to put out the effort necessary to keep, through the condition of enjoyment.

Man must act in order to uphold principles in order to survive. Pleasure or delight serves as both a motivation to keep acting and an emotional reward for good action.

In addition, because enjoying has a metaphysical meaning for man, being in a state of enjoyment allows him to directly sense his own effectiveness, competency, and ability to deal with reality, uphold his principles, and live. The sensation of "I am in control of my existence" is implicitly contained in the experience of pleasure, just as the emotion of "I am helpless" is implicitly contained in the experience of sorrow. Pain is equivalent to the sense of impotence that pleasure implies.

Thus, pleasure acts as the emotional fuel for a person's existence by allowing them to personally experience the sensation that their life has value and that they themselves have value.

As we've discussed (Chapter Five), a person's values—not necessarily his conscious, professed ideals, but the actual values of his inner life—determine what he seeks for pleasure.

Because emotion has no volition of its own, it cannot correct a man if he chooses values incorrectly. A man's emotional mechanism won't save him if his values are such that he loves things that, in actuality, will cause him to perish; instead, it will push him farther down the path of destruction since he will have turned it against himself, against reality, and against his own life. Man's emotional mechanism is similar to an electronic computer: he can program it, but he can't change how it works. If he chooses the wrong programming, he won't be able to avoid the fact that the most self-destructive desires will feel as urgent and intense to him as actions that could save his life. Of course, he has the ability to alter the code, but only by altering his values.

A man's core values reveal how he perceives himself and the world, whether consciously or unconsciously. They are an indication of (a) his level and type of self-worth or lack thereof, and (b) the degree to which he views the cosmos as open to his understanding and action or closed—that is, the degree to which he maintains what may be referred to as a "benevolent" or "malevolent" view of life. As a result, a man's pursuit of pleasure and happiness is deeply psychologically revealing because it is an indication of his character and soul. The "soul" of a man is his consciousness and his fundamental principles.

Man can feel life's satisfaction in primarily five (interconnected) domains: successful job, interpersonal connections, leisure, art, and sex.

The primary domain is productive work, which is crucial to a person's sense of efficacy and, by extension, to his ability to fully appreciate the other aspects of his existence.

I've previously stated that one of the primary traits of a person with high self-esteem who believes the world is amenable to his efforts is the great joy he finds in the constructive use of his mind—the pleasure he finds in exercising his intellectual and creative faculties. The soul of a person who prefers to work only on the routine and familiar, who tends to enjoy working while semi-dazed, and who finds happiness in being free from challenge, struggle, or effort, reveals a different kind of soul: the soul of a person who is profoundly low on self-esteem, to whom the universe appears unknowable and vaguely threatening, and whose main driving impulse is a longing for safety, not the safety won through effectiveness.

The soul of a person with little self-worth, who never expected the universe to treat them well, is revealed by someone who finds it incomprehensible that work—any form of work—can be enjoyable, who views the effort of earning a living as a necessary evil, who dreams only of the pleasures that begin when the workday ends, the pleasure of drowning his brain in alcohol or television or billiards or women, the pleasure of not being conscious.

The soul of a person who is so profoundly devoid of self-worth and so gripped by existential dread that his only means of self-fulfillment are to vent his resentment and hatred toward those who do not share his state, those who are able to live—as if, by destroying them, he will somehow be able to achieve efficacy—is revealed by the person who finds pleasure not in achievement but in destruction.

An intelligent, assured man is driven by a love of ideals and a desire to uphold them. A neurotic is driven by dread and a desire to run away from it, to the extent that he is neurotic. The items that each kind will seek out for pleasure as well as the type of pleasure he will feel reflect this variation in motivation.

For instance, the emotional quality of the pleasure felt by the four men in the aforementioned description is not the same. Any form of enjoyment has a quality that is determined by the mental processes that give rise to it, those that surround it, and the kinds of values it is based on. Just as the pleasure of reaching true values, of acquiring an authentic sense of effectiveness, and the "pleasure" of temporarily lessening one's experience of fear and powerlessness, are not the same, neither are the "pleasures" of utilizing one's consciousness appropriately and being unconscious. The self-respecting man enjoys the pure, unadulterated satisfaction of employing his faculties effectively and of realizing values in reality—a joy of which the other three men can have no conception, just as he has no inkling of the hazy, murky state they refer to as pleasure.

This idea holds true for all types of enjoyment. Thus, in the realm of human relationships, a different kind of pleasure is felt, a different kind of motivation is involved, and a different kind of character is revealed, by the person who seeks the company of intelligent, honest, and self-respecting men who share his exacting standards—and by the person who is only able to have fun with men who have no standards at all because they allow him to be himself; or by the persuader.

The desire for pleasure is an expression of the rational, psychologically sound man's desire to enjoy his mastery over his existence. The craving for pleasure is an attempt by the neurotic to escape reality.

Now think of the realm of entertainment, like a party. A sensible man appreciates a party as an emotional reward for success, but he can only do so if it includes delightful activities like visiting friends, meeting new people he finds interesting, and participating in talks where something worthwhile is being said and listened. However, a neurotic can "enjoy" a party for reasons unrelated to the actual activities going on; he may hate, despise, or fear all the people there, he may act foolishly and feel ashamed of it in private, but he will feel that he is enjoying it because people are emitting the vibrations of approval, or because being invited to this party is a social distinction, or because other people appear to be gay, or because the party has spared him, for the duration.

Being intoxicated undoubtedly provides the "pleasure" of avoiding the obligations of consciousness. And so too are the kinds of social events that exist solely to express hysterical disorder, in which the attendees stumble around in an inebriated stupor, prattling loudly and pointlessly, and reveling in the illusion of a world free of reason, logic, reality, and consciousness.

In this regard, look at the contemporary "youthniks"—if I may use that term—and, for instance, how they dance. Instead of genuine smiles of happiness, one too frequently observes vacant, gazing eyes, jerky movements, and bodies that appear to be dispersed, all of which are trying very hard—with a kind of flat-footed hysteria—to project an air of the meaningless, the senseless, and the mindless. The "joy" of unconsciousness is this.

Or think about the more low-key "pleasures" that many people have, such as family picnics, ladies' tea parties or "coffee klatches," charity bazaars, and vegetative vacations. The majority of these events are times of peaceful monotony for everyone involved, where the value is in the boredom. For these individuals, boredom entails the lack of the novel, the thrilling, the unfamiliar, and the demanding in favor of security, the known, the ordinary, and the routine.

A challenging pleasure is what? A form of enjoyment that calls for the use of the mind—not in the sense of solving problems, but rather in the sense of exercising judgment, awareness, and discrimination.

Works of art provide man with one of life's fundamental pleasures. When art is at its best, when it projects things "as they may be and ought to be," it can give people invaluable emotional energy. But once more, how one reacts to a piece of art relies on one's own beliefs and ideals.

A man might seek the projection of the noble, wise, effective, dramatic, purposeful, stylized, ingenious, and challenging; he can seek the joy of appreciation and the satisfaction of looking up to admirable ideals. He can feel himself warmly warmed by projections of the known and familiar, seeking to feel a little less of "a stranger and afraid in a world

[he] never made," or he can seek the satisfaction of contemplating gossip-column variations of the neighbors, with nothing demanding of him in thought or value standards. Or, he can enjoy art that tells him that man is evil, that reality is unknowable, that existence is unbearable, that no one can help anything, and that his deepest fear is common; he can feel comforted by the thought that he's not as bad as the dope-addicted dwarf or the crippled lesbian he's reading about.

All art implicitly expresses a worldview, and the type of art that will pique an individual's interest is heavily influenced by that worldview. In stark contrast to the soul of the man whose favorite play is Waiting for Godot, the man whose favorite play is Cyrano de Bergerac has a very different soul.

One of the greatest pleasures a man can experience is pride, or the satisfaction he derives from his own accomplishments and the development of his own character. He enjoys celebrating the accomplishments and qualities of another person out of admiration. Romantic love is the purest manifestation of the merger of these two emotions—pride and admiration—at their most extreme. Sex is the celebration.

In Chapter Eleven, we'll go into more depth on the psychology of sex and romantic love—and how those concepts relate to self-esteem. But for the time being, a few broad remarks are required to wrap up our analysis here.

A man's perspective on himself and the world shines out most clearly in this area—in his romantic-sexual responses. The lady who embodies his deepest ideals is the one he falls in love with and has a sexual attraction for.

A man's romantic-sexual responses are psychologically telling in two key ways: the person he chooses as his partner and the significance of the act in his eyes.

A man who is confident in himself and in love with life has a strong desire to connect with people he can admire and fall in love with on a spiritual level. He will be most drawn to someone who has a strong sense of self-worth and an unwavering appreciation for life. For such a man, having sex is an act of celebration, a compliment to both himself and the lady he has chosen, and the pinnacle of personally and concretely feeling the value and joy of life.

Man's nature compels him to need such an encounter. However, if a man lacks the self-esteem to earn it, he will try to fake it instead. He will choose his partner (subconsciously) based on whether or not she can assist him in doing so, giving him the appearance of happiness and self-worth that he does not actually have.

So, if a man is attracted to a woman who possesses intelligence, self-assurance, and strength, if he is attracted to a heroine, he reveals one kind of soul; if, however, he is attracted to an irresponsible, helpless scatterbrain, whose weakness allows him to feel masculine, he reveals another kind of soul; if he is attracted to a frightened slut, whose

Of course, the same rule holds true for a woman's romantic and sexual preferences.

For someone whose desire is fueled by pride and admiration, for whom the pleasurable self-experience it affords is an end in itself, the sexual act has a different meaning than for someone who seeks in sex the validation of their masculinity (or femininity), the alleviation of their despondency, a buffer against their anxiety, or an escape from boredom.

Ironically, those who are referred to as "pleasure-chasers"—men who appear to live for the now and are only interested in having a "good time"—are mentally unable to view pleasure as a goal in and of itself. The neurotic pleasure-seeker believes that by acting like there is something to celebrate, he will be able to convince himself that there is.

The fact that most of his joys are pleasures of flight from the two pursuers whom he has deceived and from whom there is no escape: reality and his own mind—is one of the characteristics of a man lacking in self-esteem—and the true punishment for his psychological default.

The neurotic is in a deadly conflict because, by his very nature as a man, he is forced to feel a desperate need for pleasure as a confirmation and expression of his control over reality—but most of the time, he can only find pleasure in an escape from reality. This is because the purpose of pleasure is to give man a sense of his own efficacy. That explains why his joys don't satisfy him and instead make him feel guilty, frustrated, hopeless, and ashamed rather than proud, fulfilled, or inspired. A man with self-esteem experiences pleasure as a reward and a confirmation. Anxiety, the shaking of the flimsy foundation of his false sense of self-worth, and the sharpening of the ever-present fear that the structure will collapse and he will find himself face to face with a stern, absolute, unknowable, and unforgiving reality are the effects of pleasure on a man who lacks self-esteem.

One of the most frequent concerns of people seeking psychotherapy is that nothing can make them happy and that they can never truly appreciate anything. This is where the pleasure-as-escape policy will inevitably lead.

A rare moral and psychological accomplishment is to maintain an unclouded capacity for enjoyment of life. Contrary to common assumption, it is not the right of the unthinking, but rather the reward of self-esteem.

CHAPTER EIGHT

Pseudo-Self-Confidence

Anxiety versus Thought

The presence of self-esteem does not automatically shield a man from making mistakes that could have unpleasant emotional repercussions. These mistakes could be about life, about other men, or about the best course of action to take. Infallibility is not a given of reason.

However, a strong sense of self-worth gives a person an invaluable tool for combating errors. When a person's worth and the power of their brain are unquestionable, they are free to use all of their knowledge and intellectual abilities to the goal of finding the truth and solving issues. So to speak, his consciousness's base is firmly in place.

In contrast, one of the most detrimental effects of low self-esteem is that it tends to hinder and undermine a man's ability to think clearly, robbing him of the full force and value of his own intelligence.

When a man lacks self-esteem, his consciousness is dominated by fear: fear of the facts about himself that he has avoided or suppressed; fear of reality, to which he feels inadequate. The opposite of thought is fear. If a man feels that reality is the enemy of his self-esteem (or his pretense at self-esteem), if he feels that the most important aspects of reality with which he must deal are hopelessly closed to his understanding, if he faces the most important issues in his life with a fundamental sense of helplessness, if he feels that he dares not pursue certain lines of thought because the unworthy features of his own character that would be brought to light, then these fears act as a barrier

Lack of self-esteem can negatively impact a man's thought processes in a variety of ways.

A man who approaches life's fundamental issues with an attitude of "What do I know? Me, the judge? Who am I to decide? "—is initially intellectually undercut. If a person believes that their thinking is doomed to failure, they will either stop thinking altogether or will stop thinking extremely persistently. A mind does not battle for what it perceives as being impossible.

A man's behaviors will typically confirm and support his poor self-image if he believes himself to be powerless and ineffective, creating a vicious cycle. By the same logic, a man who is assured of his effectiveness would typically behave in an effective manner. The way a guy views himself has a significant impact on his motivation, whether for good or negative. The influence of it that is most noticeable right away is in the caliber and ambition of his thought.

Although a man's self-esteem and self-image do not directly influence his thought process, they do have an impact on his emotional motivations. As a result, a man's feelings have a tendency to either encourage or discourage thought, leading him toward reality or away from it, toward efficacy or away from it.

Numerous men end up being psychological prisoners of their own bad self-perception. They define themselves as weak, mediocre, unmasculine, cowardly, or ineffective, and this has an impact on how they perform in the future. Most men do not maintain their self-image in conceptual form or recognize its repercussions conceptually, therefore this process takes place subconsciously.

Even if males are capable of acting in a way that challenges their negative self-perception—and many do, at least occasionally—their attitude of acceptance toward their current circumstances tends to keep them from doing so. They give in to a damaging sense of determinism about themselves, believing that being weak, average, or unmasculine, for example, is part of their "nature" and cannot be changed. Men with enormous talent who are struck by this fatal error may only be able to function to a small portion of their ability.

A generalized sense of guilt or unworthiness can considerably skew the introspection of a man who struggles with self-esteem when he tries to pinpoint the driving forces behind his actions in a particular situation or issue. He might be lured to the most harmful, the one that casts him in the worst possible moral light, rather than the one that makes the most sense and explains his actions. Or, if he is faced with the unfair allegations of others, he would feel disarmed and powerless to refute their assertions; instead, he might accept their accusations as genuine, frozen and worn out by the question "How can I know?"

In this context, it is instructive to keep in mind that one of the common tactics used in "brain-washing" is to instill or provoke some form of guilt in the victim. This is done on the theory that a mind that is troubled by guilt is less likely to exercise independent thought and is more open to indoctrination and intellectual manipulation. Self-confidence is tamed by guilt.

The underlying idea is not brand-new. It has been used by religion for a very long time (Chapter Twelve).

When a guy has poor self-esteem and puts in place numerous irrational defenses to shield himself from the realization of his shortcomings, he inadvertently inserts distortions into his thinking. In order to maintain his irrational defenses, the defenses erected to support a tolerable form of self-appraisal, he regulates his mental processes not by the goal of accurately perceiving reality, but (at best) by the goal of gaining only those types of knowledge that are compatible with the maintenance of his irrational defenses.

He makes reality conditional in an effort to pretend to have a higher sense of self than he actually does. He maintains that some factors are more significant to him than reality, facts, and truth as a general rule for how his mind works. After that, his consciousness is significantly and dangerously pulled by the strings of his desires and fears (especially his fears); they become his lords, and he must adapt to them rather than reality.

He is so compelled to maintain and strengthen the same anti-rational, self-defeating policies that initially caused him to lose confidence in himself.

Consider the situation of a man who strives to get a sense of personal value from the near-delusional image of himself as a "great operator" in business, a brave and cunning "go-getter" who is only one deal away from a fortune. This individual lacks genuine self-esteem. In one "get rich quick" scam after another, he continues to lose money and lose, ignorant to the evidence that his schemes are unworkable, ignoring unfavorable details, bragging extravagantly, and focusing only on the mesmerizingly bright picture of himself as a wonderfully skilled businessman. He breaks cognitive contact with reality in order to defend a self-perception that the facts of reality cannot support, moving from disaster to disaster with his gaze inward out of fear that he will one day realize that the self-perception that feels like a lifeline is actually a noose suffocating him to death.

Consider, for example, a middle-aged woman whose sense of self-worth is critically reliant on the idea of herself as a glamorous, youthful beauty. This woman sees every wrinkle as a metaphysical threat to her identity and, in an effort to protect it, enters into a string of relationships with men who are more than 20 years younger than her. She presents an ever more frantic gaiety, rationalizing each relationship as a grand passion, avoiding the personalities and motivations of the young men involved, and suppressing the embarrassment she feels around her friends. She dreads being alone, constantly craves new admiration, and runs faster and faster from the haunting, relentless pursuer that is her own emptiness.

Pretense, self-deception, and "role-playing" are such unavoidable aspects of most men's life that they have all but forgotten (if they ever did) what it means to take reality seriously and to have an unwavering regard for the realities of reality. They live much of their life in a fictitious universe that they have created as a result of their neuroses, and they then wonder why they experience fear and powerlessness in the outside world.

As long as there are factors in one's mind that take precedence over the realities of the situation, it is impossible to maintain one's ability to think clearly. As long as one is implicitly committed to the idea that avoiding certain realities is necessary to maintain one's self-esteem, there is no way to sustain the unbroken force of one's mind.

The misery, frustration, and fear that define the psychological state of the majority of men attest to two facts: that self-esteem is a fundamental need without which man cannot live the life that is appropriate to him— and that self-esteem, the conviction that he is capable of handling reality, can be attained only by the consistent exercise of the one faculty that allows man to comprehend reality: his reason.

Self-Confidence Versus Pseudo-Self-Confidence

A lack of self-esteem results in feelings of anxiety, insecurity, and self-doubt as well as a sensation of being unsuited for life and inadequate to live. Anxiety is a psychological alarm signal that alerts the body to impending danger (Chapter Nine).

The majority of people will feel this type of anxiety, but to various degrees of intensity.

The majority of men never acknowledge the significance of reason to their life, do not evaluate their own level of devotion to reason, and are not aware of the topic of self-esteem in the contexts described here. They simply recognize a tremendous need to be in charge, in control, and good—good in a fundamental level that they cannot articulate. However, a psycho-epistemological failure, or a failure in the correct use of their consciousness—a default on the responsibility of reason—is the root of that shapeless anxiety and shame that haunts their existence. They pay a price for that default in the form of the worry they feel.

Since self-esteem is a basic requirement of the human mind and cannot be ignored, men who do not develop self-esteem, or who do not develop it to a substantial degree, try to fake it in order to conceal their lack of it and find safety from their inner dread behind a façade of pseudo-self-esteem.

In order to reduce anxiety and give oneself a false sense of security, pseudo-self-esteem, an irrational pretense at self-value, is a non-rational, self-protective technique. It is intended to satisfy the demand for actual self-esteem while allowing the true causes of its absence to be avoided.

By avoiding, repressing, rationalizing, and otherwise suppressing thoughts and feelings that could have a negative impact on his self-appraisal, as well as by attempting to derive his sense of efficacy and worth from something other than rationality, some alternative value or virtue that he experiences as less demanding or more easily attainable, such as "doing one's duty," being stoic, altruistic, or financially successful, a man can maintain his pseudo-self-esteem.

The neurotic bases a significant portion of his life on this intricate self-deception process, which is also the source of his motivation, ideals, and aspirations. Knowing "what makes him tick" or the nature and structure of a particular man's pseudo-self-esteem is equivalent to understanding the driving force behind his behavior.

Since he builds his self-esteem on his resolve to know and act in line with the facts of reality as he understands them, there is no conflict in the psychology of a man with authentic self-value between his recognition of the truths of reality and the preservation of his self-esteem. Since his pretense at self-esteem is bought at the cost of evasion, of persistent blind spots, and of cognitive self-censorship, reality appears to the man of pseudo-self-esteem as a threat, as an enemy; he feels, in essence, that it's reality or his self-esteem. This is why a man could be completely clear-headed and rational in a situation that has nothing to do with or poses no threat to his fake self-esteem, yet blatantly illogical, evasive, defensive, and foolish in one that does. Suspension of consciousness is his usual response to any prospective attack on his phony self-esteem. Such an assault serves as a psycho-epistemological disintegrator by causing worry. As a result, he continues the same psycho-epistemological self-sabotage that led to his original failure of self-esteem.

One index of mental health and illness that might be seen as a result of this occurrence is: A man is psychologically healthy to the extent that he does not experience conflict between his ability to perceive reality and his desire to uphold his self-esteem; the extent to which this conflict does exist indicates the severity of the man's mental disorder.

It takes more than just evasion, repression, etc. to give a neurotic the appearance of self-worth; this is just one aspect of his self-deception. The other component is made up of the values he settles on as a means of developing a feeling of self-worth. A man with genuine self-esteem is motivated differently than a man with fake self-esteem in terms of how they make decisions about values.

A person who is growing healthily experiences great joy and pride in both his mental labor and the successes those efforts enable. He will desire a difficult, laborious, creative existence because he will be confident in his capacity to deal with reality's facts. Whatever his intelligence level, creativity will always be his greatest love. A person who is self-assured will be drawn to other people who are also self-assured because they provide him the chance to be admired. He will seek out people and things he can respect in order to experience the satisfaction that his own character and accomplishments may bring to others. His foundation and driving force in the world of work and interpersonal interactions is a strong sense of effectiveness, which leads to a love for existence and the fact that one is alive. He is looking for ways to convey and objectify his self-worth (Chapter Eleven).

Fear, not confidence, serves as the man without self-foundation worth's and driving force. His main objective isn't to survive but to get away from his fear of dying. His overarching objective is safety, not creativity. And what he really wants from people is not the chance to be admired, but rather an escape from moral principles and moral judgment, as well as a guarantee that he would be accepted, comforted, and taken care of—metaphysically speaking—in a terrible universe. His ideals are a confession of his lack of self-worth rather than an expression of it.

Abstract values, not the precise goals a man will pursue, are determined by his self-esteem or pseudo-self-esteem; the latter come from a variety of elements, such as his intelligence, knowledge, ideas, and personal environment. A man with strong self-esteem, for example, will want intellectually difficult job, but whether he decides to work in business, science, or the arts depends on more specific, less fundamental factors. Similar to this, a man with false self-esteem will want people to shield him from reality; but, other things will decide whether he feels more at home among the academic set, the country club set, or the underworld set.

The idea of motivation by love versus motivation by fear separates the fundamental motivation of a man with self-esteem from that of a man with pseudo-self-esteem. Fear of not being fit for existence against love of oneself and of existence. Motivated by confidence as opposed to terrified.

Consequently, the following is a further index of mental health and illness: When a man operates under the tenet of motivation by confidence, he is psychologically sound; when he does so under the tenet of motivation by fear, he is mentally unwell. A man lives negatively and defensively to the extent that he lacks self-esteem. His main motivation when deciding on his specific beliefs and objectives is not to provide himself a fulfilling living, but rather to protect himself from anxiety, painful emotions of inadequacy, self-doubt, and guilt.

The pursuit of enjoyment is not a man's top priority in an emergency scenario where his life is in physical danger, such as when he has a serious illness, but rather eliminating the threat by getting better and reestablishing the conditions that would allow him to pursue fun again. But for a man who lacks self-worth, life is essentially a constant emergency, and he is constantly in danger psychologically. He never achieves normalcy and never feels free to enjoy life because he approaches risk by trying to convince himself that it doesn't exist rather than confronting it logically and attempting to eliminate it. He will never succeed since A is A and facts cannot be changed by willful ignorance, but the majority of his avoidances, suppressions, and self-defeating behaviors are directed in this direction.

The dominant psychological factor in such an individual is fear. Fear controls his motivational behavior in the same way that it controls his psycho-epistemological behavior, undermining his ability to perceive clearly, distorting his judgments, limiting his cognitive ambition, and pushing him to ever-wider evasions. Fear also controls his motivational behavior by sabotaging his normal value-development, stunting his proper growth, and pushing him toward goals that will support his pretense of efficacy, leading him to passive conformity, hostile aggression, or autistic

These values could be referred to as "defense-values" A defense value is one that is driven by fear and intended to boost a false sense of self-worth. In essence, it serves as a rationale replacement and a means of survival. It is a tool for reducing anxiety.

Such a value is harmful, not necessarily because of what it is, but because of the reason someone would choose it. The reason for the value's selection may not be illogical, even though the value itself might not be. A logical value might be productive work, but it is not rational to use one's work as a way to hide one's defects, shortcomings, or problems. Defense values are frequently unreasonable in both senses, as in the situation of a guy trying to gain control over others in order to feel less anxious.

The degree to which defense-values serve as the foundation of a man's soul indicates how low his self-esteem is. The method through which defense-values and false self-esteem grow, as well as the psychological crisis they can trigger, are demonstrated in the following case.

Consider the case of a person who, as a child, exhibited the typical antipathy to mental effort: one who rebelled against the responsibility of thinking, one who resented the necessity of judgment, one who preferred a non-demanding state of mental fog, and one who drifted at the mercy of unexamined emotions. He tries to avoid them as much as possible whenever thoughts of fear or inadequacy break through his chronic sluggishness and alert him of the peril of his course. He relies on the leadership and direction of those close to him in order to feel safe and secure.

His parents call him a "good" youngster because of his policy of blind obedience.

His work at school is subpar, and he harbors an unspoken grudge against the class's smarter boys. He takes pleasure in watching others act out and receive discipline from the instructor because, in his eyes, it shows that they are not "decent" guys and that, despite his academic deficiency, he is morally superior to them.

He likes to attend church, where he learns that the heart, not the mind, is what matters and that "the humble shall inherit the earth."

He rarely is aware of the processes through which he chooses his values and aspirations as he matures into adulthood. However, he moves like a somnambulist under the control of unconscious commands, and his unacknowledged sense of helplessness, dread of independence, desire for safety, and hostility toward thought guide him through all of his important judgments. These inevitably drive him to choose acquaintances with average intelligence, accept a job at his uncle's hardware business, join his father's political party, and get married to the girl who lives next door.

He responds by conjuring the idea that he is a "decent citizen," a "good provider," a "devoted, faithful husband," a "God-fearing man," and that he has done all the things "one is supposed to do" whenever he feels vaguely guilty about his inertia or whenever his wife criticizes him for his lack of ambition and nags him to demand a raise. He constantly reminds himself that his defining quality is humility and that others are at fault for failing to appreciate this and treat him with respect whenever he experiences feelings of resentment or jealously toward the men in his immediate vicinity who have achieved more in life than he has. He does this in order to psychologically tolerate his existence.

He follows the prescribed procedures at the hardware shop without taking any initiative, picking up any new skills, or stopping to think. But on occasion, he daydreams about the increased pay and status he will receive when his uncle passes away and leaves him the firm; if the moral ramifications of his wish start to concern him, he quickly shifts his attention elsewhere and avoids them.

However, he does not feel the joy he had anticipated when the long-awaited event finally occurs. He wakes up in the middle of the night the day after his uncle's burial, his heart racing wildly and a sense of extreme dread filling him. He has no idea how to explain it; all he knows is that he is overcome with a sensation of approaching doom.

His early habits of self-deception and avoidance today prevent him from understanding the source of his uneasiness. In order to avoid confronting his moral and psychological default and to dodge any potential challenge to his flimsy inner "security," he had been decreasing his perception—and the dimensions of the reality with which he had to deal—for years. In an effort to avoid the work and responsibility of thought by making humility his means of existence, he has crept through life accepting, nodding, agreeing, and obeying while trying to create a society in which this would be feasible. But now that reality has torn down those world's defenses, he finds himself in a predicament where he must exercise judgment and assume intellectual responsibility. He is torn between the ideas, "I've got to know what to do!" and "I can't!" As a result of this collision, the recurring fear he had previously managed to avoid explodes into horror—the terror of realizing that his previous means of defense are no longer sufficient to keep him safe and that he has nowhere to hide.

This man's pseudo-self-esteem was based on his humility, depending on others to solve the problem of his survival, and he chose values appropriate to this mode of existence, values intended to reassure him of the validity and safety of his course. This is similar to how a psychologically healthy man bases his self-esteem on the use of his mind, and gains an ever-increasing sense of control over his existence by choosing values that demand constant intellectual growth. He experiences the dread of a man abruptly stripped of his means of survival, forced to operate and function in reality without weapons, when he becomes the owner of the hardware store.

The unjustified compulsiveness with which defense-values are typically held is a significant trait of these values. With blind determination and fanatical dedication, men with false self-esteem cling to these ideals, much as they would to a life preserver in a choppy sea. The worry that one will not be able to live is greater than the horror of dying. Men will do anything to get rid of that agonizing emotion, even go against reason, forego their practical self-interest, and occasionally even risk their lives.

With very few exceptions, they will pay any price but the one that could save them; they won't admit that their defenses are false and seek to build real self-worth; they won't take ownership of the duty of acting like responsible adults.

There are essentially countless alternative defense-values that males can adopt. But the majority of these principles fall under one overarching category: they are principles that are often valued highly by the community or subculture in which a person lives.

Examples of typical defense-values in this area are provided below.

—The man who is obsessed with popularity, who feels compelled to win the approval of everyone he meets, who clings to the idea of himself as "likeable," who, in effect, views his endearing personality as the proof of his personal worth; —The woman who lacks a sense of self and who seeks to lose her inner emptiness in the role of a selfless martyr for her children, demanding in exchange only that her children adore her, that they respect her, that they

Religious defense values are a common type of defense value. In these situations, a false sense of self-worth is built on compliance to some religious commandment (s). Adherence to religious rites, asceticism, and systematic self-denial are all methods used to buy a sense of worthiness and calm worry. The individual who justifies his behavior by persuading himself that it "does not represent the real me" and that "the real me is my goals" is exhibiting yet another form of defense-value. Such a person maintains his or her false sense of self-worth by viewing himself or herself as an aspirer—an aspirer who is constrained from living up to his or her professed ideals by forces beyond his or her control, such as the evil of "the system," the malice of the universe, the tragedy of some unspecified "circumstances," "human infirmity," "I never got a break," "I'm too honest and decent for this world," etc. A common anti-anxiety strategy is the idea of a "true me," which has little to do with anything one says or does in reality. This idea frequently coexists with other defense-values.

Defense-values and false self-worth do not always or must collapse violently and dramatically, as in the case of the individual in the previous case study who gave in to severe fear. Often, the process of psychological erosion and disintegration is quieter, more subtle; the person involved is not brought to a moment of obvious crisis; rather, his energy is gradually depleted, he becomes more prone to fatigue, depression, and, possibly, a variety of minor somatic complaints, and his pretense at self-value becomes progressively more worn and frayed— and his life peters out in lonely, pointless misery, without climaxes, without explosions.

A guy can never replace genuine self-esteem with avoidance, defense values, or a self-deception approach. None of the self-deceit men do can buy the sense of efficacy and integrity they yearn for. Man needs to believe that he is right in actuality and right in principle, and the only way to do that is to follow a policy of reason.

Let a man tell himself that gaining self-worth does not require the fullest use of his intellect, but rather its surrender in submission to faith; let him believe that gaining efficacy does not require thinking, but rather adhering to others' beliefs; let him believe that gaining efficacy entails winning love; let him believe that his fundamental worth is determined by the number of women he sleeps with, the number of women he doesn't sleep with, the number of people he can manipulate;

Most men's lives end tragically as a result of their efforts to deny this reality.

Man's motivation depends on his level of self-esteem, whether it is present or not. The horror that haunts the lives of those who fail to acquire it, the twisting roads that that terror drives them along, and the inevitable destruction at the end are arguably the most potent testaments to the urgency of man's need for self-esteem.

CHAPTER NINE
Anxiety Disorder:
A Crisis of Self-Confidence

The Anxiety Problem

There is no more terrifying object of fear to man than fear itself—and no more terrifying fear than that for which he has no object.

It has been the fate of the majority of the human race for countless millions of men and women to live with such anxiety as a paralyzing constant of their lives. The terror of tyranny, concentration camps, war, enslavement, economic collapse, and arbitrary, unexpected violence—all emblems of a world like the one we live in now, when open force is inexorably gaining ground and reason has largely been abandoned—is one that few men today can avoid. Such anxiety can be normal and sensible, a realistically acceptable reaction to actual and present dangers. Without the presence of any such obviously visible dangers, the terror I'm referring to manifests itself. Its distinctive quality is that it seems to have no apparent cause. Only that it has struck them is known to its victims; they are in the dark as to why.

Imagine the kind of dread a man might experience while dangling perilously in space from a frayed rope over a chasm. Now remove the rope and the chasm and imagine the victim of that emotion while comfortably at home in his living room, at his desk, or strolling down the street. The acute form of pathological anxiety is what is going on.

Anxiety that is pathological is a feeling of dread that is felt in the absence of any real or perceived threat.

Ordinary fear is a proportionate and confined response to a real, external, and immediate danger, such the fear of being hit by an incoming car. Pathological anxiety differs from both those fears that are rationally grounded and affect the world at large. Additionally, it differs from objective or typical anxiety: Normal anxiety is a feeling of dread and helplessness that is directed toward a specific source, similar to fear, but the danger is less immediate and the emotion is more anticipatory, such as the feeling that might overtake a person when they see symptoms of a serious illness or might strike parents whose child is in the hands of kidnappers. When a threat is no longer present, fear and objective anxiety disappear; they are not, in fact, characteristics of the person who experiences them. However, pathological phobia is.

Anxiety that is pathological or subjective does not always take an extreme or violent form. Many of its victims only experience it occasionally as a diffuse sense of worry and fear that comes and goes predictably while following some mysterious pattern of its own. They do not experience it as an intense panic attack or as a persistent feeling of dread. It can range in intensity from mild pain to an agonizing experience that many people who have gone through it have vowed they would rather die than go through it again.

The sufferer can't put a name to what he fears; he feels afraid of nothing in particular and of everything in general; if he tries to offer a rationalized explanation for his feelings or grasps at an indicator in the outside world to prove he is in danger, his justifications are blatantly illogical; and he behaves as though what he fears is not any specific concrete danger.

Henry James, Sr., the father of philosopher-psychologist William James, provides one of the most explicit depictions of the beginning of an anxiety attack in an autobiographical chapter. The senior James gives the following account of his harrowing encounter:

One day near the end of May, after a satisfying meal, I stayed seated at the table after the family had left, idly staring at the embers in the grate, thinking of nothing and feeling only the elation associated with a good meal, when suddenly—in a lightning-flash, if you will—"fear came upon me, and trembling, which made all my bones to shake." According to all outward appearances, it was an utterly insane and abject terror without any apparent cause, and it could only be explained, in my bewildered imagination, by some damned shape sitting within the confines of the room that was invisible to me and radiating out from his fetid personality influences lethal to life. In less than ten seconds, I felt like a wreck, lowered from a state of strong, spirited, and joyous manhood to one of nearly helpless infancy. I was just able to contain myself enough to stay my seat. I had the strongest want to scream for aid to my wife from the bottom of the stairs, to run to the roadside and beg people to defend me, but I was able to restrain myself by making a tremendous effort. I made the decision to stay in my chair until I had regained my lost composure. With no relief from any truth I had ever encountered other than a very faint and far-off glimmer of divine existence, I held to this purpose for a good long hour as I measured time before deciding to give up the futile battle and immediately tell my wife what seemed to be my sudden burden of inner, implacable unrest.

To cut a long story short, I endured this horrifying mental state for at least two years while experiencing steadily greater periods of relief.

There are a lot of people in the world who have severe mental or emotional disturbances. However, these individuals make up a very small portion of all men and women who have pathological anxiety for the majority of their lives, but whose condition never becomes severe enough to attract a psychotherapist's notice or be noted in any statistical study. These people are typically seen as fairly normal by those around them, and they do not consider their psychological health to be in jeopardy just because they occasionally have episodes of unexplainable, objectless dread.

These are the people who, for example, can't stand to be by themselves, can't function without sleeping pills, jump at unexpected noises, drink excessively to calm an excessive amount of anxiety, feel a constant need to amuse and entertain, run away to too many gatherings and movies they don't want to go to, and sacrifice any remaining independence self-confidence to an obsession with what others think of them.

Clinical psychologists and psychiatrists are generally in agreement that the fundamental issue they must address in psychotherapy—the symptom underneath the patient's other symptoms—is pathological anxiety. Other symptoms, such as headaches, choking feelings, heart palpitations, digestive problems, dizziness, shaking, nausea, excessive sweating, insomnia, severe bodily tensions, and chronic weariness, might occasionally be considered direct physical effects of worry. Some of these, such hysterical paralysis, obsessions, compulsions, and quiet depression, serve as shields against anxiety. However, anxiety is always the driving force behind neurosis.

Uncertainty and fear are the key characteristics of the neurotic and his ingrained reaction to the outside world. Not all neurotics experience obsessive thoughts or compulsive behaviors, not all neurotics fear heights or wide-open areas, and not all neurotics experience somatic illnesses without a somatic cause. However, fear grips every neurotic. A happy neurotic who is confident in his capacity to manage life effectively is an absurdity.

What is pathological anxiety like, and what causes it?

In order to respond to this query, one needs first take note of this anxiety's prominent and important quality: its metaphysical nature. The fear appears to be focused on the universe as a whole and existence as a whole, as if the idea that to be means to be in imminent danger.

An intense sense of powerlessness and impotence is a core component of the anxiety experience for the anxious individual. He senses an oncoming, formless catastrophe. And he frequently experiences an original, ambiguous sensation of guilt. The shame is also metaphysical in nature; he feels wrong—wrong as a human, wrong in a fundamental level that goes beyond any specific flaw or imperfection he can point to. (Sometimes the guilt is foremost in his mind; other times it is unnamed, undifferentiated, and in essence subconscious.)

This metaphysical type of dread originates within the individual who experiences it, not in the outside environment. It is something he has done to himself, not something reality has done to him. He bears the menace and peril inside his own mind.

As a fundamental attitude, self-confidence entails faith in the effectiveness of one's consciousness. The polar opposite of this condition is pathological anxiousness. It is nature's way of telling a man that his psychological state is off and that his perception of reality is off; it is his mind's cry of helplessness and loss of control. It is a self-esteem crisis.

Pathological anxiety is the suffering of a person who is crippled or devastated in this realm, who feels cut off from reality, alienated, and powerless. If self-esteem is the conviction that one's mind is capable of grasping and judging the facts of reality, and that one's person is worthy of happiness.

Behind a terror that is perceived as metaphysical is a catastrophe that is psycho-epistemological—a flaw or default in how a man's awareness should be working.

Every time a man experiences fear of any type, his reaction reveals an assessment of some danger to him, i.e., some challenge to his principles. What is the value in the case of pathological anxiety that is being threatened? It is the ego of the victim.

The mind, the faculty of consciousness, the capacity for thought—the faculty that observes reality, upholds the internal continuity of one's own life, and creates one's feeling of personal identity—are all components of a man's ego. The terms "ego" and "mind," which refer to the same act of reality and quality of man, are used differently; this difference is due to a matter of perspective: I refer to man's power of awareness as he experiences it as his "ego."

Any challenge to a man's ego, or whatever he perceives as a risk to the effectiveness and control of his mind, is a potential source of pathological worry. Because the value at stake is inevitably the most important of all his values, this anxiety's suffering is the worst that man can experience.

Man is capable of undermining and betraying his thinking, which is his most important survival tool, because he is a volitional conscious entity. By evasion, denial, rationalization, and other techniques, he can undermine the clarity and integrity of his own mental processes, distancing himself from reality and relegating himself to a situation in which being present is equivalent to being in imminent risk of death.

Let's now analyze how a guy can undermine the perceiving-integrating function of his consciousness and induce a pathological state of anxiety.

Man must seek for an unhindered cognitive touch with reality in order to successfully navigate existence and achieve the objectives and goals that his life and well-being need. This requires him to keep his mind fully focused and to strive for the highest level of awareness with regard to his actions, concerns, and everything that has an impact on them.

If a man fails in this mission, the results are not just the existential failures and losses he experiences; the deadlier punishment is the result for his ego, for his sense of self. He is forced to experience the notion that his mind is an unreliable tool. Whatever a man may be able to fake, he will never be able to fake the efficacy that his ego lacks; if his mind is out of control, it is out of control; no amount of reasoning or denial will be able to erase this fact or eliminate its psychological repercussion, which is self-distrust.

If a man refuses to think about problems that he knows (clearly or dimly) need his attention out of laziness or fear, he may be able to deny the fact of his denial, but the contradiction between his knowledge and performance is a fact that cannot be denied; the fact does not go away; it is recorded in his subconscious—along with the knowledge that the problems he avoided have not disappeared either. Self-doubt is the outcome.

The betrayal of a man's cognitive growth stays real, as sternly and unforgivingly real as the unchangeable reality outside of his closed eyelids, if he chooses a policy of losing attention and escaping into the comfort of autistic dreams when faced with any uncomfortable part of life. Self-doubt is the outcome.

In order to escape the consequences of his actions and the psycho-epistemological policy behind them, a man who acts in accordance with his emotions rather than his convictions or what he believes to be right may disintegrate his conscious mind. However, the consequences do not go away and a ruthless computer within his brain compiles them. In the event of a conflict between his reason and his emotions, he is left with the implicit understanding that he would forfeit his reason; under duress, it is his mind, his conscious judgment, that becomes expendable. Self-doubt is the outcome.

If a man uses repression or constructs mental barriers that prevent him from understanding the nature of his own sentiments in order to avoid thoughts and wants that he perceives as endangering his self-esteem or stability, he does not cure his problem; instead, he only makes it worse. He undermines his capacity for self-reflection and problem-solving. And he is left with the impression that he is hiding a terrible foe from which he cannot flee or face, a foe whom he has attempted to subdue by turning himself blind.

If a man establishes within his consciousness the principle that it is acceptable to act with his mind unfocused, that he need not know what he is doing or why, that he need not consider the challenging, the painful, or the unfavorable—if the guiding principle of his mental activity is not "know the truth," but "avoid effort" and/or "escape pain"—then this is the secret to happiness.

One need not be surprised by most men's psychological condition or the epidemic frequency of "causeless" anxiety when one considers the degree of careless irrationality that most men tolerate in themselves and view as normal. Men have given themselves plenty of reasons to be uneasy and apprehensive about their capacity to deal with life's realities.

But it's important to keep in mind that pathological anxiety is pathological, meaning it's a sign of an unnatural and harmful condition.

This emphasis is necessary in light of the works of existentialists and some religious believers who make the opposite claim. Man's natural state is not one of constant fear. Man's lack of omniscience, omnipotence, infallibility, and immortality does not warrant his ego being overcome by a sense of inadequacy. In accordance with his own nature and the nature of reality, a reasonable man does not set his criterion of efficacy. The same is true of Original Sin: sin is not "original," it is generated. If a man feels guilty, it is not because he is guilty by nature. Anxiety is a psychological issue, not a metaphysical one.

The Characteristics of Anxiety Conflicts

A person who practices illogical mind-subverting psycho-epistemological policies condemns himself to a persistent expectation of failure.

If he doesn't do the thinking that his life and concerns require, he will be forced to face the fact that his actions are more expansive than his thoughts and that he will be confronted with demands and challenges that are beyond his capacity. He will feel both guilty and afraid for not doing the thinking because he knows that he should have done it.

Since a person's deepest sense of who they are is rooted in their method of psycho-epistemological functioning, or the ways in which their mind approaches reality, when they act against their convictions, take actions they believe to be wrong, and/or fail to take actions they believe to be right, they begin to feel not just that their actions are wrong, but also that they are wrong, wrong as people.

Even if the moral precepts he adopts are incorrect or illogical, he cannot act against them psychologically without feeling as though he has violated his own consciousness and deemed himself unfit for reality. This is because they represent his true convictions. (This is one of the reasons why adopting a set of values that is actually at odds with his nature and needs—as we will describe in Chapter Twelve—would have such terrible psychological and existential consequences for his existence.)

A guy who goes against his moral principles may experience a sense of approaching doom for another, related reason. Man cannot avoid the understanding that he requires some type of moral standards to guide him in order to interact with reality successfully and in order to exist; he cannot escape his nature as a conceptual being. This is true whether the moral ideals he adopts are irrational or rational. And underlying in this knowledge is the understanding that ethical values are a necessary part of his life on earth, however dimly it may be understood or perplexed by the otherworldly teachings of mystics. His anticipation that moral and immoral actions have repercussions, even if he cannot always predict them, is a corollary of this understanding. Although this expectation is frequently avoided and suppressed, if he takes activities that he views as good, he expects to benefit existentially or psychologically; if he takes actions that he views as harmful, he expects to suffer existentially or psychologically. As a result, if and when he compromises his own values, all he has left is the idea that he is in danger and that someone or something is going to get back at him.

To assume that this mindset is solely the result of religious influence would be a grave error. The problem is far bigger and more complex. It comes from man's implicit knowledge that he needs some overarching principles to direct his behavior if he is to live successfully. (Regarding religion, it simply stands for a misguided and foolish attempt to satiate this need—or to capitalize on it.)

Pathological anxiety is a conflict-filled sensation that always reflects conflict. However, not all disputes lead to pathological anxiety. Conflicts by themselves are not abnormal. Neurotic anxiety involves a specific type of conflict, and the ego's encounter with that conflict is what triggers the acute anxiety episode.

Let's look at three distinct cases of anxiety attacks to better understand the nature of the conflict and how it manifests itself.

1. For twenty years, the same unremarkable, gentle clerk has worked in the same job. The frequency with which he has been passed over for promotions makes him feel ashamed and degraded. He does not voice his displeasure to his bosses, but rather to his wife, who he constantly berates for not giving him a job with greater authority and responsibility.

He is a man who has done the least amount of thinking that is conceivable, who has never desired to think, and who secretly desires nothing more difficult than his current job, which provides him with security and protection for his mediocrity. He avoids and hides this reality.

Then, one day, he receives word that he will receive a significant promotion. He seemed grateful and happy to hear the news. But later that night, he starts to complain about strange sensations in his head and a heaviness in his chest that hurts. He wakes up in the middle of the night with violent anxiousness.

In the days that follow, he starts to fret and express concern about his children's academic performance, then he complains about how poorly insured the house is, and ultimately he starts to sob that he is losing his mind. The subject of his advancement, however, does not come up in his conscious thought.

What set up his fear? The two absolutes, "I must know what to do" (i.e., "I must know how to manage the obligations of my new position"), and "I don't (and can't)," collided in that moment. Although the struggle is unconscious and suppressed, it is nonetheless present and devastating. The dispute has the impact of shattering the man's illusion of control over his life, hence escalating his worry.

The news of the promotion in this instance served as the catalyst for the quarrel. However, the man's psycho-epistemological policies are the root of this conflict and many others like it.

Observe the conflict's nature: it is a battle between a value imperative—engaging the man's sense of his own worth, or pretense of it—and a failure, flaw, or inadequacy that he perceives as a violation of that imperative. He thus goes through a crisis of self-esteem.

2. A young woman is brought up in a strict religious environment where she learns from an early age that she is inherently immoral. She is asked to examine her conscience every night for any moral transgressions she may have committed during the day. Her mother emphasizes the

imperturbable sanctity of family life and the depravity of sex outside of marriage particularly in her upbringing.

The girl does not contest or disagree with her parents' moral beliefs; it is not her practice to consider moral matters independently.

As she gets older, she learns that her peers do not hold the same opinions as her parents, and in college, she adopts a more "liberal" stance on sex in an effort to "belong," or to be accepted by her "peer group." After a few unsuccessful attempts at romance that were never sexually consummated, she ultimately starts an affair—with a married man. The idea that she is hopelessly in love helps her to some extent manage her guilt over the affair.

However, the religious convictions she had internalized as a child are still present, albeit being largely suppressed. One evening when she is walking back to her parents' house from a date with her lover, a number of long-avoided ideas and long-denied worries suddenly burst into her conscious awareness. She passes out on the doorstep. When she comes to, the memory of that fleeting instant is erased, and she discovers herself in the middle of a severe, "causeless" anxiety attack.

She is torn between the two absolutes of "I must not (have this affair)" and "I am (and will continue to)."

The conflict is between her activities, which go against the value-imperative, and her sense of personal worth and self-esteem (or pretense at it). She thus goes through a crisis of self-esteem.

3. After ten years of marriage, a man falls in love with another woman. He has delayed admitting his marital unhappiness and his feelings for the other woman for a very long time. But with time, the inhibition wears off, and he increasingly finds himself daydreaming about the other woman.

He has reserved his conscious thought for his work and has let his feelings guide him in the conduct of his personal life. He does not deliberate about the matter. In order to avoid making a rash decision, he simply lets himself and the issue float in the hopes that "somehow" he will come up with a solution.

Unexpected events bring him and the other woman together one night, and he starts an affair with her. His feelings forced him to start an affair even though he had no intention of doing so. He feels bad but suppresses his feelings of remorse and drifts on, dodging the other woman's inquiries regarding their future while still waiting for a solution to appear.

His wife makes the decision to travel to see her parents. He has the thought—which is more of a longing than a thought—that if the plane crashes, he would be free and would not experience any more issues as he stands at the airport watching the jet take off.

But the thought is abruptly driven from his consciousness, along with an outburst of animosity toward his wife that he would never have before acknowledged being capable of feeling.

He is suddenly unable to tell the difference between the colors of the traffic lights as he drives home, everything in his field of vision appears to be swimming, and he is experiencing excruciating pains that seem to be emanating from his heart. He believes that a heart attack will cause him to pass away. But the anxiety that has erupted inside of him is an attack on his self-esteem.

"I must not," and "I did, and I do, and I shall" (desire for my wife's demise) collide.

The conflict is between a feeling, a want, and a value-imperative that engages his sense of personal worth and self-esteem (or pretense at it). He thus goes through a crisis of self-esteem.

There is a conflict of some kind in every occurrence of pathological anxiety, such as "I must" or "I should have" and "I cannot" or "I did not"; or "I must not" and "I do" or "I did" or "I will." There is always a tension between some value imperative—which is fundamentally and profoundly connected to the individual's perception of himself and inner equilibrium—and some failure, inadequacy, action, emotion, or desire, which the individual perceives as a violation of that imperative, a violation which the individual believes expresses or reflects a fundamental and unchangeable fact of his "nature."

Different psychologists and psychiatrists with various theoretical approaches have provided various descriptions of the mechanics of the anxiety process. But if one reads the case histories, they themselves report—or any of the case histories relevant to anxiety in the numerous textbooks available today—one can very clearly see the general pattern indicated above, even though the details may vary depending on the specific situations.

Making improper generalizations is one of the most frequent mistakes theorists make when interpreting the anxiety process. For example, they can mistake a specific case of pathological anxiety for the abstract prototype of all pathological anxiety.

For instance, Freud argued that forbidden sexual desires that burst through the wall of repression and cause the ego to feel threatened and overpowered are the cause of worry in the final version of his theory of anxiety. In response, Karen Horney said that while this may have been true in the Victorian era, the advent of antagonistic impulses is what causes anxiety now.

In actuality, the underlying idea at play is manifestly more expansive than either of these justifications. Pathological anxiety is, once again, a crisis of self-esteem, and its causes can be as varied as the reasonable or irrational principles that underlie a person's own self-evaluation.

It is important to remember a few details regarding the nature of these anxiety-inducing confrontations.

1. The conflicting value imperative may be rational or irrational; it may be in line with reality and human nature or it may be at odds with both.

2. The value-imperative involves a norm, expectation, demand, or claim that the individual believes should be within his volitional capacity to satisfy, whether correctly or incorrectly. Although not necessarily held consciously, this notion is implied by the fact that the issue at hand is a value-imperative and that the person believes himself morally responsible if he fails to meet it.

3. The individual unconsciously views his moral transgression as deterministically representative of his "true" self.

4. The conflict as such usually arises subconsciously; nevertheless, it is possible for some of it to be conscious or partially conscious.

The anxiety is frequently sustained by the huge psycho-epistemological chaos that is at the root of the conflict and prevents it from being resolved, so this last statement does not imply that if and when the conflict becomes fully conscious, the worry would automatically vanish. Additionally, the release of one repressed conflict frequently causes the release of other repressed conflicts that are anxiety inducing.

However, there are instances where the anxiety does go away after the primary conflict is acknowledged—especially when it appears to be a problem that can be easily resolved.

Guilt

The element of guilt is one of the most important components of anxiety, whether it is acute or chronic. The degree of guilt that is consciously felt and the level of worry that is consciously felt do not always match. Guilt consciousness might be suppressed. The degree of the guilt, however, might not be equal to the intensity of the fear for another reason.

Even though they haven't done the necessary thinking or reached the level of psycho-epistemological clarity that their lives need, people who haven't intentionally broken their moral values, tried to trick reality, or gotten away with the irrational seem to feel the least guilty.

Those who do act against their moral convictions experience a heavier guilt, and the severity of the guilt typically reflects the gravity of the violation and/or the extent of the harm caused by their acts. But in this case, a crucial distinction must be drawn.

There are others who do attain and retain a significant level of independence in their value judgments; if they transgress their own moral standards, they feel shame as well as worry, but they do not, in fact, "feel guilty all the way down." They do not feel worthless; their remorse is narrow and constrained. Their psychological sovereignty—the fact that their moral concern is genuine and first-hand—protects them. A man is still maintaining a strong grip on his self-esteem if he believes, in essence, "It was unworthy of me to fail my own standards in this manner."

Then there are those whose intellectual sovereignty is really absent. For this psychological type, i.e., individuals with an authoritarian moral stance, the worst guilt is saved. In these situations, the moral convictions of the individuals are strengthened by the approval of "important persons" rather than by reason. There is also no healthy inner core of sovereignty to shield rule-breakers from feelings of metaphysical worthlessness when they break the rules. They are nothing more than their evil deeds to themselves. This is one of the causes of pathological anxiety, which frequently manifests as a fear of social rejection. They see "Others" as the voice of impersonal reality judging them. Guilt is most frequently a conscious component of the anxiety experience in these people. Additionally, these people are more prone to experience the most extreme anxiety.

Depression and Anxiety

One of the worst effects of pathological anxiety is how it ruins a man's ability to think clearly and objectively. One way that problematic psycho-epistemological behaviors have a tendency to perpetuate themselves is in this way. Such policies cause anxiety, which fosters evasion and repression as countermeasures, as well as the development of more complicated neurotic defensive mechanisms that require psycho-epistemological self-sabotage to be sustained (Chapter Eight).

Self-doubt has a negative impact on one's ability and can also make one more doubtful. The unstable sense of self that the neurotic has is destroyed by anxiety, and any unstable mental confidence he may have had is undermined. His cognitive frame of reference's steadfastness and objectivity are compromised when such confidence is. Because consciousness is given priority over existence, there is a noticeable tendency to lose the distinction between the subjective and the objective, between that which pertains to consciousness and that which pertains to existence. This leads to the cognitive distortions that are so characteristic of neurosis.

Man has a tendency to give in to the direction of his emotions when he has questions about the effectiveness of his thinking because emotions seem to have a certainty and authority that his intellect lacks. This is how a man encounters the process of giving the subjective over to the objective. His feelings are never a more unreliable guide than when he is experiencing worry, but they are never a replacement for rational thought at any moment.

Neurotics utilize a wide range of tools and strategies to protect oneself against anxiety because the sensation of it is so terrible in and of itself. The majority, if not all, of these defenses are fundamentally based on evasion, repression, and rationalization.

The neurotic can shrink the sphere of his concerns and commitments to avoid the challenges of the unfamiliar; he can create a fantasized self-image to protect him from a self-evaluation he dreads to acknowledge; he can repress the reality of his objectionable actions; he can disown his guilt feelings; he can deny or rationalize his fear; he can seek to distract himself by the frenzied pursuit of various activities.

Other neurotic symptoms frequently develop as a result of the repression of the anxiety problem and the tensions that underlie it. In the current situation, neurotic depression is one of these symptoms that deserves special consideration. (I do not mean to imply that every depression is necessarily a defense against anxiety; however, I am only concerned with depression in this context to the extent that it constitutes such a protection.)

Anxiety and depression both have normal and pathological forms. Depression is a reaction to the actualized destruction or loss of value, whereas anxiety is a reaction to the threatened destruction or loss of value. Depression is focused on the past, whereas anxiety is anticipatory and directed toward the future.

When depression has no connection to any object loss or when its severity and length are egregiously out of proportion to the loss, it is considered pathological.

Despair, inactivity, a sense that effort and action are pointless, that nothing is worthwhile, as well as sentiments of self-rejection and self-condemnation, are all traits of neurotic depression. How do anxiety and depression connect to one another now?

Anxiety is caused by urgent demands, claims, or self-expectations that a person feels unable to meet. For instance, it may be necessary for him to have specific knowledge and be capable of handling specific responsibilities. It may also be necessary for him to act, react emotionally, or live up to certain standards and ideals. He is involved in a dispute. Let's say he tries to suppress the conflict and the guilt it causes in order to deal with it and lessen his discomfort. Instead of it, he feels a sense of inactivity, futility, and overall worthlessness on the conscious level of his awareness.

If one carefully examines his statements that he is "no good," that life is terrible, and that he is "hopeless," one can find another message to be interpreted in his words: Do not put any demands or expectations on me. He is above moral demands since he is inherently worthless; there is no "I must" for him. He "resolves" the dispute that causes him distress in this way.

In other words, he avoids confronting his real issue by trying to prepare for the worst and make it inevitable. He claims to reject his self-esteem, but he is still secretly using neurotic methods to keep it safe.

This is one of the ways that depression may be selected as an anxiety substitute subconsciously. It's not the only pattern, though. Here's one more.

While still connected to the previous pattern, this one operates more subtly. Repression produces it as a byproduct. Imagine a man who, rightly or wrongly, accepts certain moral standards or value-imperatives as essential criteria of his personal worth—but who, in a crucial way, finds himself unable to uphold them. Or imagine a man who has a strong desire for something that he believes to be immoral and, as such, is impractical to assert or pursue. The struggle is suppressed. Since it is suppressed, there is no way to resolve it; he can either review his standards to see if he was mistaken, or he can't come up with any logical solutions for the failures, actions, or desires that go against his self-expectations.

He is left with the stifling, draining feeling that he must carry and live with this unnamed, unchangeable, irreparable burden for the rest of his days. His anxiety has diminished or been gone. He might be relatively guilt-free of conscious wrongdoing. But what he actually feels is a wearying despair that renders his will to action useless.

He no longer has the chance to find happiness or self-worth. However, they are a man's motivations. If the first thing to ask a patient about their anxiety during psychotherapy is, "What is your crime?" —When a patient is depressed, the first thing to ask them is frequently, "What do you want that you think is immoral and unattainable?"

The depressed person needs to be willing to suffer anxiety in order to regain his mental health. He needs to be ready to let go of the "comfort" of despair and face his anxiety-inducing situations in order to resolve them and move on.

Imagine a man getting lost in a large, snowy, northern area with nothing but unending, bleak snow all around him. He is aware that there is a camp far in the distance that he must reach since doing so will save his life. But because of his exhaustion and extreme cold, all he wants to do is lie down and rest. However, he is aware that if he does, he will pass out and die. Moving is painful, but remaining stationary means that hope is lost.

Like that man is the person who is caught in the middle of worry and sadness. In order to achieve safety, effectiveness, and health, he must be willing to endure worry, to push himself forward, to keep looking and going. He must also fight the illusory comfort of despair.

Anxiety is nevertheless a sign of life, of struggle and conflict, and thus, of potential success. Depression, though, is a surrender to failure.

A final remark regarding the biological importance of guilt and worry. Just as a doctor works to relieve his patient of physical pain, a psychotherapist works to release his patient from the hold of anxiety and guilt, which are painful and impair clear, objective thinking. But just as physical pain serves as a necessary survival function by alerting a man that his body is in danger, so too can worry and guilt serve the same purpose for a man's intellect and person.

A man's unreasonable psycho-epistemological practices occasionally have indirect effects that are detrimental to his existence. A man may engage in self-destruction if there were no early signs of danger or disaster, and there would be nothing to stop him or suggest that he should reevaluate his way of doing things—until it was already too late.

Man is free to disregard danger's warning signs, but they exist because doing so will result in a consequence from which he cannot escape. Pathological anxiety is therefore paradoxically both the protector and the enemy of man. A man's self-betrayed ego becomes its own avenger if he abdicates his duty to reason.

It is not necessary for a guy to have resolved all of his psychological issues before he is free from fear and guilt. But he must change his policy of allowing certain other concerns to take precedence over his perception of reality's facts, which is the root of his issues. The vital first step in the process by which a man frees himself from fear and guilt is the desire to face his issues, to look at reality, and to restore his ego to its proper function as an instrument of cognition. Psychological liberty will result if and to the extent that this determination is sustained and put into practice.

CHAPTER TEN

The Metaphysics of Social Relations

Social Metaphysics: What It Is and Where It Comes From

A process of developing a strong, positive sense of personal identity—the sense of being a clearly defined psychological entity—is a logical extension of the process of developing self-esteem.

His faculty of consciousness and his capacity for thought make up a man's "I," his ego, and deepest self. A man's knowledge increases during the course of his lifetime, his convictions could shift, and his emotions could fluctuate, but the thing that knows, judgments, and feels is the one thing about him that never changes.

The most fundamental form of self-assertiveness in man is his decision to think, to accept the facts of reality, and to assume responsibility for judging what is true or false, right or wrong. It is his commitment to his own mental strength, acceptance of his own nature as a reasoned human being, and intellectual independence responsibility.

Suspension of consciousness is the very definition of selflessness. A man abdicates his responsibility for thinking, acquiring knowledge, and making decisions when and to the extent that he decides to forgo these tasks. To give up thought is to give up one's ego and declare oneself unfit for life and incapable of handling the realities of reality.

A child's apparent joy in the use of his mind, his desire for the novel, the uncharted, and the challenging, his refusal to accept on faith the platitudes of his elders and his persistent use of the word "why?," his boredom with routine, his indifference toward the undemanding, his obsession with questions, and his hunger for that which will necessitate the fullest use of his abilities and thus enable him to achieve are all signs of healthy self-assertiveness.

Above all, as he matures and develops, a youngster of this type creates his own objectives. He doesn't rely on others to tell him what to enjoy; he doesn't expect or want advice on what to do with his time, what to admire, what to pursue, or, years down the road, what vocation to choose. He wants and needs his elders' assistance in giving him wise direction and instruction, but not in giving him pre-made goals and values. He is a self-generator when it comes to choosing ideals, and he enjoys the responsibility rather than being afraid of it. A solid, fulfilling sense of personal identity is created as a result of this philosophy, this attitude toward life and toward oneself.

A commitment to independent thought and the possession of a comprehensive set of values both result in a strong sense of self. A man views his values as an extension of himself, as an essential component of his identity, and as something that makes him who he is since they are what drive his emotions, decide his goals, and give direction to his existence.

Accepting intellectual responsibility for one's own existence is a prerequisite for healthy development toward psychological maturity. The range of thought, knowledge, judgment, and decision-making required of him at the age of twelve is greater than that required at the age of five; the range required at the age of twenty is greater than that required at the age of twelve. As a human grows to adulthood, reality confronts him with increasingly more complex challenges at each succeeding stage of his development. The accountability required of him at each step requires both cognition and evaluation; he must become knowledgeable about the facts, make value judgments, and select goals. The decision to act as an intellectually independent, self-reliant individual is not "wired in" to his brain by nature, therefore accepting full responsibility for this duty is not automatic. It is a challenge to which he replies voluntarily, that is, by choice—positively or negatively, with acceptance or rejection.

Positive responses have the effect of fostering a sovereign awareness that is self-assured. Negative responses have the effect of creating a psycho-epistemological reliance.

There are at least four things that can influence someone's decision to forgo exercising their independence and cognitive self-reliance, albeit they do not have to.

1. Thinking is mental activity; it involves effort.

2. A consistent method of thinking precludes allowing oneself to indulge in impulses or emotions that are inconsistent with one's knowledge and convictions.

3. The human mind is flawed; he may make a mistake at any stage of the thought process, and if he acts on that mistake, he may experience suffering, failure, or even destruction.

4. His independent thinking may cause him to disagree with others' perspectives and assessments, which may result in hostility.

Different elements may be at play at different times because the default under discussion does not consist of a single option or a single instant, but rather a continuous sequence of choices in a long succession of situations. In the case of a specific person, one of these elements may occasionally have a tendency to predominate.

The dread of the fallibility issue—fear of being wrong, fear of failure, fear of the hazards of acting on one's own imperfect judgment—is by far the most prevalently active component, which logically implies: fear of a universe in which success is not always guaranteed. One's susceptibility to the other three variables is often increased by this fear. The intellectual self-assertiveness that forms the basis of psychological sovereignty is given up through a succession of successive surrenders to such dread and withdrawals from life's difficulties.

Some kids react timidly and fearfully the first time they are given blocks or other construction toys; they see the situation not as a fun challenge or a chance to develop their skills, but as a threat to their "security," an enemy who makes them feel powerless by forcing them to deal with the unfamiliar. They set up a fundamental sense of helplessness that tends to stay with them—and to be repeatedly reinforced—throughout their life if they habitually give in to dread in situations of this nature, if they shy away from challenges rather than learn to manage them. They stop themselves from becoming into adults. The conceptual growth of a human being follows the same rule. In this area, the issue is both much, much more prevalent and lesser known.

The vast majority of men start running away from the difficulties of appropriate conceptual development very early in life without ever confronting the problem in fully recognized terms, and they die without ever realizing more than a small portion of their potential intelligence. Lack of self-worth is shown by the feeling of "What do I know? Who am I to judge or to make a decision? "is the result of too many instances where a person retreated from the duty of thought and judgment in circumstances where they did not have to, where an effort could have and should have been made but was not, and where the value of efficacy and knowledge was disregarded in favor of the value of fear and uncertainty.

Often, parents and other elders willfully or unintentionally promote this policy of self-abdication by acting in a way that discourages a child's intellectual independence and initiative and/or creates an impression of such bewildering irrationality that the child gives up the effort to understand, his incentives undercut by the perception that people are hopelessly incomprehensible. By the same token, parents help their children develop properly to the extent that they reward and encourage independence and self-reliance and behave in a consistent, predictable, and understandable way that supports and/or instills in the child the belief that he is living in a knowable environment.

Both the cognitive and the evaluative spheres of one's mental activity are negatively impacted by a person's retreat from the responsibility of intellectual progress and his default on the process of correct conceptual maturity. The evaluative domain, however, suffers the most destruction. Many people who aren't inherently anti-effort and who could even actively enjoy the process of thinking show a much higher level of independence when it comes to cognitive challenges than when it comes to value issues.

The conceptual chain connecting normative abstractions to their foundation in perceptual reality is extensive and complex, and they are situated on a higher, more advanced level of the hierarchy of man's concepts than many (though definitely not all) of his cognitive abstractions. Many men find this reality unsettling and frightening since it calls for more faith in their own minds' abilities than they now have.

Furthermore, and this is a very important point, the dread of depending on one's own judgment in matters of values is felt most keenly because decisions made in this area have a direct impact on one's life and well-being. Compared to the majority of their cognitive errors, men's evaluative errors have a significantly greater and more destructive impact on their daily lives. The highest type of intellectual independence—and the one most despised by the vast majority of men—is the habit of making decisions for oneself, acting purely on one's own reason and understanding, about the principles that should govern one's life, the goals in which to seek happiness. (It should be noted that such intellectual independence does not preclude the potential of learning from other men, but it does preclude the act of replacing their judgment for one's own.)

Another factor contributing to the dread of independence being greatest in the area of value judgments is the likelihood that one's independence in this area may put them at odds with other males. Men may not always harbor personal hostility because of cognitive differences, but they frequently do because of value differences, especially when fundamental concerns are at stake. Independence in the area of value judgments is therefore more mentally challenging. It should be acknowledged that the desire to have a peaceful and charitable relationship with his fellow men is a rational one and is not, per se, a breach of proper independence because man is social by nature and has many advantages to gain from doing so (advantages related, among other things, to the superior manner of survival possible to him under a division of labor). Only when a man submits his mind and judgment to that want—that is, when he puts that desire above his view of reality—does it become such a rupture. A psychologically sound man refuses to pay the price of "harmony" with his fellow men if and when that price involves giving up control of his intellect; nothing can benefit him at such price.

Another reason may also be at play for certain people who fear intellectual independence. A man can only accomplish the process of rational thought and judgment by himself. Even if thinking is an individual, lonely process rather than a social one, men can learn from one another but cannot share the act of thinking. There are men who fear independent thought and judgment precisely for this reason: it forces them to experience the fact that they are not and cannot be merely indeterminate constituents of a vast social ooze; it forces them to feel their own separateness as living entities; it forces them to understand the respect in which every man necessarily is an island unto himself; it makes them aware of the responsibility they must bear for their own existence.

To individuate, to forge a unique, individual identity, is to think, judge, and select one's values. However, there are those men who, despite how loudly they may scream to their psychiatrists that they are plagued by a sense of inner emptiness, do not want personal identity in their deepest emotions.

The struggle to escape the obligations of being a human is what this psychology symbolizes as the most fundamental type of rebellion against one's nature as a man, more especially against the responsibility of a volitional (self-directed and self-regulating) consciousness.

There are many gradations of intensity for the fear of intellectual independence. What effects does it have on a person's psychology when it is the main factor?

Reality's facts cannot be avoided, and neither can man's nature or the means of survival that nature demands. The job and purpose of consciousness in a living organism is to guide every kind of organism that has awareness in order to survive. A person can only survive and function in the world by using the minds of others: by their judgments, conclusions, and values. This is because if a person (in effect) rejects his unique form of consciousness, decides that thinking is too much work, and/or decides that choosing the values needed to guide his actions is too frightening a responsibility.

He is aware, whether consciously or unconsciously, that he lacks the knowledge necessary to make judgments in the face of the numerous options that are presented to him every day of his existence. Others, however, appear to know how to survive and carry on, so he feels that the only way to remain is to imitate them and adhere to their beliefs. They know—they will save him the trouble and the risk; they know—somehow they have control over that enigmatic unknowable: reality.

He doesn't start out choosing to be an intellectual dependent; instead, he fails to take on the burden of independent thought and judgment, leading to his eventual forced dependence. He is guided to mold his soul into the likeness of a parasite that is unfathomable in any other living species: a parasite of consciousness rather than the body.

A man with self-confidence and independent thought engages with reality, with nature, and with an objective world of facts; he views his intellect as a survival tool and cultivates his capacity for thought. However, the psycho-epistemologically dependent person lives in a world of people rather than a world of facts; people are his reality rather than facts, and reason is not his means of survival. His attention must be on them since they are the ones who see reality, thus it is on them that he must understand, appease, fool, control, or obey. His accomplishment of this work serves as a barometer for his effectiveness—his capacity for life.

Since he cut himself off from objective reality, he has almost no alternative benchmark for what is true, right, or deserving of value. His greatest and most pressing need is to understand and successfully meet the needs, requirements, terms, and values of others. His replacement for self-esteem is the momentary relief from tension that receiving other people's acceptance brings him.

I refer to this as the "Social Metaphysics" phenomena.

One's conception of the nature of reality is their "metaphysics." For the psycho-epistemological dependent, reality is people because in his mind, in his reasoning, and in the automatic connections of his awareness, people take the place of reality that reality occupies in the mind of a rational man.

The psychological condition known as social metaphysics describes a person who views the minds of other people as his ultimate source of knowledge rather than objective truth.

Psychological Social Fear

It is important to note that the social metaphysician's dependence on other men is not, at its core, material or financial; rather, it is deeper than any practical or tangible consideration, with the material forms of parasitism and exploitation that some men engage in merely being one of its effects.

The fundamental reliance of the social metaphysician is psycho-epistemological; it is a parasitism of cognition, judgment, and values—a desire to operate within a framework created by others, to live by the direction of rules for which one does not bear ultimate intellectual responsibility—a parasitism of consciousness.

Since the pseudo-self-esteem of the social metaphysician depends on his capacity to deal with the world as perceived by others, his fear of rejection or condemnation is a fear of being judged as being unsuited to reality, unfit for existence, and without personal value—a verdict he hears whenever he is "rejected.""

The following example demonstrates the nonvenal, nonpractical nature of the social metaphysician's dependence:

Consider the situation of a multimillionaire social metaphysician who is overly worried about what everyone, including his office boy, thinks of him. He is motivated to win the office boy's favor; he waits impatiently for any hint of a personal reaction; and any sign of the boy's disinterest or disliking causes him to become concerned or unhappy. He discovers himself engaging in compulsive "charming" in an effort to win the child over. In every practical, business sense, the child is his inferior; nonetheless, the multimillionaire believes that he must win the boy's devotion. He has nothing to gain from the boy's favor, neither money, counsel, prestige, or economic advantage. What meaning does the boy have for him, then? He doesn't want to appease or enchant the office lad as a real person, but rather as a representative of all other people and all of mankind. His impulse is not driven by the implicit belief that "This office lad is a possible provider who will look out for me and lead me," but rather by the belief that "I am likable in the eyes of others. Non-me people think well of me and think I'm a decent person."

The social metaphysician is prepared to belong to others in order to belong with them. However, he condemns himself to a life of ongoing insecurity and a profoundly humiliating fear of other men because he is seeking a means of survival that is contrary to the nature of man and because the intellectual sovereignty he has given up is a necessary component of mental health and self-esteem. One of the most terrible features of his situation is the shame he experiences—the feeling that he is effectively living under blackmail.

However, he rarely describes the nature of his shame and terror—he would find it too humiliating. He frequently tries to rationalize his dread by making an appeal to purportedly "practical" factors, insisting that his fear is a proper response to an actual risk in an effort to maintain his false sense of self-worth. This is one of the methods men employ the most frequently to mask their moral cowardice and fear of becoming independent.

The examples that follow demonstrate this approach in diverse contexts from various walks of life. They demonstrate how men fabricate irrational dangers or grossly exaggerate insignificant ones, sell out any genuine rationality they may possess, aid in the spread of values that are inimical to their own, and develop a vested interest in believing that people are inescapably bad, that human existence is bad, and that the good has no chance on earth because of this.

Think about the situation of an atheist philosophy professor. He is aware of the complete inadmissibility of the arguments for the presence of God, believes the idea of a supernatural being to be destructive and senseless, despises mysticism, and sees himself as a supporter of reason. But he avoids discussing the debate between atheism and theism in his books and talks, won't publicly state his position on the matter, and goes to church every Sunday with his parents and other family members.

He does not admit to himself that his motivation is fear, that he is scared to face his family, friends, and coworkers alone, that any violent conflict makes him anxious, and that he is yearning to be "accepted." Instead, he tells himself that admitting he is an atheist will damage his career (evading the fact that many professors are known atheists and their careers are unaffected by it). He tells himself that he doesn't want to upset his ailing parents because they are devout Christians and would be horrified by his lack of faith (evading the fact that he is not obliged to "convert" his parents, merely to state his own convictions, and that a man who takes ideas seriously does not sacrifice his own judgments, which he knows to be rational, in order to placate people whose beliefs he knows to be irrational).

His justifications protect him from a complete understanding of his betrayal. But because it cannot be completely blocked out, he is forced to battle private thoughts of self-disgust; in response, he curses the evil of "the system" and of reality because he can't have both his treason and his self-esteem.

Think about a successful playwright who decides to write a play about a significant issue that demands and merits a somber dramatic presentation, only to discover that his point of view will enrage a sizable portion of the population. In order to avoid anyone taking his beliefs seriously or being upset or antagonistic, he chooses to write the play as a comedy, making "good-natured fun" of the things he considers to be bad.

He doesn't tell himself he fears being thought of as "unfashionable." Instead, he convinces himself that significant plays that tackle divisive topics are noncommercial, and he writes off the many exceptions as "freaks" who don't need to be explained.

However, he is unable to completely escape the fact that he has abandoned the motivation behind his decision to compose the play in the first place. In response, he denigrates the "stupidity" and "poor taste" of the general public in an effort to combat his unsettling sense of moral uncleanliness.

Consider the situation of a scientist who despises the obscurantist terminology that pervades his field and the "postulates" that underlie it and who is logically convinced that many of his most esteemed colleagues' hypotheses are incorrect. However, he twists his thinking to use that jargon in his works, softens his criticisms in every way he can, and tries to smuggle his own views into the brains of his readers in a way that no one will notice how much he deviates from accepted wisdom.

He doesn't admit to himself that he is terrified of being labeled a "outsider" or that he desperately craves the respect of men who, in his opinion, are arrogant incompetents. Instead, he rationalizes to himself that he is "playing it smart," that he would define terms when he becomes famous, and that the "practical" "The best approach to become well-known and a great innovator is to blend in with everyone else.

The understanding that this was not the perspective on science with which he began, and that the youth who had been himself would find it weird to be informed that devotion to truth is shown by promoting deception, cannot, nevertheless, be completely drowned. So in retaliation, he curses the evilness of a cosmos where the idea of a "fashionable inventor" is absurd.

Finally, consider the situation of a businessman who understands that capitalism is the only ethical and fair social structure. He is aware of the knowledge, independence, and commitment required for industrial production. He also knows that he works hard for his money. He enjoys his work and is quietly proud of it. However, he publicly apologizes for his success, donates money to academic institutions explicitly dedicated to the eradication of businesspeople, accepts the government's appropriation of his wealth and violation of his rights without moral objection, and begs the general populace to pardon him for the sin of ability.

He does not tell himself that, despite the fact that it has never made sense to him, he is afraid to challenge the dominant, religion-derived value system that paints his way of life as ignoble, self-centered, and materialistic; he does not tell himself that he cannot bear to feel alienated from all of those who support that value system; and he does not tell himself that the responsibility of making independent moral judgments fills him with dread. Instead, he convinces himself that his actions are entirely driven by the need to safeguard his financial interests, that it is "shrewd public relations" to support academics who support the status quo so they will perceive him as a "nice man," and that it is "poor business" to pursue disapproval. In order to appease them, he must tell them that he only works to serve them, and he must restrain them by assuring them that their right supersedes all other rights. This is because his secret fear is that the masses are unthinking brutes who are the ultimate masters of reality and can kill him and take over his property whenever they please. This is "hard-headed realism," he explains to himself.

However, he is unable to completely ignore the unsettling sense that his appeasement is not motivated by the reasons he claims, and that his "practicality" and "cynicism" are actually hiding something worse. Therefore, in retaliation, he curses human irrationality and the evil of a world that requires him to be concerned with moral matters.

Men strengthen the control that fear has over their life to the extent that they irrationally give in to it. More and more objects are gaining the ability to make people afraid. Their sense of risk increases as their confidence declines. If properly opposed, social metaphysical fear can either spread or diminish, but it never stays still. The social metaphysician's sense of detachment from reality deepens with each surrender to the consciousness of others and each subsequent betrayal, and his sense of powerlessness finds reinforcement. His last remaining reserves of self-worth are depleted in order to satisfy an endless stream of blackmailers whose demands are unending; blackmailers who are any human consciousness other than his own; blackmailers who, more often than not, are as afraid of his judgment as he is afraid of theirs; blackmailers who are desperately seeking his approval; blackmailers who are committing the same type of treason and going through the same humiliation. The cruel irony is that each side believes they are acting out of "practicality," which is what drives their grotesque farce of a life.

Social Metaphysical Personalities

Social metaphysicians come in a wide variety of forms because the term "social metaphysics" is quite broad. However, there are some characteristics or signs that all social metaphysicians share: (a) the lack of a firm, unwavering concept of existence, facts, and reality as distinct from the opinions, judgments, and feelings of others; (b) a sense of fundamental helplessness or inefficacy, a sense of metaphysical inefficacy; (c) a profound fear of other people and an implicit belief that other people control that unknowable realm: reality; and (d) a self-esteem—or, more precisely, a pseudo-self-esteem—that is (This last sign does not only apply to social metaphysicians.)

The most fundamental of these characteristics is the absence of a solid, independent perception of objective reality, which renders the other characteristics necessary.

The consciousnesses of others fill this hole, and it is this void that causes the dismal sense of estrangement that is the constant torment of every social metaphysician.

It's crucial to note that one's failure to assume responsibility for thinking is the root cause of both the experience of self-alienation and the sensation of being alienated from reality and the world around one. Both the suspension of one's ego and of adequate cognitive engagement with reality occur at the same time. Flight from one's own is flight from reality.

The most prevalent and readily recognisable type of social metaphysician is the person whose values and perspective on life are a direct reflection and product of his particular culture or subculture. Social metaphysics represents a flight from the responsibility of independent judgment (particularly in the realm of values) and represents an attempt to live through and by others. This is the individual who is now occasionally labeled a "conformist." This type will be known as the Traditional social metaphysician.

This person does not attempt to explain why; rather, they accept the world and its prevalent ideals as-is. What's real? It's true what other people say. Which is correct? What other people think is correct. How ought one to live? as other people live. Why does one need a job to survive? mainly because one should. Why does a person marry? mainly because one should. Why do people have kids? mainly because one should. What draws a person to church? Oh, please refrain from getting into a religious discussion; you might upset someone.

This is Peter Keating, George F. Babbitt, and the Organization Man. For this individual, reality exists "is the person whose sense of identity and personal worth is explicitly a function of his capacity to satisfy the values, terms, and expectations of those omniscient and omnipresent "others"—the "significant others" of his social environment. I am "how you desire me"—that is how he defines himself, that is how his "genetic code" works "managing the growth of his soul.

The conventional social metaphysician is the kind of person who gives the theory of environmental determinism a veneer of plausibility. Such a man is a byproduct of his upbringing, but by choice.

Such a man might become a scientist in a society that values research; if scientists are expected to think independently and occasionally oppose the opinions of their colleagues, he might do so; he might make an effort to be a "individualist," and he might even find new knowledge. If he is taught that the era of the lone inventor is over and that all future scientific advancement rests on "teamwork," he will try to prove his credentials as a scientist by demonstrating his prowess in "human relations" rather than through the quality of his thought.

He could start a firm and possibly function constructively in a society that prizes initiative, ambition, and business acumen. He might even be successful in building a fortune. He can choose to travel to Washington instead of a society where these things are undervalued.

The conventional social metaphysician is the first to rush to a psychiatrist, crying that he has lost his identity because he no longer recognizes himself in a culture like the one we currently live in, one with disintegrating values, intellectual chaos, and moral bankruptcy—where the familiar guideposts and rules are vanishing, where the authoritative mirrors reflecting "reality" are splintering into a thousand unintelligible subcults, and where "adjustment" is becoming harder

Without this kind of person, no dictatorship could come to be or continue to exist. He is the man who "swims with the current" and is swept into the depths of a more statist society. He is the man who, in response to warning signs of impending danger, closes his eyes out of fear that he will be forced to make his own independent value judgments and realize that his world is not safe, that he must take action and protest, that his leaders' objectives and policies are evil, and that "significant others" are incorrect. In order to avoid the fear of realizing to whom and to what he has given his existence, he assures himself in the middle of atrocities that the authorities "must have their reasons." This same man will occasionally rebel in hysterical indignation, usually when it is too late, when the atrocities have come too close and cannot be escaped any longer. He may die purposefully in protest, screaming at the enemy's malevolent omnipotence and wondering what or who had enabled the enemy's power.

Of course, conventional social metaphysicians differ greatly from one another in terms of their intelligence, honesty, ambition, competence, and independence (within the limits of "the system"). Additionally, there are notable disparities in the selection of authority that conventional social metaphysicians make based on their discriminating and judgment in cultures with a range of values and models.

The Conventional type is the most obvious and straightforward species of social metaphysician; he serves as, in a sense, the paradigm case—the fundamental pattern, example, or prototype that may be used to understand other species of social metaphysician.

A man with sovereign consciousness and good psychological health rests his sense of self on his commitment to knowing what is true and right in fact and in reality, and to behaving in accordance with that knowledge. Contrarily, a social metaphysician substitutes other people's consciousnesses for reality as the domain and object of his ultimate concern; his pseudo-self-esteem depends on understanding and acting in accordance with others' perceptions of what is true and right; as a result, the approval he receives from others serves as the barometer and evidence of his effectiveness and worth. However, he is not assured to succeed because failure is always a possibility and effort, danger, and struggle are all unavoidable in dealing with objective reality. This does not go unnoticed by the Conventional type, but he accepts it. But what if a social metaphysician feels unqualified for the job, just as he does for dealing with reality? What if he considers the difficulty and the requirements to be too much? Then, in order to prevent the collapse of his false self-esteem, a new line of neurotic defenses and self-deceptive behaviors may be formed. This behavior can be seen in another category of social metaphysician, known as the Power-seeker. This type has a very strong sense of terror toward other people. He finds this anxiety intolerable, and as a result, he responds with an overwhelming feeling of hatred. The people who cause his anxiety are the targets of the hatred. His main emotional characteristics are resentment and hatred. (These feelings, naturally, are frequently present in conventional social metaphysicians as well, but they do not drive their development and objectives in the same way; they do not serve as the primary source of their motivation.)

This kind finds the conventional social metaphysician's path to pseudo-self-esteem to be too terrifyingly unstable and unsupportable due to the looming threat of failure and defeat. The Power-seeking social metaphysician experiences crushing feelings of inferiority because he is too doubtful of his capacity to win the admiration and love he craves. Additionally, he is enraged by the humiliation of his need—or, to put it another way, his unrequited dependence. He yearns for freedom from the uncertainties of social metaphysical rivalry in a "free market," where he must gain men's voluntary respect. In order to give people no choice, he intends to lie, control, and coerce their thoughts. He aspires to a position where he can compel love, respect, and obedience.

Consider King Frederick William of Prussia as an illustration. He was known for beating his peasants while yelling, "You must not fear me, you must adore me!"

Any tyrant, including those like Hitler, Stalin, Khrushchev, Castro, and Mao, has this mentality. If you can't join them, lick them is the mantra of this man.

Such men's hate of other people finally extends to reality as a whole, to a cosmos that denies them the ability to have both their irrationality and their self-esteem, a universe that inexorably connects irrationality to suffering and shame. It becomes a burning need, a desire to experience the only kind of "efficacy" they can project, to defeat the reality they have never chosen to accept, to defy reason and logic, to succeed at the illogical, to get away with it. Social metaphysicians believe that reality is made up of other people, hence their ultimate purpose is to force their will on others and force them to create an environment where their irrational will can operate.

The following spectacle can be used to gauge the degree of such men's detachment from reality and the degree to which objective facts have no status in their consciousness: The brute knows that the scene is a fraud of his own staging, that the mob is there only by virtue of his soldiers' bayonets, but his chest still swells with satisfaction as, self-hypnotized, he basks in the warmth of his victims' "adoration" as he stands on the balcony of his palace, the blood of millions dripping from his fingers. (This is the being that other social metaphysicians, who are also cut off from reality, refer to as practical.)

Power-seeking social metaphysicians are experts on fear because they have the best understanding of this emotion through introspection. The presence of someone who lacks fear deprives them of their sense of efficacy, and their sense of self-identity tends to vanish in their company. Fear is the social environment in which they feel most comfortable. Self-doubt and uncertainty are manipulable, but self-esteem is not.

While the Power-seeking variety of social metaphysicians will frequently be drawn to the political or military sphere, the type may be found in every profession and on every level of society—from the CEO of a company who promotes his executives not on the basis of their ability but on the basis of their capacity for obsequiousness—to the professor who takes pleasure in undermining the intellectual self-confidence of his students by tossing off incomprehensible contradictions as knowledge. Different levels of ambition, talent, and interests undoubtedly affect how much authority someone seeks.

There is also the issue of opportunity. The Power-seeking type's options for "self-expression" are severely constrained in a politically free society. However, in a statist culture or a society that is headed toward statism, previously restrained and repressed Power-seekers begin to emerge in astounding numbers.

When asked, "What should I do with my life?" or "What will make me happy?"

—the Conventional social metaphysician searches for the solution among the normative values of his society, including respectability, material success, marriage, family, professional proficiency, reputation, and others.

I'm asking myself, "How am I going to make my existence bearable?"

—the Power-seeking social metaphysician takes aggressive and destructive action against the external target of his fear: other people—in an effort to find the solution.

Despite having the desire to manipulate other people's consciousnesses, even when the chance arises, he rarely uses physical force. He frequently chooses manipulation, deception, and trickery instead of coercion as his preferred choices. This is due to a number of factors. First off, hardly all men of this type possess the "gut" for using physical force; they cannot bear to think of themselves using such tactics. Second, methods like manipulation and deception typically do not include the same physical hazards and dangers as using violence. Thirdly, these peaceful tools may represent a more advanced, or "intellectual," type of efficacy to some Power-seekers. But it is important to understand that the motivation behind these tactics is the same as the urge to use violence: the desire to evade and subvert the free will of others, to impose one's own will on them against their wishes, knowledge, and interests, and to feel victorious by defying logic and reality. The desire to control other men is the desire to control reality and give one's desires unlimited power.

Now, think about the spiritual social metaphysician's psychology. This type does not aim to control others like a Power-seeker or to win their favor like a Conventional social metaphysician. This kind frequently accomplishes essentially nothing. He asserts or suggests that his greatest virtue is that he is too good for this world. He shouldn't be expected to live up to expectations. He shouldn't be expected to accomplish anything concrete. His friends and acquaintances must like and admire him for who he is rather than for anything he does—doing is so vulgar. He is what? After all, not everything can be communicated. Certain things, the essential ones, can only be felt.

In other words, the Spiritual Social Metaphysician's claim to respect is based on his alleged possession of a superior kind of soul—a soul that is not his mind, not his thoughts, not his values, not anything specific, but an ineffable amalgam of undefinable longings, incommunicable insights, and impenetrable mystery.

This kind of "solution" to the issue of low self-esteem will draw some social metaphysicians as long as mysticism continues to cast a shadow over our civilization. It spares them the need to exert themselves or struggle (except, of course, the dreadful struggle to preserve this fraud in their own eyes). They are aware that their fellow social metaphysicians' sense of inadequacy provides a "market" for their spiritual vocation.

However, the "market" is constrained and distressingly unreliable. The Spiritual type has a response for this, i.e., he is prepared with his justification. He justifies to himself that people aren't fine enough to appreciate the "genuine" him if and when he doesn't receive the respect and esteem, he needs. To fantasize uninterrupted and unchallenged about how he would be appreciated and loved if only people understood what he was "truly" like, deep down, he may even prefer to be alone and avoid people. (It should be noted that there are times when he is terrified that people will find out what he truly is like.) This kind frequently exhibits an excessive fantasy life in which he imagines himself to be a holy saint, an inspired leader, a celebrated poet, or (forgetting that he is supposed to be spiritual) a sexually seductive Don Juan.

A subtype of this mentality that can be referred to as the Religious fanatic social metaphysician is its extreme manifestation, carried to the brink of madness (and occasionally beyond). Such a person can completely cut himself off from society, becoming a hermit or anchorite with God serving as his "significant other" and the focus of his social metaphysical attachment. He has given up on impressing other people and is now trying to impress God. The religious fanatic type is free to believe that God is smiling down at him, blessing and protecting him, responding to the true nobility of his soul, something everyone on earth is too superficial or corrupt to do, because God cannot frown at him, shun him socially, or ask why he doesn't obtain a job.

The Independent Social Metaphysician comes next. This is the so-called "false individualist," the man who challenges the status quo merely for the sake of defying it, the man whose false sense of self-worth is based on the idea that he is a rebellious nonconformist.

This is the "rebel" who regularly declares, "Everything stinks," in order to satisfy his concepts of profundity and self-expression. This person is a nihilist, a hippie, a non-objective "artist," and a "individualist" who disdains money, marriage, jobs, bathing, and haircuts to demonstrate their point. This son, whose father advised him that perhaps it's time to start making a living now that he, the son, is approaching forty, leaves home to join the anarchist movement.

This kind of individual reacts with the phrase "Whatever is, is wrong" when overcome by emotions of inadequacy in comparison to the cultural norms.

He intentionally insults others so that they won't think he wants their acceptance because he is overcome by the overwhelming feeling that no one can possibly like or accept him. He battles his sense of nonidentity by arguing that being an outsider is evidence of one's superiority because he feels so humiliated at feeling like a nobody.

He skirts around the fact that a man may be considered "outside" of society for two diametrically opposed reasons: either because his standards are higher than those of society, or because they are lower; either because he is above society, or below it; or both because he is too good, or not good enough.

The Independent Social Metaphysician views life as a struggle between his desires and those of other people. He places no value or significance on reason, objectivity, or reality as such.

His major motive is negative rather than positive; he is against rather than for, notwithstanding his claims of devotion to a certain philosophy or goal or even his stance as a devoted warrior. As if the lack of passive obedience, rather than the presence of autonomous, rational judgment, were the characteristic of self-reliance and spiritual sovereignty, he neither creates nor struggles for positive ideals of his own. Instead, he simply rebels against the values and standards of others. He tries to hide the truth of his inner emptiness by the use of this delusion.

The Power-spiritual seeker's sibling is the Independent social metaphysician. Frequently, whether a social metaphysician becomes one type or the other is simply a matter of historical accident. Nazism and communism, for example, drew in a large number of Independent social metaphysicians who instantly and painlessly transitioned to the psychology of the Power-seeking type; they discovered a form of "togetherness" for which they were eagerly willing to give up their "independence."

Social metaphysicians of the independent type typically stay on the periphery of society in a culture where reason, productivity, and plain sanity are valued highly, if only on a common-sense level. However, in a culture like ours, the pressure brought on by the intellectual void can propel them in an extended "Fools' Day" orgy from the depths of prestige to the heights of power. Then, one observes the triumphant spread of pretentiously eccentric mediocrity and the inebriated glorification of unconsciousness; one observes meaningless splashes of paint displayed on the walls of renowned museums; one looks for scruffy young men teaching Zen Buddhism in prestigious universities; one observes whims for the sake of whims, absurdity for the sake of absurdity, destruction for the sake of destruction, and becoming fad.

The Independent social metaphysicians participating may retaliate in one of numerous ways depending on when and how often this happens. They might then adopt the persona of Conventional social metaphysicians, wanting to fit in as respectable conformists inside the framework of their recently formed subculture, and they would then start to sneer at everyone who does not "belong." Alternately, they can adopt the mindset of open power-seekers, competing to be acknowledged as the new elite's leaders, plotting and manipulating to preserve their positions, and terrified lest their position be seized by more capable or aggressive rivals. Or, if they are too insecure to pursue a stable position within a subculture, they may give up on the movement or system they helped form and adopt a new attitude that would ensure their status as outcasts, allowing them to avoid experiencing the anxiety that comes with potential rejection.

The last type of social metaphysician I'll discuss is one that departs significantly from all the others in key ways. This sort is what I refer to as an ambivalent social metaphysician.

This is the person who has maintained a sizable amount of intellectual sovereignty despite making a big psycho-epistemological surrender to others' authority. The Ambivalent type retains a significantly greater degree of genuine freedom than any other species of social metaphysician, even though no one, not even the most abject conformist, can totally relinquish their intellect.

His intellectual self-abdication is much more constrained, and it frequently focuses on the most delicate area—the world of values—where all social metaphysicians are particularly at risk.

The ambivalent personality rarely questions the fundamental norms of his social surroundings, yet he frequently treats them with just token respect. He does not assert opposing ideals in the areas of life where these values apply; instead, he just withdraws, ceding control of those aspects of reality to others. Where his independence and sovereignty are strongest—at work—he prefers to confine his effort and concern.

His enslavement to social metaphysics is manifest in his subtly pervasive sense of disconnection from reality, his lack of confidence and freedom in making value judgments, his implicit belief that others are in charge of the world and that they have knowledge that is forever beyond his comprehension, and his humiliating need for "approval" and "acceptance." His superiority to other social metaphysicians is demonstrated by his greater independence as well as his desire to earn the respect he longs for through objective accomplishments, his relative inability to find true pleasure in admiration not based on standards he can respect, and his tortured disgust at his own fear of receiving negative feedback from others. The reason he never fully overcomes his fear and never sets himself free is that he never gets to the root of his issue, doesn't recognize the psycho-epistemological foundation of his betrayal, and doesn't accept full and ultimate intellectual responsibility for his own life and goals. He frequently tries to fight his fear by refusing to act on it or give in to it, exercising incredible will power and discipline.

Guys of notable accomplishments and exceptional creative originality fall into this category. The tragedy of these men is found in the difference between their personal and professional life. These are the men who lack the bravery to question the value judgments of their neighbors but have the fortitude to question the cognitive judgments of prominent persons in the world.

It is important to note that none of the social metaphysical types I have discussed are meant to be mutually exclusive classifications; a given social metaphysician may exhibit traits from multiple types. Such a typological description aims to identify, through an abstraction process, specific dominating patterns among social metaphysicians and to make those trends understandable from a motivational perspective.

Social metaphysics can take on an almost infinite number of forms. But if one understands the fundamental ideas at play, one will be better equipped to comprehend the horrifying social and existential outcomes that social metaphysics inevitably brings about. Here, it has seldom been possible to even allude to those repercussions. Such a condensed presentation cannot do justice to the entire story. But history has it recorded in blood on its pages.

CHAPTER ELEVEN

Self-Confidence and Romantic Love

The Psychological Visibility Principle

The two things that have the most potential to make a guy happy are; successful job and romantic (sexual) love.

Man takes control of his life and enjoys the satisfaction and pride of effectiveness when he uses his thoughts productively. Through romantic love, man receives the highest emotional reward for his effectiveness and worth—for his effectiveness and worth not just as a producer but also more broadly: as a person—the reward and celebration of himself and of what he has made of himself, i.e., of the type of character and soul he has cultivated.

Love as a romantic experience satisfies a crucial psychological need in men. The nature of that desire, however, cannot be understood without first comprehending a more fundamental need: man's need for human companionship—of people he can respect, admire, and appreciate, and who he can engage in intellectual and emotional interaction with. What motivates a need for human companionship? Why is it important for a man to discover people he can respect and love?

Almost everyone sees the desire for company, friendship, and love as a self-evident fundamental—in other words, as an irreducible reality of human nature that needs no justification. A made-up theory based on the idea that man has a "gregarious inclination" is occasionally put forth. However, this does not shed any light; instinctual explanations are only a means of masking ignorance. Psychologists haven't added anything to our understanding of this topic up to now.

The fact that living and interacting with other men in a social setting, exchanging goods and services, etc., affords man a means of survival immeasurably superior to that which he could obtain alone on a desert island or on a self-sustaining farm, may help to explain part of man's desire for human companionship. Man evidently finds it in his best advantage to interact with guys who share his ideals and character as opposed to those who do not. Additionally, guys who share his ideals and behave in ways that are advantageous to his existence tend to arouse feelings of kindness or affection in males.

However, it should be clear from observation and self-examination that practical, existential explanations such as these fall short and that the desire and experience of friendship and love are a reflection of certain psychological needs. Introspectively, everyone is aware of the need for a friend, someone to talk to, be with, understand, and share significant events with—the need for emotional connectedness with another person. What kind of psychological need is it that causes this desire?

In order to help the reader better comprehend the challenges the problem contains, I'll start by recounting two occurrences that were essential in helping me arrive at the solution.

One afternoon, as I sat by myself in my living room, I found myself enjoying my own company as I looked at a huge philodendron plant leaning up against a wall. It was a joy I had previously felt, but all of a sudden I wondered: What is the nature of this pleasure? What caused it?

The joy I felt was not purely aesthetic; if I had known the plant was fake, its aesthetic qualities would have remained the same, but my reaction and the unique pleasure I had would have disappeared. The fact that the plant was robustly and radiantly alive was crucial to my enjoyment. The plant and I felt a connection, almost like a kinship; in the midst of inanimate objects, we were connected by the fact that we were alive. I considered the motivation of those who, even in the most dire circumstances, put flowers in boxes on their window sills—for the enjoyment of seeing something bloom. What benefit does it have for a man to observe a successful life?

One would feel like a metaphysical alien if they were abandoned on a dead planet with all the material necessities to assure their survival but no signs of life, I reasoned. Imagine then that you came across a living plant. You would undoubtedly be excited and happy to see it. Why?

Because all life, by its very nature, comprises a battle, and a struggle implies the prospect of failure, man desires and enjoys witnessing concrete examples of successful existence as evidence that successful life is attainable. In reality, it's a metaphysical encounter. He wants to see it so that he can experience and validate what he knows intellectually on a perceptual level, the level of present actuality, rather than to calm his fears or reassure himself.

I pondered whether seeing another human may provide a far more powerful version of that experience if a plant could provide such worth to man. This is unquestionably pertinent to the psychological value that people place on one another.

My dog Muttnik, a wirehaired fox terrier, and I were playing on the floor one afternoon when I took the next essential step in my thinking.

We were mock ferociously jabbing and punching each other; what I found amusing and fascinating was the degree to which Muttnik seemed to understand the playfulness of my intention: she was snarling and snapping and striking back while being consistently gentle in a manner that projected total, fearless trust. The incident wasn't out of the ordinary; most dog owners are familiar with it. However, I had a question pop into my head that I had never before asked myself: Why am I enjoying myself so much? What makes me happy and where does it come from?

I realized that part of my reaction was just the enjoyment of witnessing a living thing establish itself in a healthy way. That, however, was not the main cause of my reaction. The relationship between the dog and I—the feeling of interacting and speaking with a living consciousness—was the crucial element.

If Muttnik were to be perceived by me as a mindless automaton whose movements and reactions are solely mechanical, my enjoyment of her would cease to exist. The most significant aspect was consciousness.

Then I pondered: If I were abandoned on a deserted island, wouldn't Muttnik's presence be of the utmost importance to me? It would, of course. because she might help me in a realistic way to survive physically? Of course not. What benefit did she then have to offer? Companionship. A conscious being that I could interact and speak to, as I was doing right now. What makes that a value, though?

I came to the realization that the answer to this question would explain much more than just a person's attachment to a pet; it would also shed light on the psychological idea that underlies a person's need for human companionship, on the idea of why a conscious being seeks out and values other conscious beings and on the idea that consciousness is a value to consciousness.

The conditions under which the solution was found lead me to refer to it as "the Muttnik principle" when I finally found it. Let's now think about the essence of this principle.

Knowing my reaction required understanding the specific type of self-awareness that went into my enjoyment of playing with Muttnik. Because of the nature of the "input" Muttnik was giving, self-awareness emerged. She replied in a lighthearted manner as soon as I started to "box," showing no signs of being threatened and exuding confidence and pleasant delight. If I pushed or jabbed an inanimate object, it would reply mechanically; it wouldn't be responding to me; there would be no chance for it to understand the significance of my actions, to understand my goals, and to direct its behavior appropriately. It was unable to respond to my psychology, or state of mind. Only aware entities are capable of such communication and response. Muttnik's actions had the effect of making me feel seen and psychologically visible (at least, to some extent). Muttnik was responding to me in a human-like manner rather than as if I were a machine.

It's important to note that Muttnik's response to me personally was one that I considered to be objectively appropriate, or in line with how I saw myself and what I was trying to say to her. If she had reacted in fear and with a cringing attitude, I wouldn't have felt pleasure since I would have believed that she had misunderstood me.

Now, why does man cherish and enjoy the feeling of psychological visibility and self-awareness that receiving the right answer (or "feedback") from another consciousness might arouse?

Consider the fact that a person's experience of themselves is typically one of a process. This is because awareness is a process and an activity, and a person's mental contents are a constantly changing stream of observations, ideas, and emotions. Man cannot consider his own mind objectively, that is, as a direct object of awareness, in the same way that he may contemplate things in the outside world.

He does, of course, have a sense of who he is and what he stands for, but this sense is more felt than thought; it is a very diffuse sensation that is entangled with all of his other sentiments and that is difficult, if not impossible, to separate out and think about on its own. His "self-concept" is not a single idea but rather a collection of pictures and abstract viewpoints on his many (actual or imagined) qualities and attributes, the sum of which can never be held in focus at any given time; it is experienced but not perceived as such.

The ideals, desires, and goals that a man develops throughout his life begin in his mind, or as data of awareness, and, to the extent that his life is successful, they are translated into action and objective reality. They then become a part of the "out there," or the world that he observes. In tangible form, they achieve expression and reality. This is how man's existence should and must proceed. However, a man's most valuable creation and highest value—his character, soul, and psychological self—cannot in the literal sense follow this pattern, cannot exist independently of his own consciousness, and cannot ever be regarded by him as a component of the "out there." But man yearns for and even requires a sense of objective self-awareness.

Man needs and wants the greatest experience of the truth and objectivity of that person, of himself, since he is the driver of his own actions and because his conception of himself, of the person he has made, is crucial to his motivation.

Man is able to see his own face as an actual object when he looks in a mirror, and he enjoys doing so since it allows him to reflect on the physical manifestation of himself. Being able to look someone in the eye and say, "That's me," has worth. The experience of objectivity is what gives the worth.

Exists a mirror in which a person can view their psychic selves? which he is able to see his own soul? Yes. The reflection is a different awareness.

Man can conceptually know himself on his own. The chance for man to perceive himself is what another awareness can provide.

That was the opportunity Muttnik gave me, in a very limited way. I was able to recognize a trait of my own personality in her reaction. However, a human being can only fully and appropriately experience this self-awareness in a relationship with another human being that has a consciousness that is similar to his own and that has an equal range of awareness.

A man's personality is a manifestation of his intelligence, psycho-epistemology, fundamental beliefs and values, and sense of life. The total of all those psychological features or characteristics that set one man apart from another is known as "personality," and it is perceived outwardly. A man's actions, including the things he says and does and the ways in which he says and does them, are an expression of his psychology. In this view, a man's identity is something that other people can perceive about him. When people respond to a guy, their response—which originates in their consciousness—is conveyed via their behavior, through the things they say and do in relation to him, as well as in the way they say and do them. He feels observed, he feels psychologically visible, and he has a sense of the objectivity of himself and of his psychological condition. He sees a reflection of himself in their behavior if their perception of him is in line with his own and is, thus, communicated by their behavior. Others can serve as a psychological mirror in this way.

A guy may feel visible in various ways in various human connections, just as there are many distinct facets to a man's personality and inner life. Depending on the person he is talking with and the circumstances of their contact, he may feel a larger or lesser degree of visibility, throughout a wider or smaller spectrum of his complete personality.

Occasionally, a man's sense of visibility relates to a fundamental quality, other times, to the nature of his intention when taking some action, other times, to the causes of a specific emotional response, other times, to a matter involving his quality of life, other times, to a matter involving his role as a producer, other times, to his sexual psychology, and other times, to his aesthetic values.

Every type of human connection and communication—intellectual, emotional, and physical—may provide a man the perceptual proof of his visibility in one way or another, or it might give him the feeling that he is invisible to some individuals. The majority of males are largely oblivious of the method by which this happens; instead, they are just aware of the outcomes. They are aware of whether or whether they feel "at home," a sense of affinity or understanding, or emotional receptivity in the company of a specific person.

Even just the sense of being regarded as a conscious entity during a dialogue with another person involves some degree of visibility. However, one expects a far deeper visibility in a close human relationship, involving very personal and sensitive aspects of one's inner existence, with a person one genuinely admires and cares about.

The prerequisite for that projection of mutual visibility, which is the essence of genuine friendship, is a major similarity of intellect, of essential premises and values, of fundamental attitudes toward life. Aristotle claimed that a friend is a different self. It was a suitable phrase. A friend responds to a man in the same way that the man would respond to himself if he were another person. The man views himself as a result of his friend's response. Through its effects on the perceiver's consciousness (and, consequently, on their behavior), he views his own person.

Thus, the desire to recognize himself as an actual entity—to experience the perspective of objectivity—through and by means of the reactions and responses of other people, is at the core of man's yearning for friendship and love.

The relevant principle, known as "the Muttnik principle" or "the Visibility principle," can be summed up as follows: The feeling of self-awareness that comes from seeing oneself as an objective existing is something that man needs and wants, and he can have it by interacting with the consciousness of other living things.

The degree to which a guy has this experience in any given relationship critically depends on two elements:

1. The degree to which he and the other person share the same thoughts and ideals.

2. The degree to which his self-image is consistent with the psychological facts; that is, the degree to which he accurately understands himself and assesses himself; that is, the degree to which his inner vision of himself is consistent with the personality that is being expressed via his conduct.

As an illustration of the first of these factors, imagine that a self-assured man meets a highly anxious and hostile neurotic; he observes that the neurotic reacts to him with unwarranted suspicion and hostility; the neurotic's attitude is, in effect, that of a brute advancing menacingly with a club; in such a case, the self-assured man would not feel visible; instead, he would feel bewildered and myst

This is one of the most devastating and painful ways that a psychologically sound person can be abused by people who are less healthy and given a bewilderingly unreasonable view of the human realm. Young people are especially vulnerable in this situation. His merits are not only ignored and undervalued; far worse, he is punished for them. One of neurosis's most pernicious side effects is frequently this. A healthy person is made the innocent target of jealousy, resentment, and hostility from others—reactions that have no discernible connection to the qualities he displays—and he typically has no way of knowing that the hostility he experiences is a reaction, not to anything bad in him, but to the good.

As an illustration of the second factor, let's say a man has a propensity to justify his actions and to boost his phony self-esteem by making completely improbable claims. His self-deceiving perception of the type of person he is contrasts sharply with the true self that is shown via his behaviors. Because the "input" he receives is incompatible with his aspirations, the result is that he feels chronically disappointed and invisible in his human connections.

When two neurotics communicate, it's possible for a form of pseudo-visibility to be mutually projected in which each participant supports the other's pretenses and self-deceptions in exchange for receiving support in return. Naturally, the "exchange" takes place subconsciously. This pattern is frequently the root of neurotic romantic relationships.

Men typically perceive the want for visibility as the desire for understanding, i.e., the desire to be understood by other people. A man wants to feel that others who are near to him, those he cares about, understand his achievement and its special significance to him, comprehend and attach value to the reasons behind his emotions. This is especially true if he is glad and proud of his accomplishment. Or, if a man receives a book from a friend and is informed that it is the kind of book he will appreciate, he feels pleasure and fulfilment if his friend's assessment is accurate because he feels seen, understood, and known. Or, if a guy has a personal loss, it is important to him to know that those who are close to him understand his situation and that his emotional state is real to them. Normal people need insight, not blind "acceptance" or unconditional "love."

The vast majority of modern psychologists believe that human beings are social metaphysicians by nature who need on the approval of others in order to feel good about themselves. However, it would be a grave error to conflate a healthy man's need for visibility with the pathological motivations of the social metaphysician.

A psychologically sound man expects others to see his value rather than invent it, so he does not rely on them to give him self-esteem. The admiration of others is valuable and important to him only if he respects the criteria by which others judge him and only if the admiration is focused on qualities that he himself regards as admirable. If other men show genuine signs of understanding and appreciating him, they rise in his estimation; his estimation of himself does not change. He aspires to the experience of interacting with other guys in a just and rational social setting where their reactions to him make sense given his own character traits and accomplishments. He has a conceptual understanding of the reality of his own deeds and character, but he wants to feel it personally via the people who share his beliefs and are affected by it.

For social philosophers, it is identification that they desire from others rather than visibility (plus the kind of pseudovisibility indicated above).

People who "act," or take on multiple personalities in various situations, condemn themselves to a life of terrible contradiction. As people, they cannot avoid the desire for visibility, but as neurotic "role-players," they fear being correctly understood, or perceived. They frequently harbor a deep hatred for those who fall for their act and secretly yearn for someone they will be unable to deceive. At the same time, they take every precaution to avoid the observant look of the person for whom their performance fails. A guy must be willing to be visible to himself if he wants to be honestly visible to others.

This final point is crucial for a person who is more innocent than a role-player. Consider the issue of the person who tends to suppress his virtues and value goals and submerge his own idealism out of desperation, moral confusion, self-doubt, or fear of being impractical and unrealistic (Chapter Five). Such a person doesn't feel visible to himself (he is not visible to himself), and his genuine soul is hidden beneath a protective layer of distance, resignation, and indifference to life, which renders him invisible to others. He will continually feel frustrated and undervalued in his connections with others until and unless he releases that soul, which means until and unless he recognizes his values, accords them the sanction of moral objectivity, and offers them suitable, objective expression in action. Since others' perceptions of him depend in part on their own values, acting to give his values objective form does not ensure that he will be seen by others; nevertheless, failing to do so ensures that he will remain invisible.

A mentally healthy man's primary concern in any human interaction—while driven by the desire for visibility—is not necessarily whether or not he is being properly valued.

The question of "What does he think of me?" is not the man with self-top esteem's priority when they first meet. Rather, ask yourself, "What do I think of him?" Naturally, his main preoccupation is with his own perception and assessment of the available information.

Man's need to see his ideals materialized in reality is accompanied by a desire to see his values embodied in the person of others, to see people who go through life similarly to him. Man can confirm his personal understanding of existence by looking at that sight.

An important source of enjoyment for a man in a relationship with someone he admires is the act of expressing his opinion, making his admiration objective, and projecting that he can see the other person. This is a crucial way for someone to experience themselves as an entity, to make their own selves objective, and to provide existential truth to their own values.

A guy might feel visible in many ways and to different degrees in various interpersonal connections, as was said above. A man does not have the same level of visibility in a connection with a casual stranger as he does with an acquaintance. Man does not have the same level of visibility with an acquaintance as he has with a close buddy.

But there is one kind of relationship that is exceptional in the breadth and depth of the visibility it encompasses: romantic love.

Romance

Every human being has a knowledge of whether they are male or female. A typical and intimate component of one's experience of personal identity is their sexual identity. No one ever experiences themselves as just a person, but rather as a male or female human being. (A person is considered to have a pathological condition when he or she lacks a distinct sexual identity.)

While one's sexual identity (his or her masculinity or femininity) has biological roots, it goes beyond simply being physically male or female to encompass how one experiences maleness or femininity on a psychological level. More broadly, it includes one's unique psychological characteristics as a man or woman.

For instance, if a man has a reputation for being honest in his interactions with others, this feature has more to do with his psychology as a person and is not sexual in nature. However, if he is comfortable with his sexual role in relation to women, this quality is particular to his psyche as a guy.

What then are the many psychological characteristics that, when added together, make up a person's specifically psycho-sexual identity, or their psychological identity as a man or a woman?

Just as one's personal identity, in a broader sense, is the product and reflection of the way one responds to one's nature as a human being, so too is one's psycho-sexual identity (also known as one's sexual personality) the manner in which one responds to one's nature as a sexual being.

How much is a person aware that they are a sexual being? What do you think about sex and its importance in human life? What does one think about their own body? (This does not mean: How does one evaluate their appearance, but rather: Is their body perceived as valuable or pleasurable?) How does one perceive the other sex? How does one feel about the physical attributes of the other sex? What distinguishes the sexual roles that men and women play? How would you rate your own sexual role, and would you feel comfortable in it? His responses to these types of queries shape his sexual psychology, for better or worse. An individual's perspective on these topics does not develop in a psychological vacuum. Contrarily, more than any other area of life, sex tends to include one's entire principles and psyche. The general level of one's self-esteem is the single most important component in shaping their sexual attitudes; the greater this level, the more likely it is that one will respond to their own sexuality in an appropriate manner, or have a healthy sex psychology.

A reasonably affirmative reaction to one's own sexual nature is the result and expression of a healthy masculinity or femininity. The following are necessary for this: a strong, affirmative awareness of one's own sexuality; a positive (guilt-free and fearless) response to the sex phenomenon; a perspective on sex that sees it as integrated to one's mind and values (rather than as a dissociated, mindless, and meaningless physical indulgence); a positive and self-valuing response to one's own body; a strong, positive response to the body of the opposite

This final aspect has to be clarified. The disparities in the anatomy and physiology of men and women lead to the distinctions between the gendered roles in sexuality. Man is physically bigger and stronger than women; he also creates and utilizes more energy, and he tends to be physically more active (for physiological reasons). In terms of intimacy, he plays the more active and dominant position; he has the most control over both his own and his partner's enjoyment; it is he who penetrates and the woman who is penetrated (with everything this entails, physically and psychologically). Both sexes should have a healthy amount of aggression and self-assuredness, but a man discovers the essence of his masculinity in the act of romantic dominance, while a woman discovers the essence of her femininity in the act of romantic submission.

Both jobs call both physical prowess and self-assurance. Fear of romantic self-assertiveness affects self-doubting men, whereas fear of romantic submission affects self-doubting women. An unconfident man fears the challenge of the woman's expectation that he be strong; an unconfident woman fears the challenge of the challenge of masculine strength.

A man must have enough self-assurance to be unrestrained, benevolently self-assured, and unconstrained in his ability to initiate and pursue love relationships. In order to play the position of challenger and responder to the guy, a woman needs to have the kind of self-assurance that allows her to be unrestricted, unabashed, and benevolently self-assertive.

(The aforementioned is not intended as a complete examination; the latter is outside the scope of this debate. It merely serves as a broad indicator of the masculine and feminine sex roles.)

It is fundamental to that which one seeks to objectify and see mirrored or made visible in human connections, just as it is essential to one's sense of self. Being viewed as, and feeling oneself as, a specific kind of man or woman is a necessary component of the experience of full visibility and self-objectification.

This is true for both those whose sex psychology is normal and people who have a neurotic sex psychology. For instance, a sadist and masochist's relationship depends on how well they are able to read one other's defects, weaknesses, insecurities, and neurotic phobias. The sadist and masochist would fear to comprehend and face consciously the nature of what is being made visible between them, in contrast to a healthy partnership, which is a significant distinction.

From the description above, it should be evident why interaction with a person of the opposing sex is necessary for the best experience of visibility and self-objectification. A close friend of the same sex with whom one shares common interests and values notices and reacts to characteristics that are specific to one's psychology as a human being rather than as a sexual being. A buddy can have an abstract perception of and appreciation for one's sexuality, but he cannot have significant personal stake in it. One can be perceived and personally responded to as both a human being and a sexual being by a person of the opposing sex with whom one shares a strong mutuality of mind and values. Thus, a key factor in the difficulties in perceiving full visibility is the distinction between how one is seen from the perspective of the same sex and from the perspective of the opposite sex.

Romantic love entails feeling seen as a man or woman, not only as a human being.

It must be emphasized that this sensation of full exposure is not an automatic fact, but rather merely a potential in regard to the opposite sex. It depends on a variety of factors, including the context or circumstances in which their relationship occurs, the nature of their respective interests, the presence or absence of emotional involvements on either side, the presence or absence of repression in one or both of them, etc., whether or not a man and woman with similar fundamental values and a sense of life will respond fully and personally to each other.

Furthermore, if there are significant and fundamental points of affinity and mutuality between a man and woman, they may be in love even when they do not fully share the same thoughts and values. They might feel visible to each other to a substantial and delightful extent, even if it is not optimal.

Love is an emotional reaction that involves two fundamental, linked aspects: one believes the object of love to have or represent traits that one greatly values, and as a result, one believes the object of love to be (actually or potentially) pleasurable. This holds true for all types of love, not just romantic love.

One perceives the loved item as having or embodying one's highest ideals and as being extremely significant to one's personal happiness in the case of romantic love, which is the most positive emotional response one human being can give another. In this context, the word "highest" does not necessarily refer to something that is noblest or most elevated; rather, it refers to what is most significant in terms of one's own needs and aspirations as well as what one most hopes to find and experience in life. The adored object is also seen as being fundamental to one's sexual fulfillment. One of the defining qualities of romantic love is the final one.

Romantic love entails the objectification of one's self-value more than any other kind of connection. (I am referring to true romantic love, not its counterfeit, infatuation; infatuation is an exaggerated, out-of-context response that entails focusing only on one or two aspects of a person's overall personality while ignoring or being oblivious to the rest, and acting as though the person were only those specific aspects.) Fundamental visibility is a requirement of romantic love. "I view you as a person, and because you are what you are, I desire you for my sexual enjoyment," is the crux of the passionate love reaction.

We must take into account certain facts about the nature and meaning of sex in order to see why this is the most profound personal tribute one person can give another and why romantic love involves the most intense expression and objectification of one's self-value.

Sex has the potential to be the most intense pleasure a person can experience. Other joys can endure for a longer period of time, but none can match its strength and intensity. Furthermore, sex is a pleasure that the person—the entire being—experiences, not just the body or the mind. For instance, the pleasure experienced when eating, walking, or swimming is mostly of the physical kind; psychological components do play a role. The satisfaction of productive work, a stimulating conversation, or an artistic performance, on the other hand, is primarily cerebral; it is a pleasure of the mind. However, sex stands out from other pleasures due to its integration of the body and mind. It blends senses, emotions, values, and thought, giving a person the most intense way to experience his or her own whole being and the closest and most personal sense of who they are. (Such is the potential of sex, provided that conflict, guilt, estrangement from one's partner, etc. do not dilute and undermine the experience.)

A direct, immediate source, vehicle, and manifestation of pleasure during sex is one's own body. And because man experiences pleasure as the good (Chapter 5), sex gives him the most direct and vivid way to perceive himself as good and valuable. Additionally, sex gives a man the most direct and vivid way to appreciate life.

In a man's mind, his belief that he is capable of living and deserving of living (his self-esteem) exists as an abstraction; it means that he is capable of upholding his ideals, and therefore of finding happiness, and that he is deserving of doing so. This conviction is directly, immediately, and sensory-based confirmed and reaffirmed by the pleasure he feels during sex.

In a man's thinking, his belief that life has value and that it is worthwhile to live it is an abstract idea. Its meaning is the belief that because of the nature of life, happiness is achievable and that it is within his reach. This conviction is directly, immediately, and sensory-based confirmed and reaffirmed by the pleasure he feels during sex.

Sex is the ultimate way for a guy to perceive his own goodness and the goodness of life.

More than any other activity, sex gives a man the chance to feel that he is an end in himself and that enjoyment is what life is all about. Insofar as and to the extent that he is able to enjoy the sex act, life is asserting itself within him, the principle that a human being is an end in himself. (Even if the reasons that drive a person to a particular sexual encounter are neurotic, and even if, right afterward, he is tortured by shame or guilt.) Unfortunately, the majority of men experience this emotion much too frequently. In sex, a guy can escape from any ill-willed feelings of life's futility or drudgery, of his own stupid slavery to inexplicable ends. Therefore, in the purest sense of the word, sex is the highest expression of selfishness.

Given the foregoing, it is easy to comprehend why mystic-religionist adversaries of man—of his thinking, of his self-esteem, and of his life on earth—have been so virulently hostile to the phenomenon of human sexuality throughout history.

The celebration of oneself and of life is so ingrained in the act of sex that a person lacking the self-worth that such a celebration necessitates and implies is frequently compelled to fake it, to perform a neurotic substitute: to engage in sex not as an expression of his sense of self-value and of the value of life, but rather as a way to temporarily feel valuable, to temporarily alleviate despair, or to temporarily escape from anxiety.

The participants in sex encounter a distinct and potent form of self-awareness throughout the act, which is sparked by both the sexual act and the verbal-emotional-physical contact they share. The nature of the interaction, the level and type of visibility they project, and how they are made to feel strongly influence the self-awareness in any given situation. The outcome is the deepest conceivable experience of self, of being spiritually as well as physically naked, and of gloating in that fact. This is true if and to the degree that the parties engaged have a strong sense of spiritual affinity (by "spiritual," I mean: pertaining to one's thoughts and ideals). The sexual encounter is perceived as autistic (at best), annoyingly "physical," or degradingly useless if and to the extent that the parties involved feel spiritually and/or sexually alienated and estranged.

The most deeply gratifying type of self-awareness is provided by sex. The highest and most intimate homage a person can give or receive is when a man and woman demonstrate their desire to have this experience via each other's person. This is the ultimate way to acknowledge the value of the person one desires and to have one's own value acknowledged. In this view, romantic love entails a strong objectification of one's own worth, which is reflected and made apparent by the loving reaction of one's partner.

The belief in one's ability to be a source of joy to the person one loves is a fundamental aspect of this experience. One has the impression that one's person, rather than just one's body, is what makes one's partner feel good. In essence, one experiences: "Because I am who I am, I can make her (or him) feel what she (or he) is feeling." As a result, one recognizes their own soul and value in their partner's expressions of feeling.

The person you most desire is the one with whom you feel the most free to be yourself, the one whom you (consciously or subconsciously) regard as your proper psychological mirror, the one who reflects your deepest perspective on yourself and of life. If sex involves an act of self-celebration—if, in sex, you desire the freedom to be spontaneous, to be emotionally open and uninhibited, to assert your right to pleasure and to flaunt your pleasure in yourself—then sex involves That person is the one who will enable you to enjoy your desired sex experiences to their fullest.

Because most people are poor introspectors and because the causes of romantic attraction (whether healthy or neurotic) between two people are incredibly complicated, most people find it extremely difficult to pinpoint the origin of their romantic-sexual decisions. The abstraction "a mutuality of mind and values" is very broad. What does it entail in more detail?

In order to respond to that query, we must take into account a fundamental idea for comprehending romantic love: the idea of "sense of life."

Romantic Attraction

A person's emotional experience of their most profound understanding of life and of how they relate to it is known as their "sense of life."

It is, in fact, the emotional outgrowth of a metaphysics—of a personal metaphysics—that reflects the subconsciously integrated sum of a person's deepest and broadest (implicit) beliefs about the universe, about life, and about himself.

Long before a child is able to think about the world and himself in philosophical terms, a feeling of existence is formed in early childhood. His explicit, avowed philosophy may give articulate, conceptual expression to his sense of life, may alter or modify it, or may be in unrecognized contradiction to it, depending on such factors as how rational he is, how conceptually reflective about his own life, and how well-integrated psychologically. The conscious philosophical convictions he acquires later may or may not be in accord with his sense of life.

A human person meets certain fundamental facts of reality during the course of his growth from birth, including facts about the nature of existence and the character of man, to which he might respond in a number of ways and to varied degrees of rationality and realism. The whole of these answers together makes up each individual's unique perspective of life.

For instance, it is an unavoidable truth of reality that thinking is required for man to exist, meaning that man needs information and that knowledge acquisition involves conceptual thought or effort. A young person does not arrive at their stance on this issue through an express decision or a single option. It is reached through the cumulative effect of a protracted succession of decisions and actions in the face of particular circumstances necessitating the need to consider.

A young individual might react positively and healthily, learning to actively enjoy mental exercise. Or he can approach intellectual endeavor unwillingly and obediently, seeing it as a "necessary evil" in essence. Another option is that he may see intellectual work with sluggish anger or anxiety, seeing it as an unfair burden and imposition, and make a conscious decision to avoid it whenever possible. In his psychology, a trend, a policy, a habit—a viewpoint or premise via implication—slowly takes shape and becomes more ingrained. All sense-of-life attitudes are developed in this way.

A person's experience of life is affected by a variety of factors, including but not limited to the following: Man is neither omniscient nor infallible, as I have emphasized throughout this book, and this is a truth of life. A young child learns very early that there is no guarantee that his effort would necessarily and automatically be successful in any given situation, in addition to the fact that his knowledge must be obtained via the process of cognition. He may voluntarily, genuinely, and bravely take the responsibility of thought and judgment, fully prepared to suffer the consequences of his decisions (and future acts), and realizing that there is no rational alternative to his policies. Or he might react out of fear and a desire to avoid responsibility, either by reducing the scope of his thought and behavior to lessen the "risks" entailed by potential mistakes or by abdicating the responsibility he fears, living off of other people's opinions, judgments, and values.

It is a simple fact of life that a man's success is not always assured, whether he is pursuing education or anything else of significance. A young person learns that life is a process of struggle and that struggle contains the risk of failure and defeat, whether directly or implicitly. The difficulties of life could elicit an outspoken and eager response from him. Or he can have a tendency to distance himself from them, seeing the need for battle and the uncertainty of accomplishment as a metaphysical tragedy.

Man must project his goals into the future and work toward achieving them. This requires that he have the capacity and willingness to postpone present pleasures when and if required, as well as to put up with unavoidable frustrations. One can maintain their ambition for ideals by accepting this reality in a realistic and unself-pitying manner. Or, he may choose to rebel against this reality, thereby stamping his foot at reality and focusing exclusively on values that are simple and quick to obtain out of animosity toward a cosmos that does not accord his wants power.

A human being will unavoidably experience some level of suffering during the course of his or her life; the degree may be minor or significant depending on a number of factors; what is not unavoidable, however, is the status that he or she will accord his or her suffering, i.e., the significance he or she will give it in his or her life and in their conception of existence. The belief that happiness and success are the norm and natural, and that pain, defeat, and disappointment are the abnormal and accidental, the metaphysically unimportant, can be maintained no matter how much adversity or suffering a person experiences. This is similar to how we rationally view health, not disease, as man's normal state. Or he can come to the conclusion that misery and failure are the fundamental aspects of life, while success and happiness are merely the transitory, abnormal, and accidental.

Man's ability to be rational or irrational and his potential for volitional consciousness are facts of his nature. Every person experiences some level of irrationality in some of those around him, which causes him pain. An individual may recognize that irrationality is incorrect, that it is an aberration and a divergence from reality. Or he might decide (in the form of an emotional generalization) that he is mistaken in thinking that people are rational and give in to a nefarious perspective of the cosmos, coming to the conclusion that man is, in all actuality, naturally irrational.

Because of the unique character of man, he must decide to value his own life and happiness enough to generate the necessary cognition and action. For a living creature, it is necessary to act in order to maintain its own life and well-being. A person may grow in the life-affirming selfishness that is characteristic of a living being; he may also develop a solemn desire to find happiness and an unwavering adherence to his own principles, which implies a proud unwillingness to treat them as something to be given up or sacrificed. Or, he may start the process of giving up his soul before it is fully formed because he is afraid of the work, the responsibility, the integrity, and the courage that such selfishness (and self-value) require. He may give up his aspirations, his happiness, and his values not to some obvious beneficiary but to his own nameless, unidentified lethargy or apprehension.

These are just a few of the fundamental concerns that go into a person's experience of existence; the list is by no means complete. In terms of sense-of-life difficulties, it should be noted that there are degree-related considerations; any potential responses can be sustained to varied degrees of intensity and consistency.

A generalized sensation about oneself, about existence, and about one's relationship to existence is the end result of such responses. A person's sense of life can either reflect unwavering self-worth and an unwavering sense of the importance of being alive, the conviction that the universe is open to the efficacy of one's thought and effort, or it can reflect the agony of self-doubt and the anxiety of feeling as though one lives in a hostile and unintelligible universe. It can represent a perspective on life that is exalted or one that is tragically doomed, one that is adventurous or one that is frustrated, one that is beautiful or one that is sordidly senseless. It might represent desire and self-assurance, hushed, romantic longing, agonized, tragic resistance, subtle, unobtrusive resignation, or forceful powerlessness.

Since all value-choices rest on an implicit perspective of the being who values and of the world in which he must behave, a person's sense of life is vital in the construction of his core values. All other emotions and emotional reactions are based on a person's sense of life; it is sort of like the central motif of his or her being.

This is especially clear when looking at his love and sexual responses.

It can be very challenging to conceptually isolate and identify one's own sense of life, just as it can be very challenging to conceptually isolate and identify another person's sense of life because it permeates their entire personality. However, in romantic partnerships, each party's affirmative response to the other's sense of life is essential to the perception of mutual visibility and the sensation of love. In romantic love, one implicitly experiences: "He or she has my perspective on life. He (or she) confronts existence the same way I do. He (or she) has the same perception of life as I have."

A sense-of-life affinity can be expressed in many different ways; however, a clear conceptual declaration is arguably the rarest. Two people learn about one another's values and dislikes via talking to one another, smiling, standing, moving, showing emotions, responding to events, etc. They also learn about one another by observing one another. They learn it from their interactions with one another, from what they say and don't say, from the justifications that are unnecessary, and from sudden, unexpected evidence of mutual understanding.

Common interests and dislikes in the arts are among the most telling indicators of a sense-of-life affinity; more than any other human endeavor, art is a sense-of-life world, and a person's feeling of life greatly influences his creative reactions.

The exchange of ideas between two people is not unimportant—in fact, it can be quite important—but merely reaching an abstract intellectual consensus on a given issue is insufficient to create a true sense of life affinity.

No fundamental and deep experience of visibility is conceivable without a strong sense of kinship. Someone with an alien way of life might admire you for a specific quality or qualities, but your sense of fulfillment, if any, would be very limited. You would sense that the other person's basic frame of reference, the basic context from which you are being viewed and evaluated, is different from your own, and that the admiration does not mean what it would mean in your own context.

Consider the scenario when someone with a self-assured, positive outlook on life is admired by someone with a fiercely tragic outlook on life, leading to the projection of admiration for the image of a valiant but doomed martyr. The object of such admiration would not feel truly seen because the image would not align with how he actually sees himself, which is not tragic.

When romantic love is maximally experienced, one is admired for the qualities they want to be adored for and—more importantly—in a way and from a perspective that is consistent with their outlook on life. Full visibility is there.

In other words, a person's psychology might be healthier or less healthy than his philosophy. A person's perception of life can be better (more appropriate to reality) or worse (less appropriate to reality) than his conscious philosophical ideas. People are frequently inclined to believe that love is incomprehensible, that it is "simply there," and that it cannot be understood rationally. This is because a person's feeling of life and professed philosophy may conflict, and because a sense of life can be difficult to discern. An individual could struggle to articulate why he feels emotionally in sync and visibly distinct from everyone else with one specific person but not with another (who, on the surface, may appear to be an equally plausible romantic partner).

Identifying the nature of the emotional cosmos that two extremely neurotic people share is difficult for them to achieve, and they have no interest in learning what components make up their shared sense of reality. This presents another challenge to comprehending the reasons behind their attachment.

The key to comprehending a romantic relationship, however, is through a knowledge of the individuals' perspective of existence and of the unique self-experience that the relationship gives them. This is true regardless of whether a romantic relationship is healthy or neurotic (or both in part). The questions to ask and the answers to give are: How does this relationship make me feel about myself? If a person wants to understand the fundamental reasons for his romantic feelings for another person. What makes the self-experience it causes in me distinctive? Why, then? What behaviors, attitudes, and traits of the person I love are crucial in enabling me to have this experience?

The answers to these questions will reveal a lot about a person, including not only the nature of his love feelings but also his self-esteem and most fundamental self-image.

CHAPTER TWELVE

Psychotherapy

Mentality and Psychotherapy

The psychological treatment of mental problems is known as psychotherapy.

As I hope to make clear, psychotherapy is best understood as an educational process in which the patient is taught how to improve the effectiveness of his thought processes and replace irrational values and premises with rational ones. This is done by first helping the patient understand the flaws in his way of thinking as well as the errors in his values and premises that are the root of his problems.

My standard procedure is to explain the following to a potential patient during an interview: "In my opinion, there are three forces or variables at work in psychotherapy. There I am—the psychotherapist. The "you" who is dealing with mental health problems exists. There is a "you" who is rational enough to recognize the issue and have a motivation to address it. In contrast to the problematic "you," psychotherapy is a partnership between the therapist and the "you" who doesn't have any problems." In order to effectively serve as a co-psychotherapist, the patient must continue to take a very active role in his own treatment. While retaining a state of mental indolence, he does not believe that he can be treated (the same passivity, in most cases, that was a crucial cause of his neurosis).

On the path to self-understanding and self-improvement, it is frequently necessary that the patient be taught a significant amount about psychology, including how the mind works, the nature and conditions of healthy self-esteem, the cause of pathological anxiety, and the relationships between anxiety, defense values, and neurotic symptoms. A patient has a propensity to view his issues and thought processes as singular, sui generis, which prevents him from thinking about them abstractly and objectively and renders him incapable of fixing them. He must develop a conceptual framework from which to perceive himself in order to recognize the larger psychological principles operating within his mind.

When a patient initially starts treatment, one of the most fundamental and vital things he or she must understand is how his or her mind and emotions are related. He frequently feels as though his terrible emotions are unexplainable; he sees himself as an unfathomable enigma. As a result, the patient's understanding that his issues are solvable and that his emotions have understandable reasons is one of the therapist's initial objectives. Understanding the connection between a patient's emotions and values—as well as between those values and thinking or not thinking—can be extremely helpful, even if the understanding is initially merely vague and abstract. He may feel more certain that his issues can be resolved as a result.

A patient is quite likely to view his neurotic feelings and desires as being a fundamental part of who he is as a person. My feelings are mine, whether they be nervous, depressed, hostile, masochistic, or homosexual. This mindset is undoubtedly resistant to therapy. In order for the patient to start thinking about his harmful feelings and desires with objectivity and detachment, it is required to create in his consciousness a sense of "psychological distance" between his mind or ego and those emotions and desires. He will be more driven to pinpoint the ideational causes of his sentiments, sort through the underlying causes, and adjust his emotional responses the more clearly he realizes that his feelings, no matter how long he may have experienced them, are not a part of his nature.

In this context, it is important to note that both the Freudian concept of an id and the Original Sin theology are horrendously damaging psychologically. They tend to confirm the patient's gloomy, deterministic views about himself and his circumstances, in addition to being unfounded and insulting to reason. Additionally, they frequently encourage the patient's tendency toward apathy and resignation under the pretext that "I can't help it." If they are taught and accept an emotional worldview that is akin to the medieval concept of demonology, men can't help it. This is the point of view that needs to be refuted.

A patient needs to learn to stop thinking of their emotions as irreducible primaries, just as they need to learn to stop thinking of their way of thinking, or psycho-epistemology, as an irreducible primary. There is nothing a man is more likely to perceive as irreducibly and unchangeably " himself" as his way of thinking—not the content of his thought, but the process. This makes the work of teaching this understanding frequently very tough. However, one of the main goals of a really effective psychotherapy must be to help the patient develop a new way of thinking. This is done by building on the patient's existing knowledge of rational psycho-epistemology.

Consider the case of a man who regularly avoids thinking about the reasons behind any emotion or desire that he suspects to be irrational, immoral, or unrealistic; he attempts to deny the existence of such feelings through the use of techniques like evasion and repression; if and when the feelings persist past his attempts to throttle them, he further sabotages his consciousness by surrendering to them blindly, ignoring his reason and intelligence, and turning to addition as a last resort. Pathological anxiety is the emotional outcome. The basic issue cannot be resolved, and the patient cannot be returned to psychological health, unless his condition is attacked fundamentally, that is, in terms of his psycho-epistemology. A therapist might theoretically be able to reduce his patient's anxiety by dealing with some of the specific irrationalities that triggered it.

There are two types of psycho-epistemological issues that are almost universal among patients and that the psychotherapist needs to address directly and thoroughly. The first of them is the patient's inability to think abstractly about himself and his problems, as well as his propensity to disregard the connection between his feelings, reactions, and overall psychological condition and any broader principles or abstract information he may possess. The patient's propensity for acting out of fear when contemplating himself, his life, and his behaviors is the second of these issues.

For instance, a patient might know, in an abstract sense, that emotions are not criteria for truth or untruth, right or wrong, or instruments of cognition. Despite this awareness, he still has a propensity to behave in some situations under the assumption that if he feels strongly about something or is afraid of it, his feeling must be justified and may be a reliable indicator of what to do. Because he does not apply his general knowledge to himself, it does not prevent this inclination. He needs to learn how to accomplish this. Or, a patient can be acting in a manner that, if seen in someone else, the patient would consider to be blatantly irrational and neurotic. But he disassociates himself from any such judgments because he has a vague impression that he is "different," i.e., that his situation has unique "extenuating factors." He has to be guided to realize the self-deception he is engaging in.

Concerning the issue of motivation by fear, I've provided numerous examples of it in earlier chapters. A patient is frequently influenced by his fears when deciding on his course of action and goals, when considering what constitutes his self-interest in various circumstances: fears of failure, fears of lowering his self-esteem (or pseudo-self-esteem), fears of evoking disapproval, and fears of jeopardizing his flimsy sense of "security." To dismantle a patient's psycho-epistemology, the therapist must first identify the nature of the patient's particular fears and how they function. The therapist must then work to convey this understanding to the patient so that the patient can become more aware of the workings of his own thought processes, better recognize his mistakes as they happen, and refocus his thinking in a more realistic direction.

The therapist will discover that he must frequently switch between psycho-epistemological errors and emotional or motivational conflicts, or, more specifically, between his patient's way of thinking and his incorrect values and premises, in order to untangle the causes of his issues. The realms of cognition and assessment have a reciprocal causal relationship. In the same way that rational thinking promotes the development of rational values, and that rational values promote rational thinking, unhealthy thinking frequently leads to unhealthy values, and vice versa.

Emotional and motivational (i.e., value) disruptions frequently exacerbate pre-existing psycho-epistemological errors and even lead to the development of new ones. For instance, the anxiety brought on by unhealthy cognitive practices triggers more and frequently worse avoidances, repressions, rationalizations, flights from reality into imagination, etc.—all of which are attempts to lessen the worry. Or, when a person with neurotic depression actively succumbs to the influence of his emotions and actively seeks out evidence of his worthlessness and depravity outside, his psycho-epistemology deteriorates as a result of his despair.

The pursuit of illogical values, however, is necessary because they are irrational, which needs further psycho-epistemological self-sabotage, additional cognitive disintegration, which necessitates the pursuit of irrational values, etc. For instance, a person whose "thinking" is dominated by social-metaphysical considerations may be persuaded to accept an entirely fictitious set of values, as in the case of the boy who grows up in a bad neighborhood and becomes a criminal; the irrationality inherent in his criminal pursuits further corrupts his thought processes, allowing him to accept ever-worse crimes.

As we've seen, a person's self-concept and self-evaluation are the key components of his psychology and the driving force behind his actions. The psychotherapist must continually link psycho-epistemological and motivational (or emotional) illnesses to the nature of the patient's self-esteem in an effort to comprehend his patient's difficulties and offer solutions.

The therapist must inquire: What function does this serve in terms of the maintenance of the patient's self-esteem (or pseudo-self-esteem) if, for example, the patient frequently avoids, represses, or rationalizes in a certain area of his life? How does the patient's perception of himself change if his thinking is completely ineffective in some areas as a result of self-defeating psycho-epistemological practices? What is the exact self-esteem deficit or area of self-doubt that blinds the patient and prevents him from letting go of such impulses if the patient is torn by urges that are blatantly unreasonable and self-destructive? What happens to a patient's already low self-esteem if he allows himself to be driven into irrational behavior by the pressure of irrational desires or fears? His neurotic barriers are intended to shield what specific self-doubts? How do his ideals and objectives in the areas of work and interpersonal relationships relate to how he sees and perceives himself? How does his sexual psychology change as a result? Effective psychotherapy depends on carefully working out the answers to these issues with the patient.

Think about a man who seeks psychotherapy with the following dual complaints: he is unhappy and irritated at work, and he is unhappy and frustrated in his marriage, and he is unsure of why. The results of the investigation show that the patient is a social metaphysician. He chose his particular career at his parents' urging, without any personal interest or desire on his part, and he chose the woman who would become his wife in a process that was essentially similar: she was widely regarded as the most attractive and desirable girl in his circle of friends and acquaintances, so winning her was perceived by him as a great personal achievement. He has lied to his wife about having affairs with other women twice during their marriage in a vain attempt to establish himself; the women had no significance to him, and the overall result of the events was to make him more anxious. A growing sensation of inner emptiness and futility, the feeling that he is achieving nothing and becoming nothing, is haunting him.

Making the patient aware of the psycho-epistemological processes by which his values and goals were selected is one of the therapist's main goals in treating such a patient. These processes include the patient's reliance on the terms, expectations, beliefs, and standards of his "significant others," the substitution of those others' minds for his own, the patient's need for approval and status as the regulator of his "thinking" (which means the destruction of thinking), and the patient's fear of independence. The patient must be helped to comprehend how his initial failure to uphold his independence caused the sense of insecurity that drove him into becoming a psycho-epistemological dependent; the manner in which each new act of surrender to the minds of others carried him further away from reality and thus lower and lower in his own estimation; the manner in which the betrayal of his autonomy and thus of his self-esteem inevitably strained his relationship with reality; and the process by which each new act of surrender to the minds of others carried him He needs to be made aware that his obstinately unthinking attempt at "independence" through his infidelities is merely another way of capitulating and giving in to others; he is still a "stranger and afraid in a world" because his thoughts and values were absent from the situation, he lacked anything of his own to express or seek, and he acted solely against the ever-present others from which he sees no way to escape. This raises the question of whether a patient's comprehension of the nature and causes of his difficulties is enough to result in a cure.

No, it is not the only thing needed; it is necessary, but it is simply the first step. The patient's fundamental illness resulted from his inability to carry out a specific type of mental action: autonomous thought, judgment, and appraisal of himself, his life, and the world around him; inability to focus his mind on the task of comprehending reality's truths. He took a psycho-epistemological default action, which led to his low self-esteem and social-metaphysical dependence. His issue cannot be solved or dealt with successfully until and unless that default is corrected in action (i.e., until and unless he learns to use his mind correctly and to be guided by it in his behavior). This calls for the long, arduous, difficult, halting, and doubt-filled process of learning to view reality with his own eyes, to evaluate what he observes, to form his own conclusions—as honestly and logically as he is able—and to take appropriate action. He cannot build the lackluster self-esteem he needs without doing this.

Although not all neurotics are social metaphysicians, the bulk of the patients the therapist sees fall into this category. Helping these patients achieve intellectual autonomy is one of the most demanding, complex, and difficult jobs of psychotherapy. I'll only list two of the most frequent issues the therapist might deal with because they highlight the type of psycho-epistemological retraining required.

First of all, the therapist needs to be ready to deal with and change a propensity that social metaphysicians almost always exhibit when making their first attempts at independence: a reliance on their feelings as the only type of autonomy they are aware of. Social metaphysicians often feel they have no other means of defying their authorities than their own erratic emotions. As a result, they pursue any desire, regardless of its validity or rationality, as long as it is not approved by those authorities. This is an attempt to escape the frame of reference of their "significant others." They frequently perceive life as a struggle between their desires and those of other people. They only care about one thing: Should I follow my own desires or those of other people? However, such a policy only modifies the way in which they are alienated from reality, leaving them just as disconnected as they were before. As a result, it does little to help them develop a true sense of self-worth and independence. If a patient is to develop true independence, healthy independence, he or she must learn to establish their mind, not their sentiments separately from their minds.

Second, it is essentially inevitable that the patient will substitute the authority of those "significant individuals" with that of the therapist in the process of trying to break free from them; he will act "rationally" and "independently" in order to gain the therapist's favor. The patient must be thoroughly informed of this pattern, and the therapist must be continually on guard against it. The following type of problem does, however, frequently occur. The patient is in a position where he has rationally (and correctly) determined that he should take a certain action, but he is also aware that by doing so, he will win his therapist's approval, and that consideration is extremely alluring to him. The question then arises in his mind as to whether he should take the action, given the presence of social metaphysical elements in his motivation. In such circumstances, he has to be taught that he should adopt a certain action if he is logically convinced that it is proper and suitable given the facts of reality, regardless of whether other, nonrational elements are also at play in his psychology. Consider the alternative: if he refuses to do what he knows to be right in an attempt to squelch any social metaphysical inclinations, then he is still putting other factors above reason and truth; in his very attempt to resist his social metaphysical dilemma, he is still being controlled by it. Regardless of how sensible the action may be in and of itself, a patient cannot properly operate on the assumption that if any planned action of his would elicit acceptance (which he still neurotically seeks), then he will abstain from executing that action. He can only get rid of his self-doubt, which is what causes his social metaphysical inclinations, by developing the ability to make and follow his own, independent, rational judgment.

Values and Counseling

The idea that morality is a matter of faith and that there is no such thing as a rational, scientific code of ethics has had terrible results in almost every area of human endeavor. The effects of this notion, however, have been particularly severe for the field of psychology.

The problem or issue of motivation is crucial to psychology as a science. As we've seen, values are the foundation of motivation. A man's premises—more particularly, his value premises—determine his actions and emotions within the context of his innate requirements and capabilities as a particular form of living organism.

According to me, one of the most compelling arguments that man needs an integrated, objective code of moral values—that a haphazard collection of subjective or collective whims and precepts will not do— and that a rational ethical system is as necessary to his psychological survival as it is to his existential survival—is the existence of neurosis, of mental and emotional disturbances.

The paradox—and tragedy—of modern psychology is that the only topic expressly excluded from its purview is values.

The majority of psychologists—both as theorists and as psychotherapists—have accepted the notion that morality is a matter of faith rather than reason, that moral values are inviolately subjective, that morality is a matter of faith rather than reason, and that a therapist must treat his patients without critiquing or challenging their fundamental moral beliefs.

This assumption needs to be contested.

The constant complaints of the neurotic are guilt, worry, and self-doubt. Such criticisms must be regularly dealt with by the psychotherapist. Patients that are tortured are experiencing moral conflicts: Is sex sinful or is it a natural human desire? — Do men have the right to follow their own interests, or is the profit motive bad? — Is it ever OK to feel extreme outrage or is it necessary to love and forgive everyone? — Must a person submit to the teachings of his religious leaders without question, or is it permissible to question their conclusions using reason? — Is divorce a viable option or is it mandatory to stay with a spouse you no longer love? — Should a woman view being a mother as her highest calling and responsibility, or can she pursue a profession on her own? — Is a man obligated to look out for his brother or does he have the freedom to pursue his own happiness?

It is true that patients frequently repress these disputes, and this repression is the main barrier to the resolution of the conflict. However, it is not true that just bringing these problems to the patients' attention will always result in their resolution. The solutions to moral issues are seldom obvious; rather, they call for a lengthy process of philosophical deliberation and analysis.

Furthermore, telling the sufferer to "follow his deepest feelings" won't help. That was typically the course of action that had initially led to his demise. Additionally, "loving" the patient—effectively giving him a moral free pass—is not the answer (which is one of the approaches most commonly advocated today). Love cannot replace reason, and the patient will not acquire the moral code necessary for his mental health if all moral standards are suspended. If the therapist, to whom the patient has turned for advice, is professionally devoted to not knowing, the impasse is complete. The patient feels confused, uncertain of his judgment, and as though he does not know what is right or wrong.

The extent to which the therapist upholds the belief that he must remain mute regarding moral matters, he passively affirms and supports the mysticism—more precisely, the religion—monopoly on morality. However, no ethical therapist can ignore the fact that a patient's neurosis frequently results from religious teachings.

In actuality, it is impossible for a psychotherapist to maintain his personal moral beliefs apart from his work. He reveals and makes the patient aware of his moral judgments by a variety of subtle cues, such as his pauses, his questions, his tone of voice, the things he says or doesn't say, the emotional vibrations he projects, etc. However, because this process of communication is subconscious for both parties, the patient is being led emotionally rather than intellectually; he does not form an independent, self-conscious appraisal of the therapist's value premises; instead, if he accepts them at all, he can only accept them on faith, by feeling, without reasons or proof, as long as the issues are never explicitly named. This effectively transforms the therapist into a religious figure—a sort of subconscious religious figure.

A therapist who takes this approach to moral issues may frequently urge adherence to and acceptance of the dominant moral ideas of the culture, without taking into account the issue of whether or not those beliefs are compatible with psychological well-being. However, even if the ideals conveyed by such a therapist are reasonable, the strategy of "persuasion" used is not, and as a result, the patient is not moved toward genuine, autonomous rationality.

A set of principles that direct one's decisions and deeds is known as a code of ethics or morality.

A conscious, logical, scientific code of ethics—a set of principles founded on reality and tailored to the requirements of man's life on earth—is necessary for effective psychotherapy.

I firmly believe that Ayn Rand's Objectivism philosophy has such a code of ethics, as I have argued in an earlier work. The reader is directed to Ayn Rand's book "Atlas Shrugged" and her collection of essays on ethics, The Virtue of Selfishness, for a thorough explanation of the Objectivist ethics.

It is not my intention to give a thorough explanation of Objectivist ethics in this context, but rather to (a) present the basis or justification for this system of ethics, i.e., how the Objectivist standard of value is derived and justified; (b) point out the general direction of this ethics; and (c) compare it to traditional religious ethics with an eye toward how each system affects mental health.

The concept of "values" is not assumed to exist; hence objectivism does not start by noticing that men have different values and presuming that the first ethical question is, "What values should man pursue?" The inquiry "What are values and why does man need them?" is where it all starts, on a far deeper level. What are the realities of existence and human nature that make values necessary and necessary?"

A "value" is anything that one works to acquire and/or maintain.

The target of an action is a value.

Value implies an explanation for the following question: of value to whom and for what? Value implies a standard, a goal, and the requirement for action in the face of a substitute. No values are possible if there are no alternatives. " An object could not have values or the desire for values if it by its very nature had no objectives to pursue. There wouldn't be any justification. And being without choices, incapable of acting, or for whose the results of any actions would always be the same, could have no purposes, no objectives, and thus no values. Purpose, and thus values, can only be made possible and required by existence.

Existence or nonexistence is the only fundamental choice in the cosmos, and it only applies to one class of objects: living things. While life depends on a particular sequence of action, the existence of inanimate matter is unaffected. Even though matter can change its shape, it cannot be destroyed. Only living things have to choose between life and death on a regular basis. The process of life is one of self-generating and self-sustaining action. If an organism fails to carry out that operation, it dies; its chemical components are preserved, but its life is lost. The concept of "Value" is only made conceivable by the concept of "Life." Only a live entity can judge whether something is nice or bad.

Only a live thing can have needs, objectives, and values, and only a living thing can come up with the behaviors required to fulfill those goals.

Plants can die, even though they lack consciousness, the ability to feel pleasure or pain, or the understanding of life and death. A plant's survival depends on a particular course of activity.

A plant needs to eat in order to survive; the nutrients it needs in the form of sunlight, water, and chemicals are the values that its nature has commanded it to pursue; its existence is the standard of value that guides its actions. A plant, however, has no choice in how it responds to its environment. It instinctively acts to further its life and is unable to act in a way that would lead to its own demise. Animals have a basic type of consciousness; while they cannot understand the concepts of life and death, they are able to experience pleasure and pain. An animal's survival depends on activities that are taken automatically under the control of its sensory system.

An animal is prepared to maintain its life; its senses give it an automatic moral code and an automatic awareness of what is right and wrong for it. It lacks the ability to circumvent it or broaden its understanding. It perishes in situations where its knowledge is insufficient. However, as long as it is alive, acting on information, automatically safe, and without the ability to choose, it is unable to disregard its own good, to choose the bad, and to act as its own destruction.

All living things—with one exception—are predisposed by nature to spontaneously initiate the actions necessary to sustain their survival given the proper circumstances and the right physical environment. Man is the exception.

Man must behave in order to exist, just like a plant or an animal, and he must acquire the values his life necessitates. However, because there is no physical environment on earth where a man could survive solely on the basis of his involuntary feelings, man does not behave or operate by automatic chemical or sensory reactions. Man is also born without any preconceived notions, thus he cannot have any preconceived notions of what is good or bad for him or what is true or wrong. The ability for man to survive is not inherent. The faculty of reason, which is the faculty that recognizes and integrates the data offered by man's senses, is man's fundamental means of survival.

For man, surviving is an issue—a challenge that must be overcome. The amount of passive sensory awareness that he shares with animals, or his perceptive level of consciousness, is insufficient to address it. Man must think in order to stay alive, which entails using a faculty that he alone possesses among all living things: the capacity for abstraction and conceptualization. The human level of awareness, which is the level necessary for man to survive, is conceptual. Man's ability to think is what determines how long he will live.

However, thinking is a voluntary act. The fact that man is a being with volitional consciousness is the key to "human nature" Thinking is not a mechanical process, reason does not operate automatically, and logic does not come to us pre-wired. Your stomach, lungs, and heart all work automatically, but your mind does not. You are free to consider or to avoid that effort at any time and in any situation of your life. The dilemma of "to be or not to be" is equivalent for you, a human being, to the question of "to think or not to think." This is because you are not free to escape from your nature, from the fact that reason is your means of existence.

A creature with volitional consciousness, a being without innate thoughts, must think out the objectives, actions, and values that will determine his quality of life. He needs to figure out what will improve his life and what will ruin it. He will perish if he goes against reality's facts. If he is to survive, he must learn the rules of conduct necessary to direct him in his interactions with the natural world and other people. He requires these values as well as a set of moral standards.

The values of other species cannot be freely chosen. Man is. "A code of morality is a set of values that people choose to follow."

The justification for man's moral need establishes the morality's goal and the yardstick for choosing moral ideals. The goal of morality is to provide each individual man with the moral framework he needs to live. But man needs a standard in order to know what are the values and qualities that will allow him to accomplish that goal. Diverse species have different strategies for ensuring their survival. The actions necessary for a fish or other animal to survive would not be necessary for a man to survive. Man must decide on his values based on what is necessary for a human being to live, which means that he must hold man's life (his survival as a man) as his standard of value. Since reason is a man's primary means of survival, this refers to living a life befitting a rational being or to what is necessary for a man to survive as a rational being.

"Everything that is necessary to the life of a rational being is good; everything that subverts it is evil." Man must act, think, and produce the values his life demands in order to survive. In terms of metaphysics, this is how people actually exist.

Man's fundamental virtue, from which all of his other qualities derive, is thinking. Thinking is the process of perceiving and classifying the world around us, of integrating our perceptions into concepts and those concepts into even larger concepts, and of continually broadening our knowledge to take in more and more of reality.

Man's fundamental vice—the root of all his evils—is evasion, the unwillingness to think, the purposeful rejection of reason, the willful suspension of consciousness, and the willful defiance of reality.

Like all other living things, man has a unique way of surviving that is dictated by his nature. Man is free to defy his nature, reject his thoughts and means of subsistence, but he is not free from the consequences, which include misery, anxiety, and ruin. It is still the faculty of reason that men are secretly relying on when they try to survive through parasitism and force, theft and brutality instead of thought and productive work: the rationality that some moral man had to exercise in order to create the goods that the parasites propose to loot or expropriate. Nothing can change the truth that a man's life depends on thinking rather than behaving impulsively or on creation rather than destruction. The principles of survival are not and cannot be mindlessness, apathy, parasitism, or cruelty; rather, they are the strategy of people who do not want to deal with the question of survival.

"Man's life" is defined as a life led in accordance with the values that enable man's existence as a species.

In the same way that man is alive physically to the degree that his internal organs work continuously to support his life, so too is man alive as a whole to the extent that his mind works continuously to support his life. The only vital organ with a volitional role is the mind, which is also a vital organ. A man who is enclosed in an iron lung and has paralyzed lungs is not actually dead, but he is not living a life that is fit for a man. A man whose mind is paralyzed voluntarily is also not.

If a man wants to survive, he must understand that reality is an absolute that cannot be avoided or escaped from and that the purpose of his mind is to see it, that this is his major obligation. Facts are facts, A is A, existence exists. He must understand that living is a process of self-sustaining and self-generated action, and that living entails the pursuit and achievement of logical ideals, values consistent with his nature and with reality. He must understand that thinking is the virtue that earns self-worth, which is the value without which none of the others are conceivable.

Man must regard these three things as the guiding principles of his life if he is to survive: Reason—Purpose—Self-esteem. Reason is his solitary source of information; purpose is the happiness he chooses to pursue with that tool; and self-worth is his unwavering conviction that his mind is capable of thought and that he is deserving of happiness—that is, deserving of existence. 11 The maxim that serves as the foundational tenet of the Objectivist ethical framework "The concept of "Value" is only made conceivable by the concept of "Life." Only a live entity can judge whether something is good or bad." The argument that a rational morality is impossibly unattainable and that values cannot be drawn from facts is debunked by this identification, which penetrates the Gordian knot of previous ethical thinking and clears the mystical haze in the sphere of morality.

Because living things must maintain their existence through self-generated action, it is feasible and necessary for values to exist. Every living species has a certain course of action that must be followed; an entity's identity dictates what it should do.

Objectivism disproves the idea—especially pervasive today—that the ultimate criterion of any moral judgment is "arbitrary" and that normative statements cannot be drawn from factual truths by pointing out the environment in which values develop existentially. It argues that failing to hold human life as your standard of moral judgment is to be guilty of a logical contradiction by pinpointing the genetic underpinnings of "value" from an epistemological perspective. Life is the fundamental value that enables all other values to exist. The value of life cannot be justified by any other value; to demand such justification—to ask, "Why should man choose to live? "—is to have lost sight of the significance, context, and source of one's notions. If "should" is separated from the idea and value of life, it cannot have any meaningful significance.

There is only one remaining alternative standard if life, or existence, is not acknowledged as one's standard: nonexistence. Death, however, is not a standard of value; rather, it is the antithesis of values. Man may choose not to hold life as his objective and ideal, but he is not entitled to the approval of reason or the right to assert that his decision is equally valid to all others. Whether or not man accepts his nature as a living creature is neither "arbitrary" nor "optional," just as it is neither "arbitrary" nor "voluntary" whether or not he accepts reality.

What are the main virtues that, in Objectivist ethics, are necessary for man to survive? Independence, prudence, integrity, justice, fairness, productivity, and pride.

Rationality is the unwavering dedication to reality perception, to the acceptance of reason as an absolute, and as the only source of information, moral principles, and guidelines for behavior. Independence is the acceptance of intellectual responsibility for one's own existence and the reliance on one's own intellect and judgment. Honesty is the reluctance to pursue values through a distorted perception of reality or by obfuscating the line between the real and the unreal. Integrity is adherence to one's conscience's assessment of behavior. Justice is the practice of recognizing men for who they are and treating them as such—rewarding pro-life behaviors and character characteristics in men and condemning anti-life ones. Being productive is the act of sustaining one's existence by the transformation of one's idea into reality, of making objectives and striving toward their accomplishment, and of creating information or things. Pride is moral ambition, the commitment to realizing one's fullest potential in one's life and character, and the reluctance to serve as a sacrifice tool for the objectives of others.

If life on earth serves as the benchmark, then morality does not reside in the man who forgoes values but in the man who accomplishes them; it does not reside in the man who rejects life but in the man who makes it possible. According to Objectivist ethics, every individual is an end in and of himself and not only a tool to further the interests of others. He is not meant to be sacrificed. He must exist for his own sake as a living thing, not for the benefit of others or for his own benefit. Man's highest moral goal is to pursue his own happiness.

Man has a serious duty when he chooses to pursue his own happiness; he must figure out what it actually takes to be happy. The majority of men have failed to take up this obligation. The idea that men can find happiness by pursuing any random desires they have is the most pervasive—and dangerous—belief there is. That notion is persuasively refuted by the fact that psychotherapy is a legitimate profession. Happiness is the result of leading a life that is appropriate for a rational being like a man and of pursuing and achieving enduring, life-enhancing values.

As a result, objectivism promotes an ethics based on sound self-interest.

What is objectively in man's self-interest can only be determined by reason; it cannot be chosen by emotion or whim. Self-destruction is a road that one pursues while acting according to their impulses and whims, and self-destruction is not in the best interest of man.

Man must ponder for his own benefit; he must not postpone thought. Man should act in his own best interest if he chooses his goals in the entire context of his knowledge, values, and life rather than acting on impulse and disregarding his long-term context. Person a productive being is in the best interest of man; trying to be a parasite is not. To live in accordance with one's nature is in man's self-interest; to live like an animal is not.

This forms the cornerstone of Objectivist ethics.

As we've seen, mental health is characterized by self-worth. It is the result, manifestation, and benefit of a mind wholly dedicated to reason. The principle that one's actions must be consistent with their convictions, that one must never attempt to fake reality or place any consideration above reality, that one must never permit oneself contradictions—that one must never attempt to subvert or sabotage the proper function of consciousness—are all aspects of the commitment to reason. These commitments include maintaining a full intellectual focus, constantly expanding one's understanding and knowledge, and adhering to these principles.

Man needs self-esteem; he has to be confident in his ability to deal with reality and to pursue and attain the values that his life demands. The antipodes of self-esteem and the symbols of mental disease, anxiety and guilt, disintegrate thought, distort values, and immobilize action. When a man with self-esteem decides on his values and goals, projects the long-term objectives that will unify and direct his actions, it is like building a bridge to the future across which his life will pass. This bridge is supported by the conviction that his mind is capable of thinking, judging, and appreciating values, and that he is deserving of doing so.

This sensation of control over reality and one's own life is not the consequence of specialized abilities, talents, or knowledge, as I underlined earlier (Chapter Seven). It is not reliant on specific accomplishments or setbacks. It reveals one's fundamental connectedness to reality as well as their belief in their inherent value and usefulness. It conveys the conviction that one is, in essence and in principle, correct regarding reality.

To the extent that a man subscribes to traditional morality, this psychological condition is rendered impossible. And this is one of the main justifications for why a psychotherapist cannot ignore the issue of moral principles in his practice.

Mysticism and the self-sacrifice ethos are incompatible with good mental health and self-esteem. These ideologies are harmful from an existential and psychological standpoint.

1. Man must use all of his intellect to maintain his life and gain self-esteem, yet morality, as men are taught, is based on and necessitates faith.

Faith is the intentional commitment to beliefs for which there is neither sensory nor intellectual support.

When a man rejects reason as his criterion for morality, he is left with just his feelings as an option. A mystic is a person who uses their emotions as tools for thought. Faith is the union of emotion and reason. The "virtue" of faith requires the willingness to suspend one's sight and one's judgment, to live with that which cannot be understood or integrated into the rest of one's knowledge, and to create an illusion of comprehension akin to that experienced in a trance. One must be prepared to suppress one's critical faculty and hold it responsible for one's guilt, drown any inquiries that arise in protest, and choke out any thrust of reason that trembles in an attempt to fulfill its due role as the guardian of one's life and intellectual integrity.

All of human knowledge and concepts are organized in a hierarchical manner. His sensory experiences serve as the basis and beginning point for human thought. From these, man develops his initial notions and continues to add to his body of knowledge by recognizing and incorporating new ideas on a larger and larger scale. To be genuine, a person's thought process must be supported by logic, often known as "the art of non-contradictory identification," and any new ideas must be seamlessly incorporated into his body of prior knowledge. To undermine the integrative function of consciousness, undermine the rest of one's convictions, and destroy one's ability to be certain of anything is to introduce into one's consciousness a major and fundamental idea that cannot be so integrated, an idea not derived from reality, not validated by a process of reason, not subject to rational examination or judgment, and worse: an idea that conflicts with one's other concepts and understanding of reality. The idea that one may give to reason what is reason's and to faith what is faith's is the greatest example of self-delusion. Faith cannot be defined or confined; to give up even a small portion of consciousness is to give up all of consciousness. Either reason is an absolute to the mind or it is not; if it is not, then there is nowhere to draw the line, no standard by which to draw it, no wall that faith cannot cross, no area of one's life faith cannot penetrate; one therefore remains rational only until and unless one's feelings dictate differently.

No system can accept faith because it is a tumor, and the man who gives in to it will turn to it in the very situations where he needs reason the most. When one switches from reason to faith, when one denies the absoluteness of reality, one undermines the absoluteness of awareness, making the mind an unreliable organ. It turns into the distortionary tool that mystics describe it to be.

2. Man's need for self-esteem includes the need to feel in control of reality, but control is impossible in a universe that, by one's own admission, contains the paranormal, the miraculous, and the causeless; in such a universe, one is at the mercy of ghosts and demons; in such a universe, one must deal not with the unknown but with the unknowable; in such a universe, man proposes, but a host disposes; in such a universe, the universe

3. For a man to have life and self-respect, reality and this earth must be the focus of his consciousness. However, men are taught that morality entails scorning this earth and the world of sensory perception in favor

of thinking about a "different" and "higher" reality that is inaccessible to reason and uncommunicable in language but attainable through revelation, through special dialectical procedures, and through that higher state of intellectual clarity known to Zeus.

The reality that is knowable by reason is the only reality that exists. If a person chooses not to perceive it, there is nothing else for them to sense; if their consciousness is not of this world, they are not conscious at all.

The only effect of the mystic projection of "another" world is to render man psychologically incapable of dealing with this one. Man did not emerge from the cave and change the physical universe such that a human existence on earth was made possible by considering the transcendental, the ineffable, the undefinable—it was not by contemplating the nonexistent.

If it is a virtue to renounce one's mind, but a sin to use it; if it is a virtue to approximate schizophrenic mental state, but a sin to be in intellectual focus; if it is a virtue to denounce this earth, but a sin to make it livable; if it is a virtue to mortify the flesh, but a sin to work and act; if it is a virtue to despise life, but

4. A man's existence and self-esteem depend on him taking pride in his ability to think and live, but men are taught that pride, particularly intellectual pride, is the worst kind of sin. Men are taught that virtue starts with humility, with the acceptance of one's mind's powerlessness, smallness, and helplessness.

The mystics question if man is omniscient. Is he faultless? Then, how could he dare to contradict God's word or that of God's servants and pose as the final arbiter of anything?

Intellectual pride does not mean omniscience or infallibility, as it is implied by mystics. Contrarily, the men who properly carry out this task feel proud since man must work to obtain information and because acquiring knowledge involves effort.

Occasionally, pride is interpreted informally to entail pretending to have accomplished things that one has not. The boaster, however, is not proud; rather, he has just chosen the most demeaning method to demonstrate his humility. He is the man who acts as though he had attributes that he does not.

A person's emotional response to their ability to uphold their principles, or their enjoyment of their own effectiveness, is pride. And mystics consider this to be wicked.

However, if self-doubt rather than self-confidence is the proper moral state for man, if self-distrust rather than self-reliance is the evidence of his virtue, if fear rather than self-esteem is the mark of perfection, and if guilt rather than pride is his goal, then mental illness is a moral ideal, the neurotics and psychotics are the highest exponents of morality, and the thinkers, the achievers, are the sinners, those who are too corrupt

Because it is the only virtue that can be practiced by men who have given up their minds, humility is unavoidably the fundamental virtue of a mystical morality.

While pride must be earned because it is the result of hard work and success, the virtue of humility may be attained with little effort and will come naturally to those who practice it.

5. A man's life and self-esteem depend on his loyalty to his principles, his mind and its judgments, and his life. However, men are taught that the core of morality is self-sacrifice: the sacrifice of one's mind to a higher power and the sacrifice of one's principles to whoever may claim to demand it.

Analyzing the nearly infinite harms that the principle of self-sacrifice entails is not required in this context. Ayn Rand's Atlas Shrugged provides a detailed exposé of its irrationality and destructiveness. However, there are two parts of the problem that are particularly relevant to the discussion of mental health.

The first is that self-sacrifice always and exclusively entails mind-sacrifice.

A sacrifice is the giving up of a higher value for a lesser or nonexistent value. Giving up something you don't value in order to get something you do, or giving up something you value less in order to get something you value more, isn't a sacrifice; it's a gain.

All of man's values are arranged in a hierarchy; he values certain things more than others, and to the extent that he is rational, his values are arranged in a rational hierarchy: he values things in proportion to how important they are to his life and well-being. He devalues anything that is harmful to his life, his wellbeing, or what he needs to survive as a living creature.

Contrarily, one of the traits of mental illness is a skewed value system; the neurotic often values the same things that will lead him to self-destruction rather than according to their objective merit in relation to his nature and requirements. According to objective criteria, he is constantly putting himself last.

But if making sacrifices is a virtue, it is the reasonable man who needs to be "cured," not the neurotic. He must learn to subvert his own reasonable judgment, to flip the pillars of his value system, to give up what his mind has determined to be right, and to reject and invalidate his own consciousness.

Do mystics assert that the only thing they ask of man is that he give up his happiness? The self-sacrifice creed demands and aims at nothing less than this: to sacrifice one's happiness is to sacrifice one's desires, to sacrifice one's desires is to sacrifice one's values, to sacrifice one's values is to sacrifice one's judgment, and to sacrifice one's judgment is to sacrifice one's mind.

What level of effectiveness, control, peace of mind, or conflict-free living will be conceivable for man if his judgment is made an offering?

The second factor that matters in this situation involves all the aforementioned ancient moral principles as well as the creed of self-sacrifice.

Men must accept the idea that there is an unavoidable conflict between the moral and the practical—that they must choose either to be moral or happy, idealistic or successful, but they cannot be both—due to an irrational morality, a morality set in opposition to man's nature, to the facts of reality, and to the requirements of man's survival. This point of view creates a fatal duality that splits man in two and requires him to make a decision between improving his ability to live and improving his worthiness to live. But for his mental and emotional well-being, he must accomplish both.

There is no conflict between the requirements of survival and morality if man views life as the good and measures his values by the criteria of what is appropriate for the existence of a rational being. He acquires the ability to live and the worthiness to live by accomplishing the first. However, there is a conflict if a person believes that giving up their life, their thinking, their happiness, and themselves is a good thing. An anti-life morality holds that man only makes himself worthy of living to the extent that he makes himself incapable of living, and that man only makes himself unworthy of living to the extent that he makes himself capable of living. Many advocates of conventional morality respond as follows: "We don't expect people to be completely moral, but individuals don't have to act out to the extreme. We anticipate that they will sneak some self-interest into their actions.

We understand that people must survive after all."

This moral code's justification is that few individuals will be suicidal enough to try to live by it constantly. Man's defense against his purported moral convictions is to be hypocrisy. What impact does that have on his confidence?

What about the victims who don't exhibit enough hypocrisy?

What about the kid who hides away in fear into his own world because he can't handle his parents' ravings that he is a sinner by nature, that his body is evil, that thinking is wrong, that asking questions is blasphemous, that doubting is depravity, and that he must follow the commands of a supernatural ghost or he will burn in hell for all eternity?

Or the daughter who, having committed the sin of not wishing to devote her life to taking care of the dying father who has only caused her to feel hatred, collapses in guilt?

Or the young person who turns to homosexuality as a means of escape after being told that sex is wrong and that women should be worshipped rather than desired?

Or the businessman who experiences a panic attack because, after being admonished for years to be thrifty and diligent, he has finally committed the sin of success and is now informed that it will be easier for a camel to pass through a needle than for a rich man to enter the kingdom of heaven?

Or the neurotic who, in a state of hopeless despair, quits up trying to find a solution to his issues because he has always heard it preached that this world is one of suffering, futility, and doom, where no man can find happiness or fulfillment?

The psychologists and psychiatrists who witness the human toll of these doctrines but who do nothing about it, who claim that philosophical and moral issues do not concern them and that science cannot make value judgments, who shirk their professional responsibilities by claiming that a logical code of morality is superior, may bear a greater moral responsibility than the advocates of these doctrines.

Authoritarianism and Its Risk

In order to maintain good mental health, a person must prioritize perception, consciousness, and reality over anything else.

If the patient wants to recover from his neurosis, he must learn to differentiate between a thought and a feeling, between a fact and a wish, and to understand that sacrificing one's sight of truth to any other factor can only lead to disaster. He must learn to find self-worth in the achievement of rational values and in the constructive use of his thoughts, regardless of his level of skill. He needs to understand that getting other people's acceptance cannot replace having high self-esteem, and that anyone who tries to do so will only experience worry. He needs to get the confidence to criticize and question the ingrained values of his culture. He must develop the ability to disbelieve people who demand his agreement on matters of faith. He needs to develop the ability to fight for and earn his own happiness. He needs to understand that doing the irrational will not help and that his misery will continue as long as any part of him harbors that desire.

He must learn to live logically, and he needs a set of logical moral rules to guide him in this endeavor. For this reason, I view Objectivist ethics as being fundamental to the practice of psychotherapy.

At this stage, it is important to express some caution regarding the way moral ideas are explained to patients.

Between directive therapy—where the therapist accepts the responsibility of his role as an educator—and authoritarian therapy, where the therapist preaches, propagandizes, intimidates, cajoles, or otherwise tries to pressure the patient into accepting certain viewpoints, there is a significant difference.

Invoking reason or the patient's "own good" as justifications for authoritarianism is a contradiction in terms. The presence of psychological issues does not give the therapist the right to treat the patient with anything less than complete intellectual respect. Given the nature of the therapist's position and the patient's self-doubt, it is all too common for the therapist to utilize subtly intimidating tactics to force the patient to adopt his or her moral or philosophical ideas. Such a procedure runs opposed to the therapeutic enterprise's basic purpose and essence. The patient's intellectual knowledge, not his or her blind faith, is what the therapist requires in order to assist the patient. Therapists are not witch doctors; they are scientists.

I should add that it would be incorrect to believe that therapists who embrace the requirement and accountability of addressing values in their profession are the only ones who are vulnerable to authoritarianism. Witch-doctrine is just as common, if not more so, among the therapists who avoid talking about values. In this regard, Freudians in particular are well-known.

Therapeutic Strategies

A thorough explanation of psychotherapy procedures is not within the scope of this book. I might write about that in a subsequent piece. I'll limit my remarks to a few broad generalizations regarding the more technical elements of therapy here.

1. Having patients complete written "homework" projects as therapy progresses has proven to be of great value to me. The patient is nearly usually required to produce a paper addressing (a) the history and evolution of his personal difficulties, starting from childhood; (b) what he thinks his problems are right now; and (c) what he intends to achieve via treatment, at the conclusion of the initial interview. After then, the patient can be given further papers to write about his connections with

his parents and friends, his sexual history, his educational and professional life, etc. Of course, such assignments are meant to be an addition to making history rather than a replacement for it. They frequently offer helpful supplementary information. In addition, the patient typically discovers that the task of outlining his life and issues on paper aids in the development of an impartial viewpoint.

Writing reports by the patient about how he comprehends the concepts he is learning in treatment and how he feels his new understanding is affecting him intellectually, emotionally, and behaviorally is frequently preferred. This can be particularly beneficial in group therapy as a way to keep the therapist updated on the condition and development of each patient. Such papers also serve as a check against any tendency on the side of the therapist to think that the patient comprehends more than he actually does. They also serve as a restraint against the patient's tendency to limit his reflection on his issues to the hours spent in therapy.

2. Assisting the patient in the process of depression is one of the therapist's most crucial jobs, given the fundamental and pivotal role that repression plays in the development (and maintenance) of psychological issues. Contradictions between a person's verbally declared ideas and his or her feelings and conduct, or between his or her emotions and behavior, or among his or her emotions themselves, or among his or her actions themselves, are some of the signs of repression that I have mentioned (Chapter Six).

The therapist's abilities are particularly put to the test while attempting to comprehend and reveal the patient's genuine ideas and feelings when they have been suppressed. He needs to be fully perceptive, emotionally sensitive, and capable of understanding implications in his patient's comments that the patient might not be aware of. For instance, the patient frequently communicates to the therapist in words one thing but in his body—through his breathing, his motions, his posture, the size of his pupils, etc.—a completely other tale. The therapist must constantly try to hone the art of questioning, which is undoubtedly the most effective method at his disposal. Of course, knowing what questions to ask first and foremost is part of the art, but so is understanding when and how to ask them. An effective therapist works to provide an environment where the patient can feel like they can express themselves freely. This is done by the therapist not projecting an attitude of all-encompassing warmth, forgiveness, and "love," but rather by projecting an attitude of respectful, benevolent interest, a sense of profound relaxation, and the conviction that truth, whatever it may be, need not ever be frightening and that freedom can only be found by facing facts.

I regret that there isn't enough room to elaborate on my belief that one of the therapist's most valuable technical skills is his capacity to remain deeply at ease while working and to communicate this state to the patient. The kind of stony, emotionally frozen distance or pedantic impersonality that many unskilled or insecure therapists adopt as a protective façade is forbidden by genuine relaxation on the side of a therapist. Such a façade is not necessary for professional efficiency and, in fact, gets in the way of it by preventing good connection between the therapist and the patient and restricting the patient's ability to express their emotions freely.

I can just mention hypnosis in passing as another effective instrument for breaking down restrictive walls. Through hypnosis, a patient can reach a state of considerably improved mental focus where previously forgotten or suppressed information is made available to him. Every therapist should become proficient in the art of asking hypnotic questions, hypnotic age regression, and other related methods.

I've said that the therapist needs to learn how to ask questions. Learning the questions he needs to help the patient ask themselves is a necessary component of that competence. It is amazing how infrequently a patient who is attempting to express his emotions asks himself, "What do I want?" This is possibly the most important question a person can ask themselves, and the therapist should teach his patient to ask it and keep asking it about every element of his life on a daily, weekly, and monthly basis. What do I hope to achieve professionally? In ten years, where do I want to be professionally? How do I want people to see my work? What about my work do I hope people will find admirable? What characteristics should buddies have? What characteristics should a romantic partner have? How do I want to feel about a potential love interest? What sexual sensations do I wish to experience? What activities do I want to do with my friends and family? What am I looking for and hoping to get out of the books I read? —in the films I watch? —in the music I hear?

Most patients initially have a great deal of difficulty responding to such queries (except, perhaps, in vague and useless generalities). However, the patient will be guided to identify not just his desires (i.e., his values), but also and equally significantly, his frustrations, his disappointments, his hurts and grievances, if he is encouraged to persist, to go on asking questions until the answers begin to emerge. There are practically endless possibilities for such inquiries; I've only mentioned a handful above.

3. It is helpful to have the patient categorize his issues into two groups. By making changes to his behavior in areas under his direct volitional control, such as lying, physically abusing one's child, sexual promiscuity, failing to look for work, seeking solace from one's problems through excessive socializing, etc., the patient may be able to immediately partially or completely correct some of his problems. Other issues, such as emotions of anxiety or sadness, abnormal sexual impulses, trouble thinking properly, psychosomatic sickness, etc. are obviously unfixable by a simple act of choice or decision. Sometimes a patient requires assistance figuring out which category a specific issue

falls under. (Not all issues easily fall into one of these categories; mild compulsive behavior, for example, is a borderline case.)

It is important to develop a strategy for how the patient will change the components of his behavior that he recognizes as being directly under his control over a given length of time. His logical behavior regulation in these areas gives him the assurance he needs to tackle issues that call for more intense therapy.

In order to successfully treat these latter issues, it is crucial for the patient to be very clear about his treatment objectives. When the objective is as simple as, say, being heterosexual rather than homosexual, being migraine headache-free, or losing weight, this task can occasionally be rather simple. However, the patient's issues are frequently more nebulous, with hazy sensations of worry or sadness, a general lack of self-confidence, and complaints that his life lacks meaning. In these situations, it's crucial to assist him in formulating as precisely as possible the requirements that would need to be met before he could consider himself "healed." He should be helped to come up with concrete, existential or psychological goals that he is to work toward. Otherwise, counseling could develop into a nebulous, protracted procedure.

It is crucial for the patient's progress and self-esteem at every stage of therapy that he engage in any voluntary acts that are within his power to address his issues. Problems are not often resolved all at once; rather, they are resolved piecemeal. One must make every effort to assist the patient in avoiding making the same mistakes that contributed to his neurotic condition in the slow, challenging process of assisting him to develop self-confidence and self-respect. Problems don't appear overnight; they develop gradually. They are then sustained and reinforced year after year by endless repetitions of the kinds of self-defeating behaviors I've covered in this book. The patient has to be made aware of the behaviors that contribute to his issues and those he could avoid. In order to stop the process, he needs to be made aware of and inspired to conduct the opposite kinds of behaviors.

Assume, for instance, that a person has a history of running away from any task or obstacle that even somewhat seems dangerous. He is passive, reclusive, doubtful of himself, and ineffective as an adult. He cannot be required by the therapist to start taking on significant tasks or obligations that are obviously out of his current comfort zone. Therefore, one should start by encouraging him to create a number of modest objectives, goals that do provide a challenge for him and cause him to feel some level of dread, but a controllable fear that he has the ability to fight through and conquer. Thus, the patient gains the capability and assurance to advance to more difficult objectives.

As we've already covered, therapy involves a variety of components, such as assisting the patient in recognizing his emotions and desires, guiding him toward more productive ways of thinking, assisting him in comprehending his conflicts, etc. However, it's crucial to encourage the patient to think about his issues in terms of solutions. What psychological or existential choices did he make that led to the development of his issue? What action does he take to maintain it? What steps may he take to stop the process? What steps can he take to achieve the kind of life that he wants?

4. This brings up a concept that is connected to the one above. One of the most frequent errors patients make is having the following attitude: I will be able to behave differently from how I currently behave after I have fully understood myself, once all of my emotional issues have been resolved, and once all of my fears have been conquered.

Here, the error lies in neglecting to acknowledge the necessity of changing one's behavior as one learns through the course of therapy. Otherwise, learning is not very helpful. Many patients assert that therapy has given them several advantages and that they have gained priceless insights, yet it is clear that their behavior is precisely the same as it was before to starting therapy. In these situations, it can be challenging to determine whether or how therapy helped the patient. The patient's emotional issues and worries won't be resolved in reality unless he changes his conduct as he gains knowledge.

What is the patient doing differently than he did before is the surest indication of a cure or improvement. The patient should be encouraged to put any new understanding he has attained into action at each stage of therapy. The action could involve switching jobs, working harder at the one he already has, acting differently with his kids, opening up to his wife about his emotions, controlling his temper, creating and adhering to a budget, returning to school, cutting ties with unwelcome friends, speaking up in support of his beliefs at a social gathering, etc. With the increased understanding he gains in treatment and the positive impact such activities have on his self-esteem, he will be able to adopt further behavioral changes in the future.

5. How much analysis of childhood events is required to address the psychological issues of an adult is a frequently addressed question. I don't think there is a universal solution to this topic that would work in every circumstance. Some issues can be resolved without ever looking into the patient's past; in other situations, further investigation and analysis are required.

When analyzing childhood events is necessary, the patient must be taught to understand that his problem is not being caused by the events themselves, nor even by the initial conclusions he drew from them, but rather by the fact that he continues to reinforce those conclusions every day of his adult life. Some people start telling themselves they are useless when they are just three years old and continue doing so every day until they are in their thirties or forties. On the other hand, there are people who form false assumptions about themselves or about life when they are young, but later change those assumptions as a result of new information and, possibly, additional evidence. As a result, they are able to avoid unpleasant experiences without suffering long-term consequences.

The patient must still understand what he is doing in the present to maintain his difficulties, no matter how informative and useful it may be for him to discover how his problems began. He is powerless to change what he did in the past. The answer rests in what he does about his past, present, and future deeds—in the new judgments he makes, the new psycho-epistemological rules he adopts, the new moral standards he picks up, and the new objectives he chooses to work toward.

CONCLUSION

I mentioned in our consideration of needs (Chapter 2) that the satisfaction of a need does not always lead to an organism's immediate or direct demise, but can instead cause an organism's overall capacity to operate to decline, as well as its efficacy and power. This is relevant to the desire for self-esteem in particular as well as psychological needs in general.

Naturally, patients do not typically die from a lack of self-esteem (although they occasionally do, as in suicide or other types of self-destructions), but the severity of that lack determines how incapable they are of living. The capacity of a man to maximize his intellectual and creative potential, to translate that potential into productive achievement, to function effectively and unhindered on the emotional as well as the intellectual level, to love and to give objective expression to his love, to explore the challenges and reap the rewards that human existence offers to man, is how that ability or inability is measured.

In the same way that a patient must be taught that his lack of self-esteem and the practices that contributed to it are ultimately to blame for his frustrations, despair, and the wreckage of his life, he must also be taught the cure: that supreme act of selfishness and self-aggrandizement that entails holding his self-esteem as his highest value and most exalted concern and understanding that each struggling step upward, taken in the name of that value, carries him further from the bondage to his past suffering and closer to the sunlight reality of the human potential.

In conclusion, having a positive self-image will help you succeed in life. It will enable you to realize your full potential and make the most of your skills, talents, and capabilities. A poor self-concept, though, will impede your development. In truth, self-sabotage tends to be the result of a poor self-concept. As a result, you'll find it difficult to carry out your plans of action and fall short of achieving the goals and objectives you've set for yourself. The effect that other people have on your self-concept is the most crucial point to make here. People frequently affect how you feel about yourself, the labels you assign yourself, and ultimately what you believe about yourself, your own capabilities, and the world around you through rejection, judgment, derision, and criticism. Your worth as a person is actually dependent on the people in your life. As a result, if you struggle with a negative self-concept, it may very well be a result of the daily interactions you have with other people.